Ethics and Finance

Ethics and Finance: An Introduction provides a comprehensive and accessible introduction to the ethical issues raised by modern finance. Drawing carefully on ethical theory and with frequent use of case studies, it includes an analysis of the global financial system and its regulation and control, as well as a detailed analysis of the financial crisis. Chapters on specific areas of finance practice cover all the major financial scandals of recent times, from mis-selling to market manipulation and from insider trading to bankers' bonuses, as well as much more positive developments. From microfinance to derivatives trading, the book provides a careful and balanced treatment designed to help finance students and practitioners approach this sensitive topic in a thoughtful and constructive way. No prior knowledge of ethics or finance is required, and the book will be invaluable to students, finance teachers, practitioners and regulators.

JOHN HENDRY is a Fellow of Girton College at the University of Cambridge, and Emeritus Professor at Henley Business School, University of Reading. He is the author of *Between Enterprise and Ethics: Business and Management in a Bimoral Society* (2004).

Cambridge Applied Ethics

Titles published in this series:

Ethics and Finance

An Introduction

JOHN HENDRY

University of Cambridge

CAMBRIDGE
UNIVERSITY PRESS

CAMBRIDGE
UNIVERSITY PRESS

University Printing House, Cambridge CB2 8BS, United Kingdom

Published in the United States of America by Cambridge University Press, New York

Cambridge University Press is part of the University of Cambridge.

It furthers the University's mission by disseminating knowledge in the pursuit of education, learning, and research at the highest international levels of excellence.

www.cambridge.org
Information on this title: www.cambridge.org/9781107024229

© John Hendry, 2013

First published 2013

Printed in the United Kingdom by TJ International Ltd. Padstow Cornwall

A catalogue record for this publication is available from the British Library

Library of Congress Cataloging in Publication data
Hendry, John, 1952–
Ethics and finance : an introduction / John Hendry.
pages   cm. – (Cambridge applied ethics)
ISBN 978-1-107-02422-9 (hardback)
1. Financial services industry – Moral and ethical aspects.   2. Financial crises – Moral and ethical aspects.   3. Financial institutions – Moral and ethical aspects.   4. Banks and banking – Moral and ethical aspects.   5. Business ethics.   I. Title.
HG103.H46   2013
174'.4–dc23

2013035266

ISBN 978-1-107-02422-9 Hardback
ISBN 978-1-107-61248-8 Paperback

Contents

Preface

When I started teaching business ethics at London Business School in the mid-1980s, it was still an emerging discipline. Twenty-five years later, it is a substantial field of inquiry, with its own well-developed research literature and countless textbooks. Courses in business ethics are offered at all of the world's leading business schools and many of those courses are required. However, despite the recent financial crisis and the ensuing popular debate, the ethics of finance is even less developed now than business ethics was then. There is a widespread view, both in the business schools and in financial firms, that ethics is somehow not relevant to finance.

Few people outside the finance community would have much truck with this proposition. Much of finance is, of course, very technical, but then so is much of medicine. That doesn't make medical ethics any less important. And while the financial sector may not impact physically on people's lives in the way that the health sector and pharmaceutical firms impact on patients, or mining impacts on employees and communities, it evidently does have a significant impact, both directly on its customers and indirectly on society at large. If business ethics matters, as I believe it does, then so does the ethics of finance.

This book is intended to serve both as a general introduction to ethics and finance and as a textbook for courses in the area. The approach is philosophical, but no prior knowledge of philosophy is assumed and I have restricted the discussion largely to applications of the main branches of normative ethics. Anyone with the logical and analytical skills necessary to master basic finance theory should be able to master the philosophy, and indeed vice versa. Compared with some texts in applied ethics, there is a lot of descriptive material and a relatively modest amount of detailed analysis. This is partly in conformity with business school pedagogies (reflected in most textbooks on business ethics), which emphasize class discussion of examples. It is partly because for readers without a background in finance, there is an awful lot to be explained. And it is partly because while some areas of applied ethics have one or two "big" issues, finance has many issues of differing kinds, and in a relatively under-developed literature, the reader cannot easily turn elsewhere for topics that might otherwise have been left out here.

Using the book as a course text. Different teachers have different preferences when setting up a course and this book naturally reflects my own, but it can be readily adapted to others. Three features in particular are worth noting here. First, the book begins (Chapter 1) with an extended case study of the financial crisis. The rest of the book can, however, be read independently of this, and some teachers might prefer to start with Chapter 2, perhaps coming back to the case study later or using it as the basis for assessed work.

Second, Chapter 3, on normative ethics, includes a substantial discussion of how we think about moral issues and of the relationship between the project of ethical analysis and the practical adoption of moral norms by societies. I find this very helpful when teaching people unfamiliar with philosophy as a discipline, but it is rather less helpful when teaching philosophy students and can probably be dropped in that context.

Third, the ethical analysis given in the early to middle chapters is generally more detailed than that given later on. The intention here is that there should be enough analysis early on for students to learn by example how to go about it, but not so much, later on, as to save them the bother of doing it themselves. A practical consequence of this is that while instructors can to a large extent pick and choose the topics on which they want to focus from Chapter 7 onwards, the material on Chapters 4–6 probably needs to be covered quite systematically.

Acknowledgements

As always, this book draws on all kinds of assistance, much of which I'm not even aware of myself. Specific thanks go to Hilary Gaskin and Anna Lowe at Cambridge University Press for making the book possible and seeing it through; to my wife Dee for once again putting up with my obsessive preoccupation with a book; to Marie Westoby for her valuable comments on two drafts and assistance with referencing and glossary; and especially to Richard Rowland, who provided particularly incisive and detailed criticism of the drafts and stimulating discussion of the argument. The faults and idiosyncrasies remaining are, of course, my own, but the work is massively better for Richard's critique. More generally, I have benefited from countless discussions with colleagues, both in finance and in applied ethics, and with students. The book was shaped and most of the case studies developed and tested while I was teaching MSc students at Henley Business School, part of the University of Reading, over the last few years. But it also owes something to earlier generations of students and especially to those in MBA programs at the University of Cambridge's Judge Business School in the 1990s and at the University of Notre Dame's Mendoza College of Business in the 2000s. To all of the above I am deeply grateful.

1 Opening case study: the financial crisis

Introduction

There have been many financial crises over the last thirty years, but the crisis that emerged in 2007 and peaked most dramatically in 2008, commonly referred to as *the* financial crisis, was like no other. By the late summer of 2008, most of the world's largest banks, and many smaller ones, were carrying massive liabilities in respect of derivative securities linked to US subprime mortgage valuations. These valuations were in free fall, but the derivatives were so complex that the banks often had only a vague grasp of their own exposures, let alone those of the many other banks with which they traded on a daily basis. A string of major banks either collapsed altogether or survived only through massive injections of government funds. And as the banks became reluctant to risk lending to each other, the banking system as a whole came perilously close to collapse. The system survived, but the crisis quickly shifted to the rescuing governments, most of which were already over-borrowed, generating a global national debt crisis. Meanwhile the uncertainty associated with the crisis led to widespread economic recession, exacerbating national debt problems and prompting further austerity measures, and deepening recession. As of 2013, the effects of the financial crisis still dominate the world economy and the politics of both Europe and the USA, and they look likely to continue doing so for many years yet.

Apart from its economic effects, the financial crisis has also impacted enormously on the way people think about finance and the financial sector. This sector has always been treated with a certain amount of moral suspicion, but events have thrown a spotlight on its practices, and many people don't like what they see. They particularly dislike the way the sector appears to continue thriving, paying massive bonuses, earning large profits and paying little taxes, while the public at large have, as a consequence it seems of the banks' excesses, to suffer unemployment and austerity. But there is also much more widespread criticism than before of the specific practices of the sector.

In this opening chapter we set the scene for the rest of the book by presenting a case study of the core events leading up to the crisis and the immediate responses to it. This case study draws mainly on the "official" account of the crisis as experienced in the USA, *The Financial Crisis Inquiry Report*, but, unlike that or the many other published accounts of the crisis, it makes no attempt either to provide a definitive account (impossible, given the space limitations) or to apportion blame.[1] In the tradition of business school case studies, it is intended simply to provide a basis for the discussion of ethical issues and not to illustrate either good or bad ethical practice.

The financial crisis

The context: easy money and deregulation

The new millennium had not started well. A technology and Internet stock market boom had peaked in 2000 and had been followed by the inevitable bust, and by a series of high-profile corporate collapses, including those of Enron and WorldCom, at that point the world's largest ever corporate bankruptcies. The 9/11 terrorist attacks had badly hit confidence and the major world economies had gone briefly into recession.

The financial sector had not come out of the dot.com bubble looking particularly good. A number of investment banks had been charged with various offenses relating to the fraudulent promotion of client company shares, and both banks and accounting firms had been deeply involved in the fraudulent misrepresentation of earnings at Enron and WorldCom. The economic impact on the sector was, however, modest. The traditional

---

[1] Financial Crisis Inquiry Commission 2011. Although the conclusions of the report are politically loaded, with a Democrat majority offering one set of conclusions and Republican minorities alternatives, the report is indispensable for its comprehensive coverage and in its concern to elucidate the facts as a basis for judgment. The Commission interviewed over 700 witnesses, received a mountain of documentary evidence and employed a staff of over 80 to sort and analyze it all and build a publicly accessible library of testimony and resources. For other accounts of the crisis, see Bitner 2008; Davies 2010; Jickling 2009; Morris 2008; Muolo and Padilla 2010; Posner 2009; Shiller 2008; Stiglitz 2010; and Tett 2009.

banking sector continued its long-term growth with barely a blip, accounting for about $7 trillion in loans and deposits by 2004. The rapidly growing shadow banking sector, made up mainly of the investment banks and money market mutual funds, was more heavily affected, but only briefly. Having roughly doubled in size in just four years from 1997 to 2001, it grew more slowly for a couple of years, but nevertheless matched the traditional sector in loans and deposits by 2004, after which its growth accelerated again at its previous rate. The financial sector was also increasingly well rewarded. While average bank pay from the 1940s to the 1980s had been roughly in line with average pay in other sectors, by the early 2000s it was almost double, with a substantial proportion of pay tied to short-term per-formance bonuses and, for senior managers, share price-based incentives.

By 2004, the major economies were out of recession and interest rates, especially in the USA, were at a record low. The low US interest rates were partly engineered by Alan Greenspan at the Federal Reserve to stimulate economic growth through domestic spending and the housing market, but they were also a natural consequence of a lot of money looking for safe investments. With oil prices double what they had been in 2001 and still rising steadily at over 25 percent a year, industrial growth in the developed world was limited, but the oil-producing countries were flush with cash. The Chinese economy was also growing rapidly on the basis of its manufactur-ing exports and building up massive dollar reserves. Much of this money was being invested back into US government bonds and other low-risk securities, pushing down interest rates across the board.

The banking sector by this stage had been heavily deregulated. In the USA, the strong regulatory framework created in the mid-twentieth century had been steadily eroded, culminating in the repeal of the Glass-Steagall Act, which had for decades prevented commercial banks from taking on risky investment banking activities. The large commercial banks, led by Citigroup, were now heavily involved in investment banking activities and had also taken over much of the savings and loans sector (the US thrifts, similar to UK building societies). The investment banks had diversified aggressively beyond their core advisory and underwriting activities into deposit taking through money market mutual funds and into speculative trading, especially in the derivatives markets, both for clients and on their own accounts. Despite a series of high-profile crises during the 1990s, culminating in the collapse of the pioneering hedge fund Long-Term

Capital Management, these markets had remained almost entirely unregulated and indeed had been formally exempted from regulatory oversight in the 2000 Commodity Futures Modernization Act.

Meanwhile, the UK and other countries had also deregulated their financial sectors, and in some of the more radical cases, such as Ireland and Iceland, this had led to the rapid growth of high-risk banking sectors out of all proportion to their host countries' economies. Internationally the Basel II rules for the regulation of commercial banks had replaced the traditional requirement that banks maintain a fixed percentage of their assets as equity capital with more flexible requirements based on the banks' own analyses of their risk profiles using a measure called Value at Risk (VaR). In the USA, a similar but looser and effectively unsupervised regime had been introduced for the investment banks.

Under these conditions, the financial sector was growing rapidly in both scale (between 10 percent and 20 percent each year) and scope (expanding into new areas of derivatives trading), and was stretching its resources to the limit to exploit new opportunities. This stretch was reflected in the banks' leverages, the ratio between their assets or liabilities and underlying equity capital. Traditionally, for every $1 million of capital, banks would borrow about another $11 million, giving them about $12 million to lend or invest (leverage of 11:1 or a capital ratio of 1/12 or about 8 percent). The change in their activities had increased the risk of their lending and investment, and increasing leverage meant increasing that risk still further. But it also meant higher share price valuations relative to a bank's capital base, and so higher stock-based compensation for the top executives. It also enabled a higher level of the kind of those risky activities – predominantly proprietary derivatives trading – that fed into the bonus pool.

Not all commercial banks increased leverage in this period: JP Morgan Chase and Wells Fargo, for example, remained relatively conservative in this respect. But the more aggressive banks increased it significantly, with Citigroup, the most aggressive of all, leading the way. The same was happening at all the investment banks and at most of the European banks. By the time of the crisis, leverages of 35:1 to 45:1 were commonplace in both commercial and investment banks, meaning that banks only had equity cover for a 2–3 percent loss in asset value. In some cases, moreover, the official figures hid higher values still, as risky assets were placed off balance sheet or parked overnight (sold and repurchased) at the end of each accounting period. For the US mortgage agencies Fannie Mae and Freddie Mac, leverages reached 75:1.

Common sense would suggest that a 3 percent dip in asset values is not that improbable and that for banks to risk insolvency as a result of it was crazy. But the statistical models used assumed: (a) that the risks to which the banks were exposed were largely uncorrelated, so that their total portfolios were much less risky than their components; and (b) that the sizes of any losses were subject to normal distributions, so that really large losses were extremely unlikely. As Nassim Taleb has pointed out, the way in which the banks' value at risk was expressed also seems designed to give the impression that things are less risky than they are. A VaR of one day, 1 percent and $10 million sounds as if a $10 million loss is very unlikely, when what it signifies is that on two or three trading days each year, *at least* $10 million will be lost. Even assuming normal distributions, the "at least" is highly significant, and if the distribution tails are longer (as critics like financier George Soros and mathematician Benoit Mandelbrot had long been insisting), it is massively so.[2]

Within the financial sector, a number of areas were particularly buoyant at this time and one of these was mortgage lending. Here US deregulation in the 1980s had been followed by a house price bubble, extensive fraud and the collapse of many of the traditional thrifts. Much of the thrifts' business had, however, been taken over by the commercial banks and, fuelled by the Fed's low interest rate policy, the market was again booming. Mortgage originations, having run at around $100 billion a year up to 2000, had risen to $300 billion in 2003, over $500 billion in 2004 and were set to keep rising. A growing proportion of these new mortgages were, moreover, subprime mortgages. Against a historic average of under 10 percent, these were accounting for 21 percent of the mortgage market by 2004, an increase from around $10 billion a year to around $200 billion a year. This growth in the mortgage market came at a time when real wages in the USA were actually falling. But with low interest rates and easy access to mortgages, even for those with a poor credit history and no earnings record, the housing sector was booming. Average US house prices doubled in the first six years of the century, and people increasingly took advantage of house price rises to remortgage and release money for spending.

---

[2] Mandelbrot and Hudson 2008; Soros 1998; Taleb 2004.

Another boom area was the sale of asset-backed securities, commercial bonds issued by the investment banks and secured on a package of underlying financial assets such as car loans, credit card debt and student loans. A substantial and growing part of this market, valued at between $3 trillion and $4 trillion, was in mortgage-backed securities, with the majority of new mortgage loans being securitized. And by 2004 these had given birth to a new kind of security, the collateralized debt obligation (CDO). A third area of rapid growth was in derivatives, including credit default swaps (CDSs). Central to any understanding of the financial crisis is an understanding of how these CDOs and CDSs worked.

The products: the strange world of mortgage-backed securities

Traditional building societies and thrifts were mutual organizations that took deposits from savers and lent to borrowers. Much of the time, no other institution was involved. For many decades, however, American thrifts have been able to sell on mortgages (i.e., the income streams from the mortgages together with the underlying security) to other institutions, notably the Federal National Mortgage Association (known as Fannie Mae) and later also the Federal Home Loan Mortgage Corporation (known as Freddie Mac). The basic idea was to encourage home ownership. Left to their own devices (and working under tight regulations), the thrifts could only lend as much as they could borrow from their savings depositors, but by buying up mortgage loans, these institutions effectively took them off the thrifts' books and so made it possible for them to make new loans without raising new deposits. The agencies repaid the thrifts the costs of their mortgages and took over entitlement both to the interest and repayments, and to the security of the properties should the homeowner default.

The original institution, Fannie Mae, started life as a government agency, but this meant that the government had to pay for the mortgages and hold them on its own balance sheet, and by the early 1970s Fannie and Freddie, though government-backed, were private corporations. They could still pass on their mortgages to a new government agency, Ginnie Mae, but they could also securitize and resell them on the markets. What this meant was that a whole load of mortgages would be bundled together and sold to a specially created company, which in turn would issue interest-paying bonds, backed by the mortgages as security, to investors. Each investor ended up, in effect, investing in a small proportion of a lot of mortgages. Because houses were seen as an ultra-safe investment, and because Fannie and Freddie were only allowed to buy "conforming" mortgages which met high underwriting standards and were therefore especially secure, these were attractive investments. Moreover, because the interest paid by homeowners on their mortgages was much, much higher than the interest paid out on other safe investments like government bonds, there was scope for all of the originating thrift (the company that first set up the mortgage), Fannie or Freddie and the securitizing company to take hefty fees and still leave investors in the mortgage-backed securities with a very attractive interest rate.

Initially, securitization was limited to "prime" or "conforming" mortgages, but in the 1980s investment banks saw a money-making opportunity and began buying up, securitizing and selling "non-conforming" loans: mortgages issued on the basis of lower deposits, or poorer credit records or ability to pay on behalf of the homeowner; mortgages on variable rates, such as teaser mortgages that offered very cheap rates for the first few years but then became much more expensive; adjustable-rate mortgages that left it to the borrower to choose how much, if anything, to pay back (option ARMs), and even allowed in the early years for repayment levels that increased the amount owed; "piggy-back" mortgages, provided on top of a conforming mortgage so as to provide a higher overall loan level; mortgages right up to or even in excess of a property's assessed value; and "no-doc" mortgages that charged high interest rates but required no evidence of ability to pay. These "subprime" mortgages were much more risky, but the interest rates were correspondingly higher and with rising house prices and the security of the underlying properties, they still seemed to be "as safe as houses." They could also be "tranched," which is where things start to get a bit complicated. To explain, let us look at a typical deal from 2006, CMLTI 2006-NC2, with a value of just under $1 billion, which was used as an illustration in the *Financial Crisis Inquiry Report*.

CMLTI 2006-NC2 was based on 4,499 mortgages that were originated by New Century Financial, a Californian mortgage lender. All these mortgages were subprime, so failed to meet normal underwriting standards (or at least what had been normal underwriting standards before the 2000s) in one way or another. They were bought up by the banking conglomerate Citigroup and were sold on to a separate company set up by Citigroup, which owned the mortgages and issued the securities. (This arrangement kept the deal off the Citigroup balance sheet, so that the debts didn't count when it came to calculating its capital ratios.) For securitization purposes, the mortgage pool was divided into 19 tranches (see Table 1.1), each of which offered investors a different interest rate and repayment schedule and a different priority claim on the flow of payments associated with the mortgages. Note that the tranches were not based on different sub-pools of mortgages, just on different risk-return relationships relating to the pool as a whole. To complete the offering, each tranche was given an investment rating by the ratings agencies (Moody's, Standard & Poor's and Fitch). This was effectively an opinion, paid for by the securitizing company, as to how safe an investment in that tranche was likely to be.

The idea behind the product was that there was a sufficient flow of interest payments from the underlying mortgages for Citigroup to take a generous securitization fee and still find investors for all the tranches, each one appealing to different investors with different risk-return profiles. The yields here were based on the London Interbank Offered Rate (LIBOR), which in theory was the rate at which banks lent to each other. It only transpired much later that the rates declared by the banks were not always those actually paid, but were systematically manipulated to their advantage.[3]

As with the banks' value at risk calculations, the ratings provided by the agencies were based on standard statistical assumptions. In this case they were also referenced to historically low rates of mortgage defaults (under, of course, very different conditions). The banks, which were paying for the ratings, also made it pretty clear what they wanted for their fees. Thus, although the underlying mortgages were all subprime, it was assumed by the ratings analysts that only very few would default and that even in that event, much of the security would be recovered. The tranching loaded the risk of default onto the lowest tranches, ensuring that the higher ones got impeccable ratings. In this case 78 percent of the securities issued by value, comprising the top four "senior" and "super-senior" tranches, were rated AAA, or as safe as government bonds. At the other end of the scale, just 1.5 percent of the value was issued in "equity" tranches, which bore no rating and, analogous to the risk capital in an enterprise, only got anything back

---

[3] See, for example, www.bbc.co.uk/news/business-19203103.

Table 1.1. *CMLTI 2006-NC2*

Tranche	Value ($m)	Value (%)	Rating	Yield	Investors
Senior					
A1	155	16.3	AAA	LIBOR + 0.14%	Fannie Mae
A2-A	282	29.7	AAA	LIBOR + 0.04%	Banks, investment funds
A2-B	282	29.8	AAA	LIBOR + 0.06%	Banks, investment funds
A2-C	18	1.9	AAA	LIBOR + 0.24%	Banks
Mezzanine					
M1	39	4.1	AA+	LIBOR + 0.29%	Banks, investment funds, asset managers
M2	44	4.6	AA	LIBOR + 0.31%	Banks, investment funds, asset managers, CDOs
M3	14	1.5	AA-	LIBOR + 0.34%	2 CDOs, asset manager
M4	16	1.7	A+	LIBOR + 0.39%	CDO, hedge fund
M5	17	1.8	A	LIBOR + 0.40%	Kleros III plus another CDO
M6	11	1.2	A-	LIBOR + 0.46%	2 CDOs
M7	10	1.0	BBB+	LIBOR + 0.70%	3 CDOs
M8	8	0.9	BBB	LIBOR + 0.80%	3 CDOs, bank
M9	12	1.2	BBB-	LIBOR + 1.5%	5 CDOs, asset managers
M10	14	1.4	BB+	LIBOR + 2.5%	3 CDOs, asset manager
M11	11	1.2	BB	LIBOR + 2.5%	Unknown
Equity					
CE, P, R, Rx	13	1.4			Real estate finance company *et al.*

Source: Financial Crisis Inquiry Commission 2011, p. 116

once all the bondholders had been paid. Between those, nine "mezzanine" tranches, 21 percent of the value, were given investment-grade ratings from AA+ down to BBB-, and two further mezzanine tranches, about 2.5 percent of the value, were given junk bond ratings.

As can be seen from Table 1.1, the senior tranches of this security were bought mainly by banks and investment funds. The more risky junior tranches were bought by CDOs, a CDO (in this case a cash CDO backed by mortgage-backed securities) being yet another form of security, put together by buying the junior tranches from a range of different securities and pooling and tranching *those*. The first CDOs had been put together by the infamous Michael Milken out of junk bonds in the 1980s, but they only really took off when used with mortgage-backed securities in the mid-2000s. To continue with our example, some of the junior, higher-risk tranches of CMLTI 2006-NC2 were bought by Kleros III, effectively a joint venture between the big Swiss bank UBS, which underwrote the venture by buying the tranches and selling them to Kleros III, and a specialist CDO management firm, which structured the deal. Kleros III bought about $1 billion worth of mortgage-backed securities in all, of which 16 percent, including just under $10 million of the A-rated mezzanine tranche of CMLTI 2006-NC2, were rated A, 39 percent above A and 45 percent below A. But because the underlying mortgages now came from across the USA and the ratings analysts' models assumed that mortgage failures in different regions would be uncorrelated, no fewer than 88 percent by value of the securities issued by Kleros III, based on mortgages that fell within the bottom 10 percent of the original subprime pool, were rated AAA. And of those that were not, at least half were purchased by other CDOs, to be pooled and tranched yet again.

As the junior tranches were sold from CDO to CDO, keeping track of the underlying securities proved difficult, but at least there were underlying securities. For the finance guys, this was an unnecessary and inconvenient constraint. Enter the CDS, a form of derivative used to hedge against the risk of a borrower defaulting on a loan. As the volume of mortgage-related CDOs grew, the banks that put them together increasingly kept much of the senior tranches for themselves. This was mainly because, in the fervour of the mid-2000s, they were less easy to sell at a worthwhile margin than the higher-risk but higher-interest mezzanine tranches. Because they were seen as ultra-safe, however, the banks were happy to keep hold of them, the cost of doing so being worth it for the fees they generated from selling the mezzanine tranches. To hedge these investments and to prevent them from impacting on their required capital ratios, they purchased CDSs, mainly from a financial products subsidiary of the giant insurance company American Insurance Group (AIG). Effectively, for a small premium, they insured themselves against the risk of defaults on the underlying mortgages.

One of the truisms of finance is that anything that can be used for hedging can also be used for speculation, and the investment bankers soon realized two things. First, unlike a real insurance contract, a CDS doesn't require ownership of any underlying property. A CDS involves somebody paying a premium and receiving a payout if a specified loan defaults, but that somebody need have no relationship with the loan in question, and many people can take out CDSs on the same loan. Second, once you have a market for CDSs, they can be used to construct new securities with all the properties of a CDO, but without actually needing to buy the underlying mortgages, which by the mid-2000s were in short supply: though lenders were furiously creating new ones, lending to anyone they could regardless of ability to repay, they were limited by the number of homes in the USA. In a synthetic CDO, investors effectively buy and sell revenue streams and risks modeled on those that *would* be associated with a specified pool of mortgages, but without anyone concerned having to own the mortgages: just a sophisticated form of betting on the returns from the mortgage pool. Going back to CMLTI 2006-NC2, for example, one of the lower-grade mezzanine tranches, valued at about $12 million, became a reference security for four times that value of synthetic CDOs, parts of the performance of which were modeled on its performance.

Like ordinary CDOs, synthetic CDOs have a number of tranches with different risk-return properties, and these are defined so as to mimic the performance of a notional pool of real mortgage-backed securities. But since these reference securities are not owned, the synthetic CDO has a rather different structure, with three parties to the deal:[4]

- "Funded" investors buy the equity and mezzanine tranches of the deal, paying the CDO vehicle the capital and receiving the stream of payments they would have paid and received in respect of the reference securities if

---

[4] For a specific example, see Box 8.4.

they had been owned. They also take liability for any losses they would have made on the reference securities in a real CDO, typically achieved by their selling CDSs on these securities to the CDO vehicle.

- "Unfunded" investors take the part of the buyers of the senior tranches of a regular CDO, but since there are no underlying securities, there is no need for them to put money up-front (hence the term "unfunded"). Instead, they receive premiums from the CDO vehicle modeled on the difference between the interest they would have earned from the reference securities in a real CDO and the interest they would have had to pay on a loan to buy them. They also take liability, just as the senior tranche holders would in a real CDO, for any losses that would have been made on the reference securities beyond those covered by the mezzanine tranche holders.
- "Short" investors buy CDSs on the reference securities from the CDO vehicle, the premiums received effectively paying for the CDSs it buys from the funded investors and for the premiums it pays to the unfunded investors.

The end result is that if the assets perform, the funded and unfunded investors get the same returns as from a real CDO, with the short investors paying the bill. If they fail, then the funded investors initially, and the unfunded investors if things go really badly, are liable, just as in a real CDO, with the payments going to the short investors. Either way, the sponsoring investment bank and CDO managers get a good fee. Unlike the supply of real CDOs, the supply of synthetic CDOs was effectively unlimited, and by 2006–7 they were dominating the CDO market.

The players

The central characters in the boom in mortgage-backed securities were the banks, and especially the investment banks, which led the securitization process. We shall come to them in the next section. There were other characters too, however, some of whom need to be introduced.

The investors

There would have been no boom in mortgage-backed securities if there had not been a demand for them. As always happens when interest rates are low, investors, in this period mainly from China and the oil-producing countries, were looking for ways to earn a higher rate of return at a relatively low risk. Since risk and return are generally correlated, this often ends in tears, but that doesn't stop people hoping. There was a lot of money out there looking for an AAA-rated investment home. The returns on government bonds were relatively unattractive and with the economy going nowhere, there was a limited supply of safe corporate bonds, driving down returns there too. Mortgage-backed securities and CDOs seemed to provide an answer, and investors couldn't get enough of them. Some of the tranches in many issues might be presold several months before the securitization process was completed. For the issuing banks, the business looked extremely profitable and they competed aggressively for it.

Of course, it was not only overseas investors who were looking for low-risk, high-return investments. Asset managers generally, remunerated on the basis of their relative performance against standard benchmarks, were strongly incentivized to earn a few extra basis points on their portfolios, and once people began to pile into the market, they didn't feel they could afford to be left out.

The originators and their agents

At the other end of the chain were the mortgage originators. Traditionally these had been thrifts, operating within the low-risk culture of a mutual organization and lending only with great care. Indeed, it was often argued that they made it too difficult for people to get a mortgage. And even though American thrifts might sell on some of their mortgages to Fannie Mae and Freddie Mac for securitization, these had to be "conforming" mortgages, subject to regulated standards of underwriting. By the 2000s, however, the vast majority of American mortgages were not being originated to hold but specifically to feed the demand for mortgage-backed securities. They were mostly originated by mortgage brokers, who were largely unregulated and who acted on behalf of the banks and investment banks that would buy, securitize and sell them on. Since the brokers were on fees and yield spread bonuses that rewarded them for higher interest charges to the homeowner, there was a strong incentive to originate subprime mortgages. And since demand from the banks was seemingly insatiable, there was every incentive to chase volume and none at all to worry about quality.

In the case of the mortgages making up CMLTI 2006-NC2, discussed above, 77 percent were broker-originated, and on half of these brokers received yield spread premiums in addition to basic fees. The average fee across all the broker-originated mortgages in this sample was about 2.4 percent of the total loan. A majority of the CMLTI 2006-NC2 mortgages were adjustable-rate teaser mortgages, the interest on which would rise significantly after the first two or three years. Nearly half (42 percent) were no-doc mortgages. And while a majority were secured by first mortgages on the property, a third of these came with associated piggy-back mortgages. A third of the mortgages were for 95 percent or more of a property's assessed value.

The regulators

In this environment, malpractice was inevitable. Indeed, it had already become a source of widespread concern in the 1990s, though with both deregulation and the expansion of home ownership being key elements of government policy, neither the government nor its agencies ever got around to doing anything about it. The scope for fraud was greatly increased by the growth of no-doc mortgages and by the 2000s it was apparent that it had reached epidemic proportions. One estimate suggested that 1.5 million loan applications annually contained some element of fraud. Another put the level much higher and suggested that 13 percent of new mortgage applications in the middle of the decade contained lies or significant omissions. By 2008, Fannie Mae was rejecting over $0.5 billion a year of mortgages sold to it by originators and securitizers as fraudulent. Steaming along on a gravy train, however, and passing their liabilities on to others, the originators no longer had any reason to closely monitor for fraud and failed to report it when they found it. The FBI, meanwhile, obsessed after 9/11 with the threat of terrorism, was understandably reluctant to devote resources to the problem.

In addition to fraudsters falsifying loan applications or preying on ignorant and vulnerable homeowners, mortgage brokers were also selling people more expensive loans than their records entitled them to, and many home loans were going to people who simply could not afford them and who had little idea what long-term obligations they were taking on. There was also ample evidence of appraisers, who assessed the value of the homes on which money was being lent, being pressured to inflate their valuations if they wished to retain the banks' custom. Here too, though, government and regulators were reluctant to act. Some states, especially those in which house prices were escalating faster than the average and where malpractice was all too evident, were keen to intervene. But in the interests of regulatory uniformity, the federal banking and thrift regulators explicitly exempted the firms they regulated from state regulation.

The general view of the regulators, here as elsewhere (in respect of capital requirements, for example), was that the banks were taking the risks and that their own risk management systems should be able to deal with them. In 2005 the Federal Reserve and the Office of the Comptroller of the Currency (OCC), the main US bank regulators, did issue draft guidelines for banks, urging them to treat subprime mortgages with caution, but the banks strongly objected to any new constraints and the Office of Thrift Supervision (OTS) backed the banks, arguing that they would discriminate against the banks, which were in competition with stand-alone mortgage lenders. Guidelines were eventually issued, but they were only guidelines and the most visible consequence was that Countrywide, one of the largest and most aggressive mortgage originators, switched its regulators from the Fed and the OCC to the more benign environment of the OTS.

The ratings agencies

As is clear from the examples given above, the ratings agencies were also key players. The new securities would only sell if they came with invest- ment grade ratings, and when banks kept senior tranches on their own books, which as we shall see they often did, they needed them to have AAA ratings if they were not to cost too much to protect, through CDSs, or not to impact too severely, through their VaR modeling, on their capital ratios. For the agencies themselves, this was a massive source of new business. Since they relied heavily on modeling rather than on deep sector knowledge, it was business they could get without much expenditure on staffing. And since the banks badly needed the ratings to come out right, and the business afforded high margins, they could make sure that the agencies were well rewarded.

To take one example, by 2006 Moody's was earning $887 million a year, nearly half its total turnover, from rating structured products such as asset-backed securities, CDOs and synthetic CDOs. Rating synthetic CDOs and so-called CDO^2s, built from tranches of other CDOs, was especially easy as they just referred back to their original CDO ratings, not to the underlying mortgages. These in turn had been based on the assumption that default risks on mortgages in different US states were uncorrelated, an assumption that made it quite easy to generate an AAA rating. When it modified its model in 2005, it based its revised ratings on the record of overall mortgage default over a twenty-year period, a period in which house prices were steadily rising, defaults were low and subprime mortgages were rare.

Of course, the ratings turned out to be wildly optimistic, and one area of contention is to what extent this was a product of circumstance – sensible ratings falling foul of extreme conditions – and to what extent it was the result of a flawed ratings system. On the one hand, the assessments, valuations and statistical assumptions underlying them were widely shared. On the other hand, there was already ample evidence of a problem. As John Lanchester points out in his popular treatment of the crisis, *Whoops!*,[5] standard economic risk assessment of the kind that was used throughout the crisis, and is still being used today, placed the stock market crash of 1987 as a 10-Sigma event, i.e., lying outside ten standard deviations of a normal distribution, which would have been unlikely had the markets operated for a billion times the life of the universe. The 1998 Russian bond default was rated a 7-Sigma event (once every three billion years). And there had been numerous cases in recent decades of 5, 6 or 7-Sigma events (all expected less than once in 14,000 years). At the peak of the crisis, 25-Sigma events (and we are now way, way beyond the number of particles in the universe) were almost daily occurrences. Any rational person, faced with these calculations, should reckon that something is wrong with the way they are being calculated.

The analysts who consistently gave bunches of subprime mortgages AAA ratings, as secure as government debt, were certainly rational people. But they knew full well that if they didn't give AAA ratings, they wouldn't get the business. And they also knew that the models they were using were standard models, that the analysts in rival firms would come to the same view and that by going with the flow and taking the fees, they were unlikely to come in for any criticism. Given their balance of incentives and the

---

[5] Lanchester 2010.

culture of the industry in which they worked, it would have been personally riskier to say "no, those should not be AAA rated" than it was to do what they did.

The insurer

Another key player was the main provider of CDSs, the large multiple insurer AIG. The world's largest insurer by market capitalization and one of only a handful of corporations with its own AAA rating, AIG used this rating to access cheap funds that it could then invest in more profitable businesses than its core insurance. In the late 1990s, it had launched a finance subsidiary, AIG Financial Products (AIGFP), that quickly became a major dealer in derivatives and dominated the market in CDSs, which banks bought initially to hedge their loan risks and so reduce their capital requirements. Like most of the other players in this game, AIGFP managers were heavily incentivized to make new sales. The bonus pool amounted to 30 percent of new earnings and the CEO reportedly earned over $200 million in five years.

In 2005, AIG lost its AAA rating after it was charged with manipulating earnings. The same year, some of its executives also realized belatedly that it was over-exposed, as some 80 percent of the mortgages it was insuring were subprime. But it kept writing CDSs. Indeed, it greatly increased its exposure before it eventually withdrew from writing new business and it saw no need to hedge its own risks by re-insuring. CDSs contributed to the market in mortgage-backed securities in three ways. First, for the few months between mortgage origination and securitization, when the banks carried the loans on their own books, they might buy CDSs to hedge against any losses, mainly to preserve their capital ratios. Second, when banks kept senior tranches of mortgage-backed securities and CDOs on their books in the longer term, they might similarly use CDOs as a hedge. Third, as the CDS market grew, hedge funds and other speculators with no assets at risk began to buy CDSs as a way of betting against the mortgage market. As a particular example, Goldman Sachs, which appears to have been AIGFP's largest customer, took out CDSs on the securities referenced by its synthetic CDOs. This mimicked the action it would have taken on a comparable real CDO had it held the bulk of the underlying assets, but since there were no real assets involved, it was effectively a form of speculation.

The banks

At the center of all this were the banks. They issued the securities, they paid the ratings agencies, they lobbied the politicians to minimize the impact of regulation and they either worked directly with the mortgage brokers or with corporate originators, like New Century, providing them with the funding facilities to bridge the gap between mortgage origination (when the money had to be paid to the borrower) and securitization (when it was received from an investor). They also increasingly failed to undertake any due diligence of their own on the mortgages they bought up for securitization: on one estimate, only 54 percent of loans met standard due diligence guidelines, but 83 percent were accepted for securitization and those that were rejected were just shuttled along to the next pool. Since any checking that was done was through sampling, there was a good chance they would find their way into the system eventually.

Banks were also increasingly buyers and holders of CDOs, as well as of the underlying mortgages. With a time lag between the purchase of mortgages and the sale of CDO securities, they naturally held inventories of mortgage loans, and since these paid high levels of interest, it was tempting to over-stock and hold on to them. By 2006, many banks were also holding on to significant proportions of the senior or super-senior tranches of their own CDOs, either on their balance sheets or, in the case of the more aggressive banks, in off-balance-sheet structured investment vehicles (SIVs). By 2007, 80–90 percent of mezzanine tranches were also being bought for repackaging in new CDOs, as banks and CDO managers looked to maintain and grow their fee income.

The reason why banks were holding on to super-senior CDO tranches was that while there was strong demand for the high-interest mezzanine tranches (albeit increasingly from other CDOs), there was now little demand for the senior tranches – or at least there was little demand at a price that made them profitable. The choice was to sell them and reduce the value of the deal (and with it the fees and bonuses earned) or to maintain the valuation but hold on to them. Since they were AAA-rated, the impact on banks' capital requirements was minimal, so holding was a realistic option and it was naturally the option favored by the managers concerned.

Finally, one of the most critical roles played by the banks was the short-term funding of asset positions.

The money flows: funding, leverage, ratings and liquidity

Almost every aspect of the system we have described was critically dependent upon short-term funding. Mortgage originators needed to fund the gap between when they lent money to homeowners and when they sold the mortgages on. Securitizers similarly needed to fund the gap between buying mortgages and selling mortgage-backed securities, between buying mortgage-backed securities or CDO tranches and selling new CDOs. When banks held on to CDO tranches, they needed funds to pay for them.

In one sense, there was nothing special about these funding requirements. The long-term assets and liabilities of banks and other financial companies are never perfectly balanced, and they are always borrowing and lending on a short-term basis. The terms of that borrowing and lending, however, depend critically on the perceived safety and liquidity of underlying securities.

The mortgage securitization and CDO business was funded predominantly through two kinds of instruments: asset-backed commercial paper and repos. Asset-backed commercial paper consists of short-term (between one day and about six months maturity) bonds issued by a borrower with securities as collateral. With repos, the securities actually change hands: the borrower legally sells the securities to the lender with a commitment to buy them back at a specified future date. Repos are typically of very short duration – a day or a week – but are regularly rolled over, the effect being to allow the lender to terminate the loan at short notice. An open repo allows the lender to terminate at any time. In many cases, repos were arranged through third parties, typically large commercial banks, which held ownership of the securities and maintained a market between buyers and sellers. When first introduced, repos were typically backed by government bonds, but they were quickly extended to other AAA securities.

With both asset-backed commercial paper and repos, the perceived quality of the underlying securities is critical. The more highly rated and the more liquid the securities, the lower the cost of the effective loan will be, and the longer the duration over which it can be held. Should the securities fall in value, however, or become illiquid, lenders will demand greater security, charge higher rates or decline to roll over the loan at all. In the case of mortgage-backed securities and especially CDOs, both were possibilities. Most of the securities in the market had been AAA-rated, but if that rating were to drop, the holders of the securities would have to either sell them – which relied on a liquid market – or pay higher charges and quite likely post additional security, most likely in the form of government bonds or other safe and liquid assets. For mortgage originators, this might not be possible, and even in the case of the banks, it would impact on their leverage ratios, already at the limits of what the regulations permitted. At this point the reputation and perceived safety of the borrower, already a factor in the terms available, becomes critical to the continuation of the lending facility. While repo lenders own the collateral and will often own collateral to a higher value than the loan, the last thing they want is the hassle of disposing of it, so by and large they will only lend when they are confident that the borrower will be able to repay when required.

Apart from its dependence on ratings, valuation was also a more general problem, especially, as we have already noted, in the case of securities retained by the issuer. Both accounting standards and Securities and Exchange Commission (SEC) regulations required that these be valued on a mark-to-market basis, but where they were not being traded, so there was no actual market, this could only be done by theoretical modeling. Since the values fed straight into managers' bonuses, the temptation was to use the modeling to push them upwards, but continued funding depended on lenders being convinced of those valuations. In September 2006, the Financial Accounting Standards Board announced a clarification of the mark-to-market rules (FAS 157), which required expanded disclosure both of the nature of assets held and of the sources of information used to value them. It also stated explicitly something that was already implicit, namely that any changes in credit risk should be reflected in valuations. In the course of 2007, lenders began asking their borrowers for disclosure of valuations based on the new standards.

We have already noted the degree to which banks and mortgage originators were leveraged, the dependence of their capital ratios on value at risk models, and their tendency to stretch their leverage to the limit enabled by these. One consequence of this was that any change in the ratings or perceived liquidity of assets held had immediate knock-on effects, not only on loans held against those securities but also on their capital requirements. Perceptions of their capital adequacy and liquidity also fed into their costs of borrowing generally, and into the margins and collateral called for by counterparties in leveraged transactions, such as derivatives trading. And these in turn impacted on their value at risk. Some of the banks' balance sheets, in short, were highly complex and finely tuned instruments, which were extremely vulnerable to disruption.

The collapse

The house price bubble peaked, in the USA and elsewhere, around 2006, and by this time the risks of the system that had been created were already becoming apparent to some. As early as 2005, one of the USA's largest CDO managers had pulled out of the business, publicly citing the deterioration in the credit quality of the mortgages coming into the market. By 2006, hedge funds were beginning to short the market or to enter into complex deals, buying some of the more secure CDO tranches while simultaneously shorting less secure tranches. Throughout the sector, individuals were alerting senior managers and regulators to rampant mortgage fraud, inadequate due diligence and growing risks. But the CDO machine – increasingly a synthetic CDO machine – kept going. The largest generator of synthetic CDOs, Goldman Sachs, was now effectively taking a short position across the mortgage market, but it continued to issue new products. Many of the banks and investment banks were now rushing to offload the lowest grades of their inventory, but they were still building up their AAA-rated inventories. Increasingly, moreover, the riskier tranches were finding their way, through CDOs bought by asset managers, into investment portfolios around the world.

In 2007, as the US housing market continued its correction, delinquencies on subprime mortgages (defaults or multiple missed payments by the borrower) began to soar. By this stage, the values of subprime securities could be approximately tracked through the ABX index, a series of standardized CDSs with open market prices. The index of CDS prices on BBB-rated tranches was already showing significant falls and the ratings agencies responded by starting to downgrade subprime mortgage-based assets, beginning with the mezzanine tiers. This immediately impacted on the valuation of these assets, and while the senior tranches at this stage retained their AAA ratings, market expectations were also pushing valuations of these down, triggering collateral calls from lenders.

An early high-profile victim of the fall in values, which gives some indication of how the system worked, was Bear Stearns Asset Management (BSAM). A subsidiary of the Bear Stearns investment bank, this operated two hedge funds that held highly leveraged investments in mezzanine CDO tranches. As values fell, BSAM managed to offload some of its CDOs as senior tranches of a CDO^2, which it sold to money market mutual funds as short-term commercial paper: in effect, it used them as security for borrowing. As for the remaining holdings, which were soon dropping quickly in value, BSAM was not only saddled with unsellable assets but also relied on them as collateral for the repo lending through which the hedge funds were leveraged. As their values were marked down by the repo lenders, the demands for additional collateral, and then for cash repayment, rose. At the same time, hedge fund investors began to redeem their holdings, also demanding cash repayment. Eventually Bear Stearns was forced to buy out the repo lenders in respect of the less risky hedge fund (labeled "High Grade") for $1.6 billion. It let the other fund go bankrupt. Meanwhile, the sale of commercial paper had only been achieved with the help of "liquidity puts" bought from Bank of America, which effectively underwrote (at a cost) the BSAM commitment to the lenders. When the holders of the paper refused to roll over their loans and BSAM could not repay them, Bank of America picked up a $4 billion tab.

From then on it was all downhill. In August 2007, with mortgage foreclosures and delinquencies increasing fast, Countrywide, which depended for its funding on asset-backed commercial paper, found that it could neither roll over that paper nor access any repo funding. Nor could it find sellers for its mortgage-backed securities. Forced to draw on emergency lines of credit, its rating and share price collapsed. Depositors literally queued up to withdraw funds. Within months, it had effectively collapsed and been taken over by Bank of America. At about the same time, across the Atlantic in the UK, Northern Rock, which had pursued a similar strategy to US mortgage lenders, came to a very similar end and was taken into government ownership.

With the markets now in blind panic, both the asset-backed commercial paper and the repo markets began to seize up, with lenders increasingly prepared to commit only on a very short-term basis if at all, and only to the highest-quality borrowers. This effectively removed the funding lines from the various SIVs that held senior CDO tranches retained by the securitizing banks, meaning that these had to be taken back onto the main bank balance sheets, weakening their financial positions and causing knock-on effects throughout the sector. As values continued to move downwards, increasingly affecting the senior AAA-rated tranches, many of the banks also had to take significant losses on their mortgage-related assets, compounding the problem. In October 2007 Merrill Lynch recorded what was then seen as a staggering $7.9 billion loss, mainly on CDOs, and reported a continuing CDO exposure of over $15 billion (in fact a net exposure: its gross CDO assets were more like $55 billion). A few days later, Citigroup reported a total subprime exposure, including liquidity puts, of $55 billion. AIG, meanwhile, had disclosed a CDS subprime exposure of $79 billion. In both of the last two cases, alarmingly, senior management stated that they had been unaware that exposure had reached these levels.

In March 2008 Bear Stearns collapsed. It was taken over by JP Morgan Chase in a deal negotiated by the Fed, but to make it happen, even at a rock-bottom price, the Fed had to take over $30 billion of its liabilities. For its size, Bear Stearns had been a very big player in the mortgage-related market, and the most obviously vulnerable. As securities values dropped, it had come under pressure from all sides. Counterparties had increased their margin and collateral requirements. Clients shifted their business elsewhere. The repo lenders on whom it depended for day-to-day working funds (over $100 billion by early 2008) and the clearing banks that mediated the repos, and effectively took the intra-day risk, had shortened their loan periods and increased collateral requirements. Though it tried to sell off assets, it was stuck in a vicious circle and eventually the repo lenders pulled the plug, leaving it without any cash at all.

Though the other investment banks were not so reliant on repos as Bear Stearns, all except Goldman Sachs had significant reliance on overnight or open repos, which could be called in at any time. Following the collapse of Bear Stearns, they were also in a goldfish bowl, under intense scrutiny. By this stage, the regulators were at last getting actively involved. The Fed introduced a program to lend government bonds and subsequently cash to the investment banks in exchange for AAA-rated mortgage-related securities, so that they would have a supply of high-quality collateral, and it also provided emergency lending to Fannie Mae and Freddie Mac. Meanwhile, the Fed and the SEC stress-tested the investment banks for both solvency and liquidity, and concluded that both Merrill Lynch and Lehman Brothers were short of liquidity. The Fed and the OCC also undertook reviews of Fannie Mae and Freddie Mac, and found that they were virtually insolvent. Both had been buying and guaranteeing ever-riskier loan products, and in search of volume had been charging guarantee fees below what even their own risk assessments suggested.

In early September, Fannie Mae and Freddie Mac, with $5.5 trillion of assets between them, were taken into government administration. The crisis then accelerated. CDS prices on Lehman's debt had suggested since the spring that the market thought it likely to fail, and while it was still reporting confidently on its position at the end of August (and claimed to have passed its own liquidity stress tests), no-one believed in its underlying asset valuations. Estimates of the degree to which its assets were over-stated ranged from $20 billion to $70 billion as against reported capital of just $28 billion. Lehman had actually raised both capital and liquidity over the previous months, but as with Bear Stearns it was under pressure on all fronts. Over the summer, its repo facilities were steadily withdrawn and by mid-September the firm was bankrupt.

This time, after much discussion, the Fed decided not to come to the rescue. Over a long period of time it had consistently bailed out any bank getting into trouble. With its interventions to save Countrywide and Bear Stearns, the expectation had been established that it would always step in when needed, and it had become increasingly worried that with this expectation the banks would not put their own houses in order. In this case it tried to facilitate a takeover by one of the large commercial banks, but pointedly refused to give any guarantees. A buyer would have to take on all the (unknown) risk and no bank was prepared to do that. On Sunday September 14, with JP Morgan having announced that it would not provide intra-day repo funding for the next day, Lehman filed for bankruptcy. On Monday September 15, Bank of America, which had been touted as a possible buyer, instead took over the other at-risk investment bank, Merrill Lynch.

Meanwhile, AIG, which had not only failed to cover its rapidly growing CDS liabilities but had also invested heavily in – and lost heavily on – mortgage-related assets, was also going under. By September 12, calls for collateral from its CDS counterparties had reached $23.4 billion, an amount that while impossibly large was dwarfed by its potential liabilities. It had $4.6 billion of commercial paper due or coming due that it could not place. The lenders of its $9.7 billion in mainly overnight repos were beginning to panic. And the ratings agencies were warning of an imminent downgrade in its credit rating, which would spark an estimated $10 billion of additional collateral calls. As the weekend arrived, the firm thought it had perhaps a week's worth of liquidity left. By Monday, when the downgrades were announced, it was clear that this was an over-estimate. By Tuesday, the Fed had agreed an $85 billion government loan, which was later to grow to over $180 billion. Not only was AIG way too big (and too interconnected) to fail, its main creditors were all American banks and investment banks, which also had to be protected. These were now paid in full using government funds.

By the end of the week, the crisis had hit the big British banks, with HBOS having to be rescued, with government encouragement, by Lloyds TSB. A week later, the giant thrift and mortgage originator Washington Mutual (WaMu) was seized by the government and put into receivership, its banking operations being sold to JP Morgan Chase. By the end of the month, Wachovia, a large commercial bank but one that, like Countrywide and WaMu, was heavily exposed to option ARMs, had also gone under, being absorbed by another of the giant banks, Wells Fargo. The European Fortis bank and the British Bradford & Bingley had also been taken into government ownership. Early October saw the collapse of the Icelandic banks and government rescues through large equity stakes of the largest British banks, RBS (owner of NatWest) and Lloyds and HBOS (still in the process of merging).

With no-one quite sure where mortgage-related liabilities might be lurking, the crisis continued. With repo lending drying up almost completely and the derivatives markets grinding to a halt, the fundamentally sound investment banks Morgan Stanley and even Goldman Sachs came under pressure and switched their status to bank holding companies. This brought them under Federal Reserve regulation, but also gave them access to Fed funds, without which Morgan Stanley would have come close to a forced sale. By November, the giant Citigroup was also in danger of imminent collapse. Not for the first time in recent decades, it survived only thanks to large-scale government assistance.

After-effects

In the years immediately following the crisis, the banking system stabilized, though it remained heavily indebted to the public purse and in some cases under state ownership. The banks scaled down their most risky activities, shed some of their staff and reduced bonuses. On the whole, though, while shareholders lost out, the banks and their staff emerged relatively unscathed. Senior managers mainly remained in post and even when they didn't, they had accumulated earnings and pension rights that left them extremely well off.

The general population did less well. As the banks, trying to rebuild their balance sheets, cut back on spending and confidence plummeted, both household spending and business investment fell. What had started as a financial sector crisis soon turned into a severe economic recession, which in turn exposed the extent to which many national governments had followed homeowners and banks into excessive debt – even before borrowing more to rescue their banking sectors. As unemployment and associated welfare costs increased and tax revenues declined, government debt levels in many countries, even with continuing low interest rates, became unsustainable, resulting in budget cuts and austerity. This was enough of a problem in large economies like France, Germany, the UK and the USA, with strong credit ratings. It was much more of a problem in some of the smaller and, it turned out, more reckless economies like Ireland, Greece and Iceland. As pressures mounted, not only on these smaller countries but on much larger economies like Italy and Spain, it also turned out that many banks, including some of the large French banks that had avoided exposure to subprime securities, were heavily exposed to what were now high-risk government bonds, again through the medium of supposedly low-risk CDOs. And this put still more pressure on the French and other governments, which were effectively guaranteeing their banks' positions. Five years after the dramatic events of September 2008, the crisis was in effect still ongoing, with no sign of it coming to an end.

Some ethical questions

The history of the financial crisis is much too complicated for blame to be laid on any single party, though that hasn't stopped people trying.[6] At every turn in the story, however, ethical issues arise.

---

[6] See for example the majority conclusion and dissenting reports in Financial Crisis Inquiry Commission 2011. The more balanced attempts to allocate blame include Davies 2010 and Jickling 2009.

Consider first the aggressive and large-scale selling of home loan products to people who could not demonstrate their ability to repay and in many cases may not have understood the commitments they were entering into, on terms designed to entice them into heavy over-borrowing. Some people have blamed the government for encouraging more widespread home ownership and the home buyers themselves for irresponsible borrowing, but even granting that, there seems intuitively to be something wrong in the way that these loans were sold by the brokers and other originators. One question we can ask is: how ethical or unethical were these lending practices and why? Linked to this, we might also ask how ethical the banks were, incentivizing the originators in a way that positively encouraged unsound lending. They might try to distance themselves, but if somebody offered to pay children to collect apples and paid double for those in private gardens, would they be completely innocent of any stealing that resulted?

A slightly different kind of problem arises with the appraisers who inflated their house price valuations. We might expect salespeople to sell what they can, but appraisers are professionals, committed to independent judgments and bound by a professional code of conduct. They were also under strong pressure from the banks of course, but isn't not giving into such pressures fundamental in some way to professional ethics? We might ask much the same about the professional auditors who helped firms massage and in some cases massively misrepresent their accounts (Arthur Andersen at Enron, for example, or Ernst & Young, who signed off Lehman Brothers' massive over-statement of assets).

The ratings agencies were not professional firms and were not subject to either professional or regulatory discipline, but their ratings were depended upon across the financial sector. Does this influence carry ethical responsibilities akin to those of professionals, or does the fact that they only gave "opinions" excuse them from responsibility for the actions people base on them? (Auditors, too, give "opinions.") Was there anything wrong, in their circumstances, in giving their customers what they wanted and paid for?

The behavior of the banks raises all sorts of ethical questions. How ethical is it, for example, to knowingly manipulate a regulatory system in order to do things it was designed to prevent? Is this no more unethical than committing fouls at football, or is it more like cheating – perhaps like using a self-testing regime to take drugs in athletics? And what exactly, from an ethical perspective, is wrong with cheating?

Was there anything unethical in banks shifting their focus from protecting their depositors and shareholders to maximizing their risk and hence return? The shareholders weren't objecting; indeed, the banks could present their reorientation as delivering shareholder value, which is what companies are supposed to do. But did they also have an ethical responsibility to depositors? And is the fact that their strategies were driven by personal gain, through bonuses and stock incentives, relevant here?

We might also question the banks' selling securities to asset managers and others without having undertaken any due diligence on the underlying assets, and without understanding themselves the risks entailed – or, in the case of Goldman Sachs, selling their clients securities knowing full well the risks entailed and in the confident expectation that their clients would lose money. Is the financial sector one in which anything goes and the onus is always on the buyer to exercise caution, or does a bank product come with some sort of ethical underwriting? We might assume the latter in the case of personal finance products (though the banks' records are not particularly good there), but are there differences in a firm's duties to its clients, depending on their knowledge and sophistication, and if so how do these play out in the financial sector?

We might also ask questions of some of the other financial institutions. How ethical was it for the managers of a large insurance company, for example, to run up tens of billions of liabilities without reinsuring? Was this just a poor commercial judgment or was it negligence? And at what point does negligence become unethical? How ethical was it for asset managers to buy complex mortgage-backed securities, with no due diligence whatsoever, for the portfolios of their clients?

The case also raises some questions about regulation. How ethical was it for politicians to leave such a high-risk industry on which so much depended so lightly regulated and to let financial institutions choose for themselves which agency regulated them? How ethical was it for the regulators to let banks effectively set their own risk levels and to fail to act in the face of mounting mortgage fraud? What are the ethical responsibilities of a regulator?

Finally, there are even broader questions about the financial sector and, indeed, the financial system as a whole. Many people have criticized the extent of speculative derivatives trading, but is there anything inherently unethical in this, and if so what? Similarly with the incentive structures used by banks to pay their staff. There has been much public criticism of bankers' bonuses, but what, if anything, is ethically wrong with a firm paying its staff bonuses? The financial system too is contentious. On the one hand, it is defended both by its participants and by government politicians as a source of wealth creation. On the other hand, it has been criticized as a system that steers massive wealth towards the finance community while causing massive damage to the rest of the world. So is it good or is it bad? And how might we make that judgment?

In this book we shall attempt to address some of these questions and many more arising in other parts of the financial world. Sometimes a simple analysis will suggest answers to the questions, whereas sometimes it will just lead to a more careful phrasing of a question, or point to lines of argument that require further exploration and analysis. Before starting on the rest of the book, however, the reader is encouraged to think carefully about some of the questions raised above, forming a moral viewpoint and trying to understand where that viewpoint comes from and what principles underlie it. The purpose of this book is to help you to conduct an ethical analysis, not to provide ethical answers, and this will provide a basis on which to engage constructively with the argument.

2   Introduction

Finance and morality: a history of tension

In September 2008, the global financial system, which had been in a preca-
rious state for over a year, very nearly collapsed altogether. Government
bail-outs kept the banks going, but the repercussions included a prolonged
economic recession and a string of national debt crises in the Eurozone. As
ordinary people suffered from the ensuing unemployment, welfare cut-
backs and other austerity measures, the bankers and hedge fund managers
widely blamed for the crisis seemed to get away scot free and continued to
earn enormous salaries and bonuses. Not for the first time in history, there
is currently a widespread feeling that the financial sector as a whole is
deeply unethical and many of its practitioners are routinely pilloried by
press and public alike. Despite this concern, and despite a very well-
established tradition of writing and research in business ethics generally,
there have been remarkably few attempts to treat finance ethics dispassion-
ately, either in the research literature or in textbooks. This book is an
attempt to fill this gap.

Finance and ethics are not concepts that fit naturally together. As far as
its practitioners are concerned, finance is simply nothing to do with ethics.
You sometimes get people behaving badly, in finance as in any other field,
but that has nothing to do with finance itself, which is seen as a largely
technical, amoral field of activity in which questions of good and bad, in the
moral sense, simply don't arise. Whether you are studying finance or prac-
ticing it, ethics is not something you expect to have to think about. People
outside the field tend to take a slightly different view. They agree that
finance has little to do with ethics, but see this as a failing, either viewing
it as out-and-out immoral or, more commonly, seeing something immoral
in its very amorality.

From a moral perspective, then, finance is a bit like sex. For the vast majority of those engaged in them, both are ethically unexceptional, essential and indeed enjoyable parts of life, perfectly legal and perfectly respectable. For many outsiders, however, both are deeply suspicious. They may be necessary, but they are fraught with moral danger, should be strictly regulated and should be indulged in only so far as is necessary, in as straightforward a fashion as possible (no unusual positions, game-playing options or derivative trades). One difference is perhaps in attitudes to privacy. While sexual moralists are always suspicious of what goes on behind closed doors, they prefer, on the whole, that it should be behind closed doors. In questions of finance the desire for privacy seems to be wholly on the financiers' side, which can only heighten moral suspicion.

Moral doubts about finance are nothing new; they are as old as finance itself. Even before the advent of a monetized society, we find prohibitions on the charging of "interest" on the lending of foodstuffs from one season to the next, and in the Old Testament, usury, or lending with interest, whether the loan is of food or money, is forbidden amongst the Jews – though in dealings with foreigners it is allowed. This norm was carried through into both Christianity and Islam and ironically led to the emergence of the Jews, who were treated in both Christian and Islamic societies as "foreigners," as moneylenders. Shakespeare's Shylock, merchant of Venice, provides an exemplary illustration both of the Jew as financier and of the financier as morally repellent.[1]

Meanwhile, the first ever monetized society seems to have been that of classical Greece in the early sixth century BCE, and in the plays of Aristophanes and the philosophical writings of Plato and Aristotle, written at the height of that civilization about 200 years later, we find four ethically charged characterizations of the object of finance: money. First, money is seen as homogenizing and demoralizing, reducing all goods and all values to its own purely quantitative measure. Second, it is seen as dehumanizing, replacing thick personal relationships based on kinship and reciprocity with impersonal financial relationships of monetary exchange. Third, it is seen as desired, even though it is in itself artificial and of no value. And, fourth, both money and the desire it inflames are seen as unlimited. Whereas one can only eat or drink so much, or indeed have so much sex,

[1] Visser and MacIntosh 1998.

the appetite for money is insatiable: the more you have, the more you want.[2] An early statement of this last point is found in Aristophanes' satire *Wealth*, where two of the main characters run through a long list of all the good things in life, noting of each one that you can have too much of it, but when it comes to money, "give someone thirteen talents and he'll want sixteen. Put sixteen in his pocket and he'll yell for 40 ... and then he'll start whinging that he can't survive on that." As the god, Wealth, says: everyone claims to be virtuous, but "the moment they grab hold of me, the moment they become wealthy, that's when they become unbearably and utterly evil."[3]

For the philosophers Plato and Aristotle, goodness was associated with limits. Money, being unlimited, was morally suspect, and for Aristotle the practice of making money from money by lending at interest (the earliest form of finance), being something that was both unnatural or artificial and unlimited, was especially so.[4]

The concept of usury is complex and the moral norms associated with it have often been confused. At some times and in some societies, any lending at interest has been condemned, while in others only lending at excessive interest has been considered usurious. At some times, usury has been considered sinful, at others merely uncharitable. In some societies, a fine distinction has been drawn between the legitimate charging of interest for putting money at risk and the illegitimate charging of interest without risk, while in others any use of money to make money has been outlawed. Throughout the development of modern society, however, three things have remained unchanged. First, people have always needed to borrow. Kings have needed to borrow to make war, governments to build infra-structures, entrepreneurs to buy stock or invest in equipment, and the poor or unfortunate to get them through their misfortunes. Second, people have only been prepared to lend, local or family charity apart, at interest, and the poorer the borrower, the higher the interest. There is in reality no such thing as a risk-free loan, and the higher the risk of non-repayment, the higher the interest needed to cover that risk. Third, despite this, lending at interest and especially at high rates of interest has always been considered morally doubtful.

---

[2] Seaford 2004, Walsh and Lynch 2008.   [3] Aristophanes, *Wealth*, Lines 108–9, 196–7.
[4] See, for example, Aristotle, *Politics*, Book 1.

Nowadays, lending at interest, which was for centuries a crime in many European countries, is illegal only in Islamic societies – and even they have developed complex institutions that effectively allow such lending as a form of risk-sharing. But it still gives rise to ethical issues. As we shall see, interest rates that are thought to be excessive are still morally condemned, even when they are economically justified. And there is also a more modern concern with irresponsible lending. This is reflected, for example, in the perception that one cause of the recent financial crisis was excessive mortgage lending that lined the bankers' pockets while putting millions of homeowners at risk of default.

The moral disapproval of making money from money, first found in Aristotle, is also reflected in more modern attitudes. In the nineteenth and early twentieth-century USA, "speculation," associated mainly with speculative trading in grain and grain derivatives, became a term of moral opprobrium much like "gambling" (which is indeed what it was) or "liquor." Derivatives markets continue to be viewed with deep suspicion by those outside the finance community.

The association of finance with insatiable greed, first satirized by Aristophanes, has also endured. Another morally loaded word of the nineteenth century was "promotion," which typically referred to the selling of shares by greedy stockbrokers in speculative and risky new corporations, especially during stock market bubbles, to innocent widows and other vulnerable parties. More recent concerns have focused on the promotion of penny shares (low-price shares, typically in little-known companies) at one end of the spectrum and of junk bond issues at the other. The junk bond promotions of Michael Milken and others in the 1980s will be forever associated in the public eye with the fictional character Gordon Gekko's assertion in the movie *Wall Street* that "Greed is good." Critics will also point to the same (immoral) culture of greed amongst the Enron energy traders at the turn of the millennium, who were unhesitatingly prepared to black out California in pursuit of profit.

The financial shenanigans at Enron at the turn of the millennium brought down not only the corporation itself but also its auditors, Arthur Andersen, a firm that had long been renowned for its ethical probity. The scandals at WorldCom and Tyco, which struck around the same time, were also associated with financial misdemeanors. The decade since has seen a range of high-profile cases of insider trading, endemic mis-selling of both investments and insurance, and fraudulent product promotions. At the time of writing, in the long wake of the 2008 financial crisis, the harmful effects of economic recession are widely blamed on unethical behavior in the financial sector, from the aggressive marketing of subprime mortgages to their securitization and sale as junk products masquerading as low-risk investments.

People are particularly concerned, in this context, that while banks have had to be bailed out by taxpayers, bankers' bonuses have continued at what, to members of the public, seem quite obscene levels; that while many banks have quickly returned to profit, they seem to be paying very little in the way of taxes; that many of the leading players in the financial sector also seem to pay little or no taxes in the countries in which their profits are made; and that leading up to the crisis, the banks seem to have had no qualms about selling their customers products they knew to be worthless. There is a growing and well-founded suspicion that the gains from money invested in mutual funds and personal pension schemes go almost entirely to the fund managers and not at all to the investors or pensioners. There is anger that the speculative dealings of bankers have brought about a situation of near-zero interest rates, in which honest pensioners who have carefully saved for their retirement are deprived of their expected income while people and firms who have gone deep into debt seem to be getting off scot free. And there is anger, too, that while the recession has sent many small businesses into liquidation, most of the banks whose perceived irresponsibility set things off were deemed "too big to fail" and were helped out of their difficulties. Taking stock of the last few years, many people see one set of rules for the financial sector and another for everyone else.

In this environment, the world of finance cannot escape ethical scrutiny. But it is important that this scrutiny should be reasoned and not just take the form of emotional reactions. Finance itself, which is arguably the most logically disciplined of all the social sciences, sets high standards in this respect, which we need to follow. It is also essential that, in looking at ethics and finance, we recognize and take account of the ways in which the practice of finance is different from the social practices that mostly shape our moral views. In the rest of this chapter we shall look more closely at what distinguishes finance from the everyday moral world and excites the moral suspicion with which it is customarily viewed. We shall then run briefly through the different aspects of finance to which ethical critique can be applied and set out the plan for the book.

Finance and amorality: theory, technique, abstraction

One of the reasons why finance arouses such moral suspicion in the population at large is because it is a very different kind of activity from the "everyday" activities around which our moral norms are formed. In this respect, it is very different from sex, with which we compared it in the last section. Sex arouses some people's moral anger in part because it is concerned with things that matter a lot emotionally to them: with personal relationships, love, childbearing and so on. Homophobes object to homosexual activity because they find it repulsive, but also because homosexuals don't find it repulsive, because they don't feel the same emotions as they do. People whose sexual activities or proclivities arouse moral disgust are often portrayed as inhuman in the sense of being somehow "wrongly assembled" humans. Finance, in contrast, is seen as morally suspicious in part because it is disconnected from the emotions, because it is seen as inhuman in the sense of not being human at all.

If we ask more specifically how the domain of finance differs, in morally related ways, from the domain of everyday life, three things stand out. In the first place, finance theory, which informs and underpins contemporary finance practice, is based on a model of the world in which our usual conception of morality has no place. We shall explore this in the next section, but very briefly financial economics is built on the assumption that people are opportunistically self-seeking and will do whatever they can to maximize their monetary wealth. Critically, this assumption carries no moral connotations. If people will lie to get what they want, for example, that is from a finance perspective a simple fact of life. Finance theory is concerned with economic values. It takes no account, in any way, of moral values.

In the second place, in its preoccupation with money, finance is constantly abstracting from the everyday world of people and things. Financiers don't deal with material products, or the people who make or consume them, but only with financial interests in such products. The decisions of business executives working in the "real" economy impact directly on the physical world. The decisions of financial intermediaries, buying or selling stocks and shares, options or currency futures, are one step removed from that reality. Of course, financial firms have customers and employees whose livelihoods are affected by the firms' activities, but their primary focus is on the world of money, which is essentially artificial, a medium through which things and values are represented rather than a thing or a value in itself.

In the third place, as a highly technical activity – an activity, indeed, that is simply unintelligible to most people – finance tends to be demoralizing in at least two ways. First, it consists in the application of a set of rational "scientific" laws which are themselves without moral content. To use an engineering analogy, a decision to manufacture or deploy a missile system might have a moral side to it, but there is a sense in which the design and manufacture of the system, the engineering, is morally neutral. Similarly, whatever one may think about derivatives, the development of a computerized system for options trading is a purely technical affair. Second, immersion in the technology tends to be all-absorbing and to crowd out anything that cannot be expressed in the technological language. Finance activities are in many ways like games, played according to complex rules, and absorbed in these games the players, like the players in many games, do not typically look beyond these rules. Indeed, the abstract nature of finance accentuates this tendency. For those playing the various games involved in "running money" (the colloquial term for investment management), the fact that the money has an exchange value adds to the excitement, but doesn't necessarily change the nature of the game. The aim is simply to win within the rules and playing with tokens or with Monopoly money wouldn't fundamentally change things.

In seeking to understand the relationship between finance and morality, this last point is especially important. In the public mind, finance has always been and will always be associated with monetary greed. But if finance practitioners are greedy, it is probably for the winning at least as much as for the money.

None of these considerations necessarily rules out a moral perspective. We can ask about the purpose of financial activity and its place in a morally desirable society. We can ask about the spirit in which the game is played and the ethics of competition. And we can ask about the responsibilities of financial intermediaries to the technically less literate clients whose money they manage. But these questions all have more to do with the contextualization of the activity than with the activity itself, which remains in some sense separate, in the minds of its participants, from the moral realm of everyday living. In the following sections we shall explore this in some more detail.

Finance theory and human motivation

Finance theory is a subset of applied economics and part of the applied social sciences. Like all social sciences, it deals with the behaviors of humans, behaviors that are generally far too complicated and uncertain to be modeled accurately in the way that we might model an atom or the solar system. Planets and electrons are hard enough to predict, but they don't trip over, forget things, change their minds, fall in love, fantasize, get angry, argue and make up, and all the other things that humans do on a daily basis. In order to generate scientific predictions in such a complex world, all the social sciences have to make radically simplifying assumptions about human behavior and institutions, and finance is no exception. Financial behaviors are in fact easier to model and predict than most – at least in the aggregate, which is generally what matters. Money is, on the face of it, a simple quantity, and decisions about financial matters tend to be quite calculative and unemotional. Assumptions are still needed, however, and they are not entirely uncontroversial.

To set the assumptions of finance theory in context and illustrate the importance of assumptions generally, consider simple neoclassical economics, the theory of prices. This is the theory represented by intersecting supply and demand curves as learned by every beginning economics student. As a general approach to prices, this is both immensely powerful and intuitively compelling. If the demand for something goes up (or down) and the supply remains fixed, the price will rise (or fall) to the point at which supply and demand are balanced. The same is true of a change in supply conditions. As a general model, this is simple and attractive. If we want to make the theory rigorous, however, the assumptions it requires turn out to be quite extreme. It is, for a start, a static theory, which applies only to equilibrium states. It assumes that there are no trading costs and that all the actors involved have perfect information on everything, past, present and future, including each other's actions under any possible eventuality. Under such conditions, every conceivable possibility can be taken account of, and all transactions for all time can take the form of bilateral barters conducted now. There is actually no place for firms and no need even for money.

Much of contemporary finance theory is a product of attempts through the middle half of the twentieth century, and especially the 1960s and

1970s, to explain why firms do exist and, in the process, loosen and make more realistic the assumptions of neoclassical economics. The key elements here were the introduction of information and transaction costs.[5] But once you abandon the assumption of perfect information about what people will do, you also need a theory that will *predict* what they will do: you need, in other words, assumptions about human motivation and behavior.

We shall return to how finance theory treats the firm when we look at issues of corporate governance in Chapter 9. Essentially it treats it as a nexus of contracts between different involved parties, but for various reasons it privileges one party, the shareholders, and focuses on their particular perspective. In this section we shall concentrate on the more general assumptions about human behavior that permeate the whole of the finance discipline.

Human actors, according to finance theory, are self-seeking, opportunistic, rational and competent monetary wealth-maximizers. As self-seeking actors, they are assumed to follow only their own narrow interests, free from any constraints of duty or altruism. In principle, self-interest need not exclude altruism – I might get pleasure from helping others – but it is extremely difficult to build that into a predictive quantitative model. In practice, the assumption is always applied in the form of a very narrow and monetary self-seeking.

For the same reason, people are also assumed to act opportunistically, or without moral scruples, lying and cheating if necessary, for example, if they can get away with it, in order to maximize their financial returns.

The senses in which people are assumed to be rational vary across different theories and applications. In some contexts they are considered strictly rational calculating machines, taking account of any informational uncertainties through probabilistic calculations. In others they are considered as more boundedly rational, saving on the costs of information retrieval and calculation by copying each other or following simple rules of thumb.[6] In behavioral finance they are considered as flawed calculators who proceed

---

[5] See Milgrom and Roberts 1992. For the classic papers, see Putterman and Kroszner 1996.

[6] The concept of bounded rationality is due to Simon (1955) and was introduced to describe a situation of radical uncertainty, in which it is literally impossible for someone to know, let alone evaluate (probabilistically or otherwise), all the relevant information about a situation. In such a situation, it is rational to base decisions on imperfect

with strictly rational calculative intent, but are in practice subject to a variety of cognitive biases, such as conservatism, over-confidence in private information or forecasting ability, belief persistence, etc.[7]

As competent actors, people are assumed to be able in practice, should they choose, to specify and achieve their objectives. If they are financial traders, for example, and their interests will be served (through the bonus structure) by a particular pattern of trading, it is assumed that they will follow this pattern and execute it competently. If they are CEOs and their interests will be best served either by maximizing shareholder wealth (and being rewarded with incentive pay) or by some other strategy (which might entrench their position and future earnings, for example), it is assumed that they will not only make the appropriate choice but will also carry it out as well as it could be carried out. This assumption is rather strong, but it is necessary to ensure that the assumed motivations will flow through to outcomes.

Finally, as monetary wealth-maximizers, people's fundamental aim, the object of their self-interest, is assumed to be to obtain as much money as possible. Economists in other fields might take account of other factors, but in financial economics no other interests or desires count.

As a minimal set of assumptions from which to derive financial predictions, this is actually a very reasonable starting point, and within the world of finance it is almost completely uncontroversial. We know that the assumptions are not strictly accurate: people do have moral scruples, they do sometimes behave altruistically, they are not perfectly competent and they do value things other than money. But these are not things we can build into financial models. In many cases they are not obviously relevant to financial behaviors. And in many other cases individual deviations from the assumed norm may well average out and disappear when we look at the aggregate behavior of a large population. It is worth repeating, moreover, that within finance the assumptions carry no moral connotations. The aim is to describe how people behave when engaged in financial activities, not how they behave in their families or communities and certainly not how they *should* behave in any context.

information, even if you have no idea of what you might have left out and can put no probabilities on your forecasts.

[7] Shleifer 2000. The key underpinning of behavioral finance is provided by Kahneman and Tversky's work on cognitive bias: see Kahneman *et al.* 1982, Kahneman 2011.

For many critics of finance, however, the assumptions are nevertheless contentious, for two main reasons. First, there is concern that, in educating finance students, what starts out as an average empirical behavioral norm will come to be seen as an acceptable moral norm. If this is how people behave, it is OK to behave in this way. Research has shown that economics and business students do behave, in game-playing situations, in a more self-interested and less altruistic way than students from other disciplines. And people find this troubling.[8]

Second, there is a concern that theory may carry over into practice in another way, through policies based on finance theory. Of particular concern here is executive pay. Finance theory suggests that the most effective way to get CEOs to effectively pursue the interests of their shareholders is by tying their monetary self-interest to that of the shareholders through incentive pay. The assumption is that unless incentivized, they will pursue their own interests rather than those of the shareholders, but that this tendency can effectively be trumped by using the incentive carrot of stock options.

The problem is that the assumptions can all too easily become self-fulfilling. Dutiful stewards, who start out motivated to do a job to the best of their ability and who are arguably the most valuable kind of managers, both to the corporation and to society at large, find their "good" motivations (in moral terms) crowded out by "bad," purely mercenary ones.[9] And generous monetary incentives attract into senior management positions people who *are* motivated by the money, rather than by the sense of achievement associated with a challenging and high-profile job. More broadly, policies and regulations that accept the hypothesis of self-interested behavior, and even promote it as working, through efficient markets, to the benefit of society as a whole, inevitably devalue more traditional altruistic stances and so act to demoralize society. In recent decades the pursuit of self-interest has become socially legitimate in a way never seen before, and while this certainly cannot be blamed wholly on finance, the political pervasiveness of economic thinking and assumptions has equally certainly played its part.[10]

[8] See, for example, Frank 2004, McCabe and Trevino 1995.   [9] Frey 1997.
[10] Hendry 2004.

The nature of money

A second way in which finance differs from the world of everyday moral judgments is in its exclusive concern with money. As we have already noted, money has long been associated with insatiable greed and the absence of moral limits. Because its value is primarily an exchange value, it isn't naturally limited in the way that physical goods are, and however much we may have of it, we always seem to want more. As an exchange value, moreover, it acts as an ideal measure of achievement, a way of keeping the score. So if we're competing in a field in which money does provide a measure, even if we reach a point at which extra money really wouldn't be of much use to us, we may still want to make more, and in particular to make more than our peers or competitors, because that is what winning the game is all about. And in its abstraction from physical, social and emotional realities, finance is a kind of game.

We know, of course, that money is not a measure of everything: "Money can't buy me love," to quote the famous Beatles song. And in most fields it's not seen as an adequate measure of recognition either. Whether making love, making music or making dinner, most people, beyond a certain level of affluence, would rather have recognition than cash. Being valued is not the same as being paid, and being paid may even devalue an activity by seeming to prostitute the person. The cash earned from playing in a function band may be an economic necessity, but it's no substitute for the applause earned from playing in an art band, and musicians generally look down on function bands.[11] In the limited, abstracted world of finance, however, money *is* the measure of everything.

One danger of working in such an abstract world is that when moral issues do arise, they aren't recognized, partly because people aren't looking for them and partly because the language – in this case the language of monetary calculations – has no way of expressing them. Just as money can't buy love, or goodness, or right or wrong, it also can't easily measure or represent them in a net present value calculation.[12]

---

[11] George Simmel, in the classic treatment of this topic, used the example of mediaeval minstrels: Simmel 1990, pp. 405–7.

[12] We can try to include these things in an economic utility function and some economists argue that we should do so. See, for example, Frank 1985, Layard 2005. But it is not a natural thing to do.

More subtly, but insidiously, monetary measures also have a bias towards the short term. This is not intrinsic to the nature of money, but arises from the rapid growth in both complexity and uncertainty as timescales extend. Complexity arises as the number of possible outcomes expands. Uncertainty arises because in many important respects the future just cannot be predicted, even in probabilistic terms. We might try to predict the probability of one particular event (an earthquake, a change of political regime, a debt default, an assassination) and assess its impact on what concerns us, but the future is made up of countless such events, many of which are entirely unpredictable and which no-one has foreseen. We simply cannot mathematically model the distant future in the way that we might the present or very near future, and since we have no way of bringing it into our calculations, it stays out of them.

Strategists sometimes try to get around this by using techniques like scenario planning to generate a qualitative space of possible world futures, looking at the implications of different combinations of possible key events.[13] Finance has no comparable techniques and it tends to take into account only that which it can confidently measure and simply ignores everything else.

This is relevant to ethics because moral considerations are very often concerned with longer-term outcomes. In the Christian tradition, morality is tied to the longest-term outcomes of all: heaven and hell. More generally, an ethical view will often ask us to set aside short-term interests and look at our own well-being in the longer term, rather than at short-term gains or pleasures.

A technical practice

Closely linked with the abstraction of monetary calculations, the third characteristic of finance that separates it off from the moral world of every-day life is its technicality. Discussion of financial matters is conducted using a specialized vocabulary, even the simplest elements of which are often meaningless or mysterious to outsiders. (Most people would need a basis point explaining, never mind a repo.)[14] Even a very basic understanding of

---

[13] See, for example, Schwartz 1991.

[14] See the Glossary for these and other technical terms.

financial portfolios and the risks associated with them requires a reasonable knowledge of probability and statistics, and many issues can only be analyzed and understood using relatively advanced mathematics. Much financial trading is done using sophisticated computer programs, designed by teams of high-powered physics and math PhDs.

This kind of technicality is far from peculiar to finance, of course. Medicine, engineering and other professions are equally technical. But in all these areas, the technicality gives rise to two kinds of moral problem: it demoralizes the practice and, at the same time, it imposes moral demands on the professionals. The demoralizing effect can be understood by looking at an activity like the development of the H-bomb after the Second World War. Nuclear weapons have the power to completely and utterly destroy the world. For many people, ordinary members of the public, the development of the H-bomb was morally wrong and the scientists engaged in it were also morally wrong. For many others, worried less about the potential destruction of humanity than about the perceived imminent threat of Soviet supremacy, their development was a moral necessity and the scientists were moral heroes. But the scientists themselves were for the most part, *in their own minds*, just scientists, technicians. The use of the bomb may have been a moral issue, but they viewed their own work – conducting experiments, solving equations and so on – as morally neutral.[15]

Similar arguments can be applied to all technical areas, and working in finance may be less morally sensitive than working on the H-bomb or in Guantanamo Bay. But quite apart from the question of whether the scientists' or financiers' claims are ethically defensible, there is a risk that when moral issues do arise, they are not noticed or are treated just as technical problems like any other. The H-bomb scientists were completely engrossed in their scientific project and problems, in a culture in which solving the next set of equations or setting up the next experiment dominated their lives, to the exclusion of almost everything outside the technical realm. Finance can be engrossing too, as beating the market absorbs and obsesses a trader in the way that proving a theorem might absorb and obsess a mathematician. And this obsession can be blinding. A physician taking part in trials to assess the effects of a new drug might put the gathering of information above the health of his or her patients. A trader trying to beat the

---

[15] For an in-depth exploration of some of the issues involved here, see Mason 2006.

market by amassing better information than his or her competitors strays into using insider information. Most moral problems in finance, and in business generally, do not arise from intentionally immoral behavior; they arise when people get carried away by their search for performance, fail to think through the implications of what they are doing or fail to notice that something has gone wrong.

The moral demands on the finance profession, as on other professions, arise because of a dependence of the client on the professional. If you go to a lawyer, a doctor or an accountant, you effectively put yourself in their hands. You engage them because they have a set of professional knowledge and skills that you don't, and you trust them to exercise these on your behalf. You *have* to trust them, because you can't monitor or check or second-guess what you don't understand, but you expect in turn a duty of care on the part of the professional.

The situation when you engage a finance professional is the same, but with the complication that from the perspective of finance theory, as discussed above, it doesn't make sense. Under the behavioral assumptions of finance theory, a finance professional might well demonstrate a duty of care (in economic agency theory we would call this a bonding cost), but only insofar as doing this maximizes his or her returns: the justification would be economic, not ethical, and serving the client would be strictly subsidiary to serving self-interest. The professions, however, are one area (management, as we shall see, is another) where these assumptions need to be qualified. There is an economic trade-off. Most of the professions effectively cut a deal with society, according to which they undertake a self-regulated duty of care to their clients in return for the right to control entry to the profession (property rights, in effect) and the ability to charge some kind of monopoly fee. People go into medicine and law, as well as finance, for the money as much as anything else. But while some professionals might see things in purely economic terms, many don't, and the expectations of society at large, as well as of clients seeking advice, is essentially a moral one. In a field like medicine, the moral perspective dominates both sides of the relationship. Most doctors not only accept but are positively motivated by a moral duty to their patients. Private physicians might recommend a higher level of care than is really needed, to the financial benefit of themselves and the colleagues to whom they refer patients, but they would not knowingly risk harm to their patients. As a general rule, they not only abide by but also strongly endorse the regulations governing their profession. However, in a field like finance, which people do not typically enter to "do good," we find an asymmetry of attitudes as well as of information. Clients expect a duty of care, society expects a duty of care, but financial practitioners don't always see things quite the same way.

Ethics and finance: a philosophical approach

The ethical issues associated with finance fall roughly into two classes. There are, first, a range of issues associated with financial activity in general: its existence and legitimacy, its contribution to the well-being and ills of society, its remuneration, and its regulation and control. For many of those engaged in finance, these should not be issues at all, and become so only because of the ignorance, envy or irrationality of members of the press or public. The fact is, though, that they *are* perceived as issues and need to be carefully addressed. The very existence of finance depends, ultimately, on a kind of license to operate and, in the face of a skeptical public and the long-standing moral doubts surrounding the field, this has to be continually politically negotiated. In Chapter 4 we shall look at the moral issues surrounding capitalism and the financial system as a whole.

In the second class are a range of issues associated with particular aspects of financial activity and the ethical risks and conflicts of interest associated with them. We shall break this down for convenience into four areas, which will be covered in Chapters 5–8: lending, trading and investment, information and efficient markets, and client relationships. In Chapter 9, cutting across these two general classes of issue, and also cutting across finance and business more generally, we shall look at issues associated with corporate governance. We shall conclude in Chapter 10 with some reflections on regulatory ethics and regulatory policy.

As we have already noted, arguments about ethical issues in finance tend to get quite emotional. Critics of the system and its practices are typically outraged rather than merely critical, and those criticized tend to be outraged in turn by the accusations made. This is characteristic of all moral issues: our morals are, as we shall see, grounded in our emotions. But emotions are not always a good guide to what is ethical. The approach taken in this book will be a philosophical one, within the rational tradition of analytical philosophy. Our concern will be to apply – or more often to prepare the ground for the reader to apply – reasoned arguments on both sides of a case, with a view to reaching a balanced and rationally defensible judgment.

In doing this, we shall not get too heavily into the niceties of philosophical argument. It is often said that if you ask economists to make predictions, you will receive as many different views as you have economists, despite the rational scientific criteria being used. Much the same is true if you ask philosophers about their theories. Philosophers are in the business of dissecting each other's arguments for flaws: disagreement is their stock in trade. It is this critical approach, however, allied to a shared commitment to analytical rigor which is philosophy's great strength. In terms of rigor, the kinds of arguments we shall apply are not unlike those used in finance itself, though in other respects they will be rather different. On the one hand, they will be much simpler in structure and will make no calls on mathematics or anything but the most straightforward logic. On the other hand, they will be more attuned to the underlying assumptions, more self-consciously aware of their own limitations. Whereas in finance the priority is to get workable answers, but at the cost, sometimes, of uncritical assumptions, our priority will be to ask critical questions, at the cost, sometimes, of any clear answers.

Another important characteristic of our approach, and one that also distinguishes it from much (though by no means all) writing in finance and economics, is that whatever our commitment to rational analysis, we shall also have to engage explicitly with people's emotional responses, and with the prevailing moral norms that both express and reinforce these. An ethical analysis that ignored what people actually feel about the morality of things might be a worthwhile critical academic exercise, but would be of very limited practical use.

We shall lay the ethical foundations of the book in the next chapter. Ethical theory is conventionally divided into two parts: meta-ethics, which is concerned with the possibility and theoretical grounding of ethical judgments (what does it mean to say something is good or bad?), and normative ethics, which is concerned with the development of rational principles by which we can make ethical judgments (what things, actions, etc. are good or bad?). In applying ethical theory to any practical situation, such as in this case to finance, it is normative ethics on which we mainly draw.

3   Ethical foundations

One of the resources we shall use in this book will be arguments drawn from normative ethics. In the first half of this chapter, we shall set the project of applied normative ethics in the context of how we think generally about ethics and morals. What are we doing when we say something is good or bad, right or wrong? How much significance should we attribute to the prevailing "morality" of society, as compared to our own feelings, judgments or beliefs, or the prescriptions of normative ethics? And how can these prescriptions be related to the practical demands of everyday decision-making? In the second half of the chapter, we shall introduce the varieties of normative ethics on which we shall draw in the body of the book.

Ethics and moral practice

Normative ethics is concerned with how we ought to live and behave. It aims to develop rules, principles and guidelines, grounded in rational argument, to help us distinguish good from bad and right from wrong. Applied ethics seeks to apply these rules, principles and guidelines to specific practical problems.

Applied ethicists take the view that normative ethics is a valuable resource for addressing moral issues and one that is worth learning about. This book is motivated partly by the thought that it is a particularly valuable resource for those, such as students of finance, who are already familiar with the benefits of rational argument and are accustomed to arguing rigorously from premises to conclusions. It is evident, however, that normative ethics is not the only resource on which people draw in their practical moral thinking and is generally not the main resource. Indeed, most people know nothing about it, but they are not obviously any the less ethical in consequence. So where and how does it fit into the wider discourse of morality?

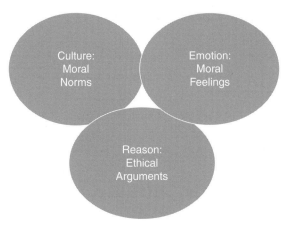

Figure 3.1   Grounds of moral judgment

The grounds of moral judgment

Suppose that I respond to some action by thinking "that action is morally wrong": what lies behind such a response? In very simple terms, we might distinguish between three possible grounds of practical moral judgment (see Figure 3.1).

First, I may think something is wrong because I feel it is wrong emotionally. I find it repugnant, or it makes me angry to see someone doing it, or I feel strong sympathy with a victim of the action. I may also feel guilty or shameful if I do it myself. If I see someone hit a child or commit an act of vandalism, it is this immediate emotional response that appears to be dominant.

Second, I may think it is wrong because it goes against the culture and norms of my society, or perhaps of a section of society with which I identify (my church, class, etc.), norms that I have consciously or unconsciously taken as my own. I may not think further than "it's wrong," but the judgment stems from norms endorsed by the traditions I have been brought up in or the authorities I respect and have learnt from. This is probably the default response in the absence of any particularly strong emotions.[1]

Third, I may think it is wrong on the basis of some kind of rational argument. I may judge it wrong because it has foreseeably bad

---

[1] For a review of the literature on how our general moral precepts are formed, see Hinde 2002.

consequences, for example, or is in conflict with criteria of fairness or equality, or seems to fall upon analysis within a particular class of actions I consider generally wrong. Note that even here, I am unlikely to refer explicitly to normative ethical theory. I will tend to rely on general rules or principles that seem to me to be self-evident, or at least uncontroversial, and my reasoning will be directed more toward the question of how a particular action is to be classified than toward any justification of the principle being used. If normative ethics is to play a part, however, this is where it will fit in.

Of course, things are not really as simple as I have described. In the first place, none of these grounds provides a straightforward or infallible guide to what is right or wrong. In the second place, they are all interdependent. It is instructive to explore these complications.

None of the ways in which we typically ground our practical moral judgments is infallible. Emotions and feelings evidently vary from person to person and they are notoriously unreliable as moral motivators. They clearly do guide our moral thinking, but they can also badly cloud our judgment. Anger can prompt us to do things we shouldn't. So can love. ("Love is blind," as the saying goes.)

Cultural norms are more consistent and may well be an adequate moral guide for most people, in most cultures, most of the time and in most circumstances. But times change, circumstances change and understanding changes, and our moral norms can be slow to adapt. In any non-primitive society at any particular time, we can readily point to established moral norms that were accepted by the vast majority but were nevertheless open to serious question. We may think, for example, of the norms relating to slave ownership in the eighteenth-century USA, to homosexuality in the twentieth-century UK or to the position of women in some twenty-first-century Islamic societies, amongst many other examples. It is also common for norms to conflict with each other. We run into situations in which we seem to have conflicting duties, for example, or have to choose the lesser of two evils.

Cultural norms also vary across social groups or institutions, raising the difficult question of which norms should prevail in a group or institution that is also part of a wider society. This is an issue in the ethics of finance and in business ethics more generally: the norms prevailing in a business corporation often seem quite different from those prevailing in the society in which it is located. Many norms become embodied in formal laws, and in some cases we can take obeying the law as a useful proxy for behaving morally, but this doesn't always work. It is evidently possible to be illegal without necessarily being immoral (low-level traffic offenses, for example), or to be immoral without being illegal (simply by being really nasty to someone).

We should also note that while emotional feelings and cultural norms generally lead us in the same direction, this is not always the case. Consider, for example, the very common case of an elderly Alzheimer's patient losing her mind, losing control of her body and wanting to die, or the less common case of an infant born with a congenital disability that will kill her within a year, during which she will experience nothing but pain. In both cases the emotions of close relatives typically lead them to want to put an end to the suffering (as we would, "out of kindness," if an animal were in a similar position), but contemporary norms and laws strongly favor the preservation of human life and so lead in the opposite direction.

The third resource, reason, is invaluable in negotiating our way through such conflicts, as well as through cultural change, but even it is contentious, as we shall see below.

Turning to the second complication, the three grounds, though very different in kind, are not independent. Our emotions are conditioned by the cultures in which we grow up (we *learn* what is disgusting or shameful) and our cultural norms are in turn conditioned by our emotions (we condemn what makes us angry). When we invoke well-internalized cultural norms, they seem to come with feelings and emotions attached. These norms and the laws that sometimes formalize them are also the products of reasoned judgments. The reasoning behind them does not always survive changing circumstances or the passage of time and accumulated critique, and it is often distorted by the interests or prejudices of those in power. But the norms would never have become established as norms in the first place if they were not in some sense reasonable, given certain widely held assumptions. When we judge that a particular cultural norm is irrational, it is generally because our underlying assumptions have changed, or because the reasons that were once used to justify it no longer carry weight or do not carry weight with us, not because there never were any reasons.

Again, reasoning on its own cannot give us answers to moral questions. Given some fundamental assumptions about, say, the nature of goodness, we can use reason to derive their consequences. But logic alone cannot give us ethical answers. Our reasoning has to start from some general principles or axioms, and these in turn have to come from somewhere.

Where that "somewhere" might be is a topic of considerable philosophic debate and contention. It has traditionally been located either in divine injunction, in human intuition or in some empirical properties of the natural world. In any scientific account of morality, however, emotions and culture tend to dominate,[2] and there is a growing consensus that ethical reasoning finds its grounding at least partly in one or both of these areas, whether in the emotions or norms of specific individuals or societies, or in those that are characteristic of nearly all humans or nearly all human societies, seen as the products of biological and cultural evolution.

As well as reaching diverse conclusions as to the grounding of ethical judgments, philosophers have also argued as to their status. When I state that "cheating is wrong," for example, it can be debated as to whether I am making a truth claim – stating my belief in a fact that could in principle be established to be objectively true or false – or merely expressing a subjective attitude or feeling: I don't like cheating and take the view that people shouldn't do it. Both these positions turn out to be difficult to defend. On the one hand, attempts to ground objective truth claims, whether in properties of the natural world, human intuition or even human evolution, run into a multitude of difficulties. On the other hand, a subjectivist view struggles to provide a sufficient grounding for the weight we attribute (or wish to attribute) to ethical statements, or for the resolution of disagreements. Indeed, it doesn't even recognize disagreements, since on a subjectivist view, if Jack says "cheating is good" and Jill says "cheating is bad," Jack and Jill are not disagreeing about whether it is good or bad as a fact, but are only approving or disapproving of it.

In their attempts to negotiate these difficulties, philosophers engaged in meta-ethics have developed a plethora of more and more sophisticated theories as to the nature of ethical judgments. For the most part, however, these impact little upon the project of normative ethics and its application. There is a widespread consensus that, however subjective ethical judgments may be, they are sufficiently objective, one way or another, to be the subject of constructive rational debate.

[2] *Ibid.*

The interdependence of the three different grounds of our moral judgments is reflected in our practical moral thinking. My response to a situation may well encompass elements of all three dimensions, and I may be hard put to determine which is dominant. In informal discussions we may also draw haphazardly on our feelings, social norms and rational arguments. In general, though, everyday public discussions of morals tend to be dominated by reference to the prevailing social norms, in the sense that the principles to which people adhere are legitimated by reference to commonly held cultural values rather than by reference to the emotions or arguments from first principles. This has certain implications, to which we shall come shortly. First, though, given the practical dominance of established social norms and the contrasting emphasis of this book on rational arguments derived from normative ethics, it will be helpful to draw out the distinction between them.

Ethics, morals and social norms

In everyday language we often use terms such as "ethics" and "morals" interchangeably. Most philosophers also slide happily between them, and when the sense is obvious, we shall do so here. Several philosophers have, however, found it useful to draw a distinction. In particular, Bernard Williams, whose work has been a major influence on contemporary normative ethics, uses the term "ethics" to refer to attempts to answer the traditional philosophical question "how should one live?" and "morality" to refer to one particular set of answers to this question, namely that which is embodied in the institutions and norms of modern Western culture.[3] I want here to make a very similar distinction, but one that is more appropriate to the study of a global practice such as finance. By "ethics" I shall generally refer to the philosophical question as to how people should live, including how they should behave to themselves *and* others, what rules or principles they should apply, etc. By "morality" I shall generally refer, given the global context of the book, to a system of norms that *actually prevails* in *any* given society, together with the socially accepted justifications of these and the attendant structures of blame, etc. So to say that an action is moral or immoral is to judge it according to the prevailing norms of a society. To say

---

[3] Williams [1985] 2006, p. 6. Note that other philosophers also distinguish between ethics and morality, but in completely different ways: there is no standard usage here.

that it is ethical or unethical is to judge it – and, at the same time, to judge those norms – on the basis of critical philosophical reasoning. This distinction reflects the ways in which everyday language does in fact distinguish morality from ethics. If we want to describe a person, an institution or a society as one whose behavior we approve of, perhaps because it differs from that prevailing elsewhere, we might call them moral but will generally use the word "ethical." However, if we want to describe a society as one in which the actual norms (whatever they are) are particularly strong or strongly enforced, we call it moralistic, and we describe someone who gives frequent or insistent voice to those social norms as moralizing or a moralizer.

In the present context, we shall come across a number of practices within finance that are widely regarded as *immoral*. Our task will be to determine whether they are also *unethical* – to judge, in effect, between those in the finance community who practice and accept them and those in society at large who condemn them. In doing this, we shall aim both to give some guidance to individual actors and also to critique and develop the social norms in play.

One feature of the norms actually prevailing in a society that is relevant to this task is that they are mainly concerned with how we treat other people rather than with how we should live more generally,[4] and this will also be our main concern here. People do criticize others for their appearance or demeanor, their private behavior, indeed, their very thoughts, and bankers and financiers come in for a fair bit of such criticism. To the collective society, however, how someone treats other people generally matters much more than whether their life is fulfilling, say, or whether they live up to their own ideals. The central issues in the ethics of finance, and the issues in which there is a broad public interest, are all to do with the ways in which the institutions, practices and behaviors of finance and financiers impact on other people.

Positive and negative injunctions

Another feature of "morality" worth noting at this stage is that it is primarily concerned with negative injunctions. Christianity, the moral norms of

---

[4] Ronald Dworkin uses this as the basis for another ethics–morality distinction, restricting morality to questions as to how we treat others: Dworkin 2000, p. 485.

which still underlie those of most Western societies, teaches us positively to love one another, but its moral emphasis has historically been on the Ten Commandments, which mainly tell us what *not* to do. The same is true of the other great religions and moral systems. Each has both positive and negative aspects: there are virtues as well as vices and commendable as well as forbidden or reprehensible behaviors. But the social norms that result are dominated by prohibitions. Even when the norms are positively expressed, the force they carry is often negative. The Judeo-Christian commandment that calls for sons and daughters to honor their parents, for example, and the traditional Chinese norms of filial piety and obedience effectively act as injunctions not to dishonor, disrespect or disobey.

This is quite understandable. Negative injunctions are typically much clearer and much easier to enforce than positive ones, and to the extent that the moral norms of a society are a means of holding it together, these are important considerations. Normative ethics, we shall find, leads to both positive and negative rules, and a positive approach to ethics has some significant advantages, especially when seeking to reconcile cultural differences.[5] But in the case of finance, as in many other areas of applied ethics, our interests lie more in what should or should not be allowable than in what might be especially praiseworthy, and we shall generally apply normative ethics to this end.

Rules and exceptions

Finally in this section, we should note that both the moral norms of a society and the ethical arguments that might support or contest these norms tend to take the form of general rules, principles or maxims, applicable across a wide range of situations. This again is quite understandable. Given the enormous range of situations that can arise in life, each with its own peculiarities, it would be quite impracticable to establish in advance how people should behave in each and every one of them. However, it has certain consequences.

An important characteristic of general rules is that they don't always give the answer we might want in particular circumstances: they may be subject

---

[5] For a good example of the use of positive ethics to overcome cultural barriers, see Appiah 2006.

to exceptions. If we consider the rule not to tell lies, for example, we might want to make an exception for "white lies." If we try to frame a more complex rule that incorporates the exceptions, however, we often get into difficulties: what qualifies as a white lie, what harms is it legitimate to avoid, under what conditions (and so on)? Once we start introducing complexities, it is hard to stop. The more practical approach is to accept the general rule as a general rule, but this still leaves us with some difficult choices. In the case of established social norms, we often find an unwritten, tacit understanding as to when general rules can legitimately be broken. People understand, without being able to frame it precisely, when a rule should be enforced and when it should not. In the same way, societies develop a tacit understanding of what is acceptable in trying to resolve questions of conflicting duties. We recognize the binds people can get into and we allow them a degree of latitude in their responses. Again, we would be unable to frame things precisely, and we would not wish to do so. The whole point is that every situation is subtly different and that any explicit prescription would fail to capture this subtlety.

Arguments from normative ethics are necessarily explicit and so much less open to such fudges. Sometimes this is precisely their strength. One of the ways we address serious moral conflicts, where different principles lead to conflicting duties, is by using normative ethics to reflect rationally upon, weigh up and refine the moral norms in play. There are indications, for example, that in the case of the elderly Alzheimer's patients referred to earlier, we are currently going through such a process, as the confusion arising from our established norms and emotional responses, affecting more and more people, becomes a social concern and questions of life and death are considered too important to fudge. But this seems in practice to be relatively rare, at least at the level of conscious, explicit reasoning. We seem to work instead, both as individuals and as societies, with relatively simple, unrefined norms, even though we know them to be imperfect.

In this context, we shall sometimes need to consider whether it is better to impose a blanket rule that generally works, even though there may be cases where it doesn't, or whether it is better to allow for exceptions. And if it is better to allow for exceptions, how should these by justified: by considering each case from first principles or by taking the general rule as the default position and placing the onus on anyone claiming an exception to justify that? The tension between general rules and specific circumstances is an issue for any kind of legal or regulatory system, including, as we shall see, for financial regulation and accounting standards where it is manifest in contemporary debates over "rule-based" versus "principle-based" regulation. It is also an issue in several kinds of normative ethics.

Normative ethics

There are many varieties of normative ethics and many versions of each variety. We shall focus here on a selection of approaches that appear to be particularly useful and relevant to our topic. *Utilitarianism* judges actions by their consequences, assessed in terms of some measure of utility. Its application typically takes the form of a kind of cost-benefit analysis, but applied to the utility function for society at large rather than to that for a particular actor. *Kantian ethics* focuses on the actions themselves and the principles that might be adopted to guide people in these actions, irrespective of their consequences. It suggests that people have an unconditional ethical duty to follow principles that are universalizable and that treat people as ends, not means. Various kinds of *contractual and consensus ethics*, mainly rooted in Kantian ideas, identify what is ethical with what people can or could reasonably agree to. *Virtue ethics* focuses on the character of the actor rather than on the actions or their consequences, and equates the ethical with what a virtuous person would do in any particular situation.[6]

In the following sections, we shall briefly introduce each of these approaches. In the final section of the chapter, we shall address the practical question of their application, looking in particular at which theory seems to work best in which circumstances.

Utilitarianism

According to *act utilitarianism*, any action that increases total utility across society is good and any action that decreases it is bad. To act ethically is to act so as to increase or, ideally, maximize total utility.[7]

---

[6] For introductions to the different approaches, see, for example, Blackburn 2003; Deigh 2010; and Shafer-Landau 2011. For authoritative online introductions to the different approaches, see Zalta ongoing.

[7] As will become apparent, I am using "utility" here in a relatively broad sense to incorporate anything we might reasonably include in a social utility function. Some

This approach is intuitively attractive, clearly capturing something important about ethics, and it seems on the face of it to offer a wonderfully simple rational procedure for resolving ethical issues. When we try to apply it, however, we run into a range of difficulties. These do not necessarily detract from its value as a theory; indeed, they bring to the fore some important ethical issues that other theories fudge or ignore. But they do make it hard to apply in many circumstances. We shall discuss these under two headings: general procedural difficulties and difficulties of definition and measurement.

From a procedural perspective, we often have neither the time nor the means to work out the consequences of our actions. Many ethical decisions have to be made more or less on the spot, when confronted with a difficult and unexpected situation – a fight, an intruder, a child in danger. It may simply not be practical to work out, even roughly, what the consequences might be before deciding what to do. It may not even be ethical. Stopping to calculate all the consequences before acting has consequences itself: the child in danger might die if you delay. And even in the absence of such consequences, stopping to calculate all the consequences before going to someone's aid is not what we normally think of as ethical behavior: in the words of Bernard Williams, it is "one thought too many."[8]

Even if we set aside the time issue, calculating the future consequences of an action may simply not be feasible. In financial economics, where all we have to calculate is the financial return on an investment, we typically assign probability distributions to the future values of key variables and estimate the expected return. But even in this context, it can be argued that we don't know, and can't know, what probabilities to use. As successive leading economists have pointed out, from Frank Knight to John Maynard Keynes to Herbert Simon, the future is *radically* uncertain, and beyond even probabilistic calculation.[9] Not only do we not know things, we don't and can't know what we don't know. In the wake of the recent financial crisis, as many writers are beginning to stress, this problem cannot be ignored.[10] When we turn from the relatively simple problem of maximizing the financial returns on an investment to the massively more complex one of

philosophers give it a much narrower meaning and would call the approach outlined here consequentialist, but not strictly utilitarian.

[8] Williams 1981a, p. 18.   [9] Keynes 1920, 1964 (1936); Knight 1921; and Simon 1997.

[10] See, for example, Skidelsky and Skidelsky 2012 and Turner 2012.

maximizing the utility of society as a whole, radical uncertainty becomes even more of a problem.

Herbert Simon's response to the combined problems of radical uncertainty and the limits of human cognition (even if we had the information, we couldn't possibly process it), in the context of business administration, was to argue that a rational manager would not attempt to calculate everything, but would "satisfice" (a combination of "satisfy" and "suffice") using simplifying assumptions and procedural algorithms to reach conclusions that were good enough to work with. Contemporary utilitarians, similarly, turn to rules and algorithms to overcome the procedural problems associated with calculation.

Indirect act utilitarians share something very similar to Simon's concerns about the limitations of human cognition and forecasting. They recognize that maximizing the utility consequences of every individual action is completely impracticable and that trying to do it is likely to be counter-productive.[11] The best way to maximize the utility of our actions, they suggest, is to critically analyze a range of typical actions; to use this analysis to develop simple guidelines as to our general behavior; and to follow those guidelines. Sometimes the individual actions that result may not be utility-maximizing, but overall this is the most effective way in practice to maximize the utility consequences of our actions.

Rule utilitarians follow a very similar approach, but instead of developing guidelines or rules on the basis of the consequences of typical actions, they focus on the consequences of the rules themselves. They seek to establish the general rules or social norms which, if followed by everyone, would maximize overall utility. The weight of analysis here falls on the rule, and the consequences of the general observance (or attempted observance) of one rule, or one set of rules, as compared with some alternative. The requirement for the individual actor is simply to follow the rules that have been established in this way.

The rules and guidelines put forward by both indirect act utilitarians and rule utilitarians tend to be quite general and straightforward. In practical terms, they need to be internalized and followed routinely, and complex rules or rules subject to many exceptions would be badly suited to this purpose. The rules also tend to correspond closely to the typical moral

---

[11] See, for example, Hare 1981.

norms of a society: "don't tell lies," "don't hurt people," "don't cheat," etc. However, a case can also be made for more controversial rules, especially on the basis of rule utilitarianism. The rules "give everything you don't actually need to the poor" at one extreme and "act according to your narrow self-interest in economic affairs" at the other, while radically different in their implications, are both plausible candidates for utility-maximizing rules.

The second set of difficulties with utilitarianism concerns definition and measurement. First, for utilitarianism to work *in practice*, there must be some broad consensus as to how utility is defined – what, in the language of economics, goes into the utility function. Is monetary wealth an adequate measure of utility or should we also (or only) take account of happiness, or pleasure, or Amartya Sen and Martha Nussbaum's notion of capabilities, which includes measures of freedom, human rights and equality?[12] If pleasure counts, will any pleasure do, or only "healthy" pleasures? Should we be looking only at the total sum of wealth, happiness or pleasure, or also at the ways in which these are distributed?

These difficulties of definition carry with them difficulties of measurement. Even if we could agree on what properties to put into the utility equation, we might not agree on how to measure and weight them. To a large extent, this is a technical issue, which complicates the application of utilitarianism but doesn't seriously undermine it. However, it highlights a more fundamental difficulty in reaching consensus on what really counts. For example, since we have, in principle at least, to reduce all factors we take account of to some common currency in order to add them up, what price do we put on a life? Is the life of a young Wall Street banker with future expected earnings of $200 million worth 20,000 times the life of a middle-aged Indian peasant with future expected earnings of $10,000, or is it worth exactly the same? More generally, are all lives of equal value or are some more valuable than others? If the question were put to them in these simple terms, most people would probably say that all lives are equal, but if we look at the policies of governments and corporations around the world, many of which are framed at least partly on utilitarian grounds, we seem to find an almost universal assumption that some lives are more valuable than others.

In many applications of utilitarianism, these difficulties of definition and measurement are not a major problem. They do not impact seriously on the

---

[12] Nussbaum 2000; Sen 1985.

philosophical arguments underlying the theory, and so long as we apply it carefully – making sure, for example, to take account of *all* those affected by a rule,[13] and to take account of the indirect effects, such as the effects of setting a good or bad example or the social effects of a particular welfare distribution – we shall often reach much the same conclusion on any plausible definition or measurement of utility. There will inevitably be cases, however, that are sensitive to the measures we adopt, and others in which the definition of utility is both critical and contentious. These are, of course, the most interesting cases to explore, but they need special care.

As a final general comment on utilitarianism, one of its most striking characteristics is that it is in one sense strictly egalitarian. Because it is concerned with the overall utility of the whole of society – indeed, the whole world – it gives no-one any intrinsic priority. Economic calculations obscure this, but if we think of utility in terms of happiness or well-being, the utility of any one individual is in principle as important as that of any other.

One consequence of this is that distant strangers, people we have never met, weigh just as heavily as people who are close to us, including ourselves. Suppose I give my mother a present on her birthday: it no doubt makes her happy, and it might make her unhappy if I didn't do it. But for the same money I could probably save the life of a child in the developing world and it is hard to construct an application of utilitarianism under which this would not be better. Similarly, it would be very hard to justify on utilitarian grounds a policy that involved paying for private healthcare or private schooling in a country like the UK when the same money could achieve far more if spent on health or education in the developing world. Indeed, it would be hard to justify not spending far more on such things generally than we do.

A recent estimate suggests that a tax of 1 percent of gross domestic product (GDP) on the wealthiest nations could double the incomes of the poorest two billion in developing countries. A simple act utilitarian

---

[13] A common student error is to focus only on those most immediately affected – for example, in assessing the ethics of a business policy to focus only on the consequences for the shareholders, employees and perhaps customers of the business without taking account of those of its competitors (which will often cancel out the former: in a competitive environment, if one firm prospers, its rivals suffer) or of the consequences for society at large (which are generally what matter most).

calculation would here argue in favor of such a taxation policy, or at the very least in favor of comparable voluntary donations. To not give a little to achieve a lot would surely be unethical. Of course, nothing is quite that simple. Even if we set aside the problems of implementation, all sorts of arguments can be made about the demotivating effects of such welfare policies, the value of individual freedom and suchlike. But here the basic calculation is so simple as to be compelling, even though most of us, when it comes to it, give our own self-interest priority over the ethical judgment.

In these respects, act utilitarianism, whether direct or indirect, is very demanding. For many of its advocates, this is one of its attractions. But its critics contend that it goes too far: there is nothing wrong, they argue, in prioritizing the interests of those close to us, or even in pursuing our own self-interest, so long as this does not actively harm other people. Rule utilitarianism is much less exposed to this criticism. One might well argue, for example, that overall utility would be maximized by rules that prioritized the well-being of one's own family, community or society, so long as they did no active harm to others.

A second consequence of egalitarianism is that act utilitarians run the risk of endorsing the maltreatment of minorities. Imagine a policy through which the welfare of the majority of a community is greatly enhanced at the cost of the persecution or abuse of a small minority. It would take some imaginative scaling of the utility attributed to different states of well-being for this not to be good on a utilitarian calculation. But even if the sacrifice of the few for the benefit of the many may arguably be right in some cases, it is surely wrong in others. As in the previous case, however, rule utilitarianism may be able to overcome the objection. A set of rules that protects the interests of minorities may well lead to greater overall utility than one that ignores them.

Kantian ethics

The eighteenth-century philosopher Immanuel Kant set out to derive ethics in the form of a "categorical imperative," or absolute demand on any human being, based only on reason and a conception of human beings as free-willed moral agents. The arguments he used are extremely difficult and not always completely convincing, but the conclusions he reached are nevertheless impressive and have remained at the heart of normative ethical debates to this day. Kant offered four different but, he claimed, equivalent formulations of the categorical imperative, two of which have been particularly influential in applied ethics.

One of these formulations is the *Formula of Universal Law*: *act only on a maxim (or personal principle) that you can also will (or rationally choose or impose) as a universal law*.

Philosophers have argued endlessly about how exactly this should be understood,[14] but it seems to capture a number of important ideas.

First, it bears some relation to the "Golden Rule," a moral norm that can be found in some form or another in most societies: treat other people as you would want them to treat you or, alternatively, don't do to others what you wouldn't want them to do to you. It is stronger than this, however, in two ways. In the first place, it is universalized. It doesn't just say "don't do to Joe what you wouldn't want Joe to do to you," but "don't do to anybody at all what you wouldn't want someone – anyone – to do to you." The particular relationship between you and Joe is explicitly taken out of the equation. In the second place, it refers to what you could *will* as a universal law, with a view to imposing it, not to what you might merely want. The criterion is meant to be objective, dependent only on reason and not on feelings, wishes or preferences.

How this works is contentious, but the core of Kant's idea is that you can only will something to be a universal law if you can will it without running into any rational contradictions. Some maxims are not universalizable because they are self-defeating (we say there is a contradiction in conception). A maxim of making promises without necessarily intending to keep them, for example, would, if universalized, deprive the practice of promise-making of any meaning. Expressing it another way, a *universalized* practice of making promises and keeping them only when it suited would defeat the purpose of the *personal* maxim of making promises and keeping them only when it suited, since no-one would take the promises seriously anyway.

Other maxims are not universalizable because they contradict the notion of humanity from which Kant starts (in Kant's terms, there is a contradiction of will). These situations are often handled more simply by the

---

[14] For an extended discussion of the various things it might mean or has been taken to mean, and how it relates to similar precepts, see Parfit 2010.

other formulation of the categorical imperative at which we shall look below, but willing as universal a maxim of harming yourself or others, for example, or of neglecting your or their development seems contrary to what human beings, as free-willed moral agents, are all about. There is a contradiction between the purpose of the personal maxim and the purpose of the human will.[15]

A second observation on the Formula of Universal Law is that while it is often applied to individual actions, it is framed, like both rule and indirect utilitarianism, in terms of general rules, principles, maxims and indeed laws. Moreover, despite the very positive phrasing, these general rules or maxims take the characteristic form of negative injunctions: they are about what is not permissible. Even a seemingly positive duty, like a duty to help others, is derived by Kant in the form of a duty not to refrain, as a principle, from helping others.

These considerations are important when it comes to application. Take, for example, the Kantian duty not to tell lies, which can be derived in the same way as the duty not to make promises without intending to keep them. Universalized lying when it suits destroys the practice of truth-telling and thwarts the very purpose of lying when it suits. Some critics argue that alternative maxims that allow for exceptions, like "tell lies when it suits you but not too often," are perfectly universalizable even though they are clearly unethical: the "not too often" would ensure that the practice of truth-telling was not destroyed. But a Kantian would respond that this last formulation is not what we mean by a general law or rule, whether in a Kantian or a utilitarian context. A rule might allow for some well-defined qualifications, but not for qualifications of the "not too often" sort. (Nor, we might say, of the "when it suits me" sort, but since they evoke a specific purpose, Kantian ethics can explicitly rule these out as leading to contradictions, in the way we have seen.)

Other critics argue that the Kantian duty not to tell lies is too strict: it makes no allowance for the exceptional cases in which it would be ethical to tell a lie. As we noted earlier, all general rules are subject to exceptions. The

---

[15] Expressing the contradictions as contradictions of purpose is potentially controversial, but it seems a fair expression of what Kant seems to have intended, and also gives the contradiction of will some force, which is difficult to achieve otherwise. See Korsgaard 1985.

way we deal with these in utilitarianism is by setting the benefits of a simple rule against the costs of it sometimes not working. The way we deal with them in Kantian applications is by invoking other ethical principles. So there is a duty not to tell lies, but there is also a duty not to hurt people and sometimes we have to choose between these. That we have to do this suggests a weakness in the Kantian logic, but we know from the sciences and social sciences that all theories are imperfect, especially when faced with the messy reality of human life, and that they can still be very useful nevertheless.

Another criticism sometimes made of the Formula of Universal Law is that it seems to prohibit maxims that seem positively good but that could not be universalized, like "give away all your money" or "stay celibate." If everyone gave away all their money, there would be no-one left to receive it, and if everyone were celibate, there would, in time, be no-one left at all. The way to avoid this difficulty is to restrict the maxims we consider, as Kant himself did, to those about what is or is not permissible. A maxim of telling lies when it suits you does not fail because of what would happen if every-body told lies all the time and nobody ever told the truth; that would dramatically change the practice of truth-telling, but would not necessarily destroy it. It fails because of what would happen if people sometimes told lies and sometimes told the truth. If people sometimes gave away all their money or stayed celibate when it suited their purposes, in contrast, there would be no contradiction. The maxim "it is not permissible to keep any of your money, for any reason" is not universalizable, but that's fine: we consider giving money away to be good for the purpose it serves, not as an end in itself. In the same way, some people's purposes are served by celi-bacy, others not.

Summing up, while indirect utilitarianism requires us to abide by rules or principles that maximize utility, the Formula of Universal Law requires us to abide by principles that can be universally imposed without contra-diction. The lists of principles that result are very similar, and very similar to the moral norms we find in most societies: don't lie, don't harm, don't steal, don't break the law and so on. But the Kantian formula gives us a different approach that we can use when utility is hard to gauge or seems to involve treating some people (because they are in a minority, for example) differ-ently from others.

The other particularly influential formulation of the categorical imperative, and the one that is probably most useful in practice, is the *Formula of
Humanity: treat humanity, whether in your own person or in any other person, always
as an end and never merely as a means.*

This formulation, which derives straight from Kant's conception of
human beings, is easier to apply, but it still needs some clarification if we
are to understand it and apply it properly. The underlying idea is that all
human beings, whoever they are and wherever they are, are individually,
each one of them, of absolute, unquantifiable value as ends in themselves.
This relates, in Kant's conception, to their being endowed with rational free
will. It also relates to the Christian idea that every human being is created by
God and created in His image (Kant's own religious background was in
Pietism, a relatively strict but very inclusive form of Lutheranism), but it can
be found equally in other religions and cultures. The injunction, then, is to
treat everybody with the deep respect that their status as human beings
deserves, to treat everyone as being infinitely valuable ends-in-themselves,
and never to let that respect lapse by treating them merely as a means to
some practical objective.[16]

The injunction does not prohibit us from treating people as means. It
does not necessarily prohibit us from employing people, or enlisting their
help, or persuading them to buy things from us, or even in certain circumstances from doing them harm. But it does prohibit us from overriding their
interests or autonomy in the process. It also requires us to place higher
interests, those relating to people's existence and growth as free-willed
moral agents, above lower ones, relating to pleasure, wealth or even happiness. To get habitually drunk, for example, would be to treat oneself merely
as a means to some instrumental objective (pleasure) and not, since it
impairs one's free will, as a proper end.

As a general ethical principle, the Formula of Humanity is unusually
positive. As with most general principles, its immediate force is negative –
don't treat people merely as means – but with that "merely," it relies heavily
on some positive conception of what is meant by treating someone as an

---

[16] In everyday language we would probably say "as a means to some practical end," but for
Kant the only things worthy of being treated as "ends" are human beings and their
goodwill. The word "end" in the formula refers specifically to a human being and not to
some general objective.

end. How much respect is enough to achieve this? Kant would say complete, infinite respect, but what that entails in practice is hard to judge. From the Kantian perspective, it is the rational intent that matters, a "good will," but it is extremely difficult to judge the intent of other people, and almost as difficult to judge our own. However, the Formula works in practice because in many cases, people's intentions are so far from ethical, in its terms, that they leave little room for debate. The argument that "my intentions are good" when people are being abused and exploited is often just not credible.

Contractualist and consensus ethics

One pragmatic way of exploring whether a principle might be universalizable would be to ask whether everybody would in fact agree to it. One way of showing respect to other people would be to consult them on one's action and take their views into account. Neither of these approaches is strictly Kantian. Kant's concern was not with whether everybody could agree to something, but with whether they could rationally will it, and if one person could rationally will it, so, on his theory, could another. His model of human interest, likewise, was quite independent of what people might think their interests to be. But the approaches lead us to a range of contractualist or consensus-based theories of ethics and political justice that are broadly Kantian in their inspiration and are particularly helpful when looking at issues of corporate or public policy.

The contractualist and consensus-based approaches we shall consider here don't go as far as basing the ethical just on what people will agree to. It's a common feature of the real world that people often don't agree, and even when they do, they're not necessarily right: they might agree because they share the same prejudices or the same delusions. Instead, the focus is on what *reasonable* people will agree to or what people will *reasonably* agree to. In Thomas Scanlon's formulation, "everyone ought to follow the principles that no-one could reasonably reject."[17] The question then is how to operationalize the notion of "reasonable." If we assume that people in practice have different interests, different viewpoints and different prejudices, and that they, and we, generally lack the Kantian detachment to

[17] Scanlon 1998, as paraphrased by Parfit 2010, p. 360.

formulate universal laws (even if that should be possible in theory), how might we overcome these difficulties?

The most influential form of contractualism is due to John Rawls, who invokes the device of a "veil of ignorance."[18] Rawls asks us to consider what conclusions would be reached by rational agents in what he calls an "original position." They know that they are members of a society but, behind the veil of ignorance, do *not* know what positions they occupy in that society. Nor do they know anything about the likelihood of their occupying different positions (they are faced with radical uncertainty in this respect) or about their own natural strengths or weaknesses.

To provide a motivational basis for people's reasoning, but also to sharpen the ethical problem, Rawls assumes for argument's sake that the agents in his original position are purely self-interested economically rational agents. He concludes, though, that under the conditions of the veil of ignorance, it would be in their rational interest to take account of the needs of every person, including the weakest and the most disadvantaged, because that just might be them. Specifically, while they might favor a system that maximized total utility, they would also impose constraints in the form of two principles of justice. Rawls's first principle of justice states that everybody should have an equal right to the most extensive basic liberties compatible with the same liberties for others. The second principle requires that any inequalities in a society should be such as to be of the greatest benefit to its least advantaged members, and that positions of advantage in a society should be equally and fairly open to everyone.

Rawls's main focus was on political justice and the purpose of his theory was to derive the basic structures of a just society. But his approach provides a useful way of looking at ethical issues, and especially of analyzing new situations in which regulatory norms and moral conventions have yet to be developed, or have developed to suit the interests of the most powerful actors rather than those of society at large. Beginning with a scenario involving and affecting a variety of people in a variety of positions, we aim to establish what moral rules or conventions would be rationally agreed to, hypothetically, by those concerned if they did not know in advance which position they occupied or which person they represented. The form of rationality assumed here is essentially instrumental, so we need to

---

[18] Rawls 1971, 2001.

assume something about their aims and objectives, but, as in some areas of economics, the conclusions may not be very sensitive to the behavioral assumptions. Because the mechanism is set up to respect the interests of others, even the assumption of narrow self-interest may lead, as in the Rawls example, to quite altruistic or other-oriented conclusions.

Other philosophers have sought to operationalize the idea of reasonable agreement by focusing on the procedural aspects of real discussions and debates. The most influential of these theories is probably the "discourse ethics" of the late twentieth-century German philosopher Jürgen Habermas, but similar lines of thought also feature in the writings of the contemporary American philosophers Amy Gutmann and Dennis Thompson on "deliberative democracy."[19] In both theories, a moral norm is valid only if all those affected could in practice agree to it. This does not necessarily mean that it serves their interests or conforms to their beliefs, but they must be able to accept that it is reasonably justifiable, at least in the circumstances and for the time being, as the result of a debate carried out according to certain rules.

To achieve this, all those affected – or, more realistically, some representatives chosen by or acceptable to them – must first of all be able to participate in discussion over the issue concerned. It is not enough to have their interests represented by an armchair philosopher, trying to work out what people would agree to under some hypothetical conditions, or by people who may not fully understand them and so not adequately represent them. Moreover, the management of this discussion must be such as to treat all contributions with full and equal respect. It is not enough to allow people to "have their say" – what they say must be taken account of and responded to. This can be challenging, especially as the very structuring of public debate and the way in which ethical problems are classified can discriminate in favor of some interests and against others (women or minorities, for example). However, this is probably not an insuperable problem.[20]

Reasonableness enters this model in the form of a requirement that all those participating in the discussion, including not only those charged with a final decision but also all those who may be affected by this decision, must

---

[19] Gutmann and Thompson 2004; Habermas 1990.   [20] See, for example, Benhabib 2003.

give reasons for their arguments, and these reasons must be both generally intelligible and generally acceptable. It is not acceptable for someone to impose a decision without giving good reasons for it, but nor can anyone affected by the decision object to it without good reason.

Finally, where deliberation fails to resolve substantial differences, the results should be treated as provisional and subject to further scrutiny. It serves no-one's interests to keep arguing continually, but respect requires that where reasonable differences or doubts persist, they should not be closed off completely.

Compared with contractualist theories, theories of deliberative or discourse ethics are more concerned with the processes by which moral norms are developed, or moral decisions made, than with the content of those norms or decisions. The purpose is, however, to reach good principles by capturing in the process a full respect for other people. Moreover, in many practical cases, process issues are a central ethical concern. This is generally the case in politics and in all those situations in which there is a significant political dimension: wherever there are different and competing interests, for example, or competing moral norms, that have somehow to be recognized and taken into account. In contemporary society, which is characterized by cultural pluralism and the erosion of tradition, this is very often the case.

Deliberative approaches are also helpful when social, economic and technological change leads to the need for new moral norms or the reconsideration of old ones. Some of the most contentious issues in contemporary morality are the product of technological developments, most obviously in medicine and the life sciences, but also in finance and business. And they are helpful for many allocation problems. Deliberative and discourse ethics suggest, for example, that major business decisions that differentially affect different stakeholders should be taken in a way that not only takes account of their possible interests but also allows them to argue for these interests, and argue for their values, in a genuine debate. There may be limits to how far this is feasible in practice, but it ties in with the common perception that while any business has at times to make hard decisions (decisions, for example, involving closure or redundancy, or decisions that set a limit on health and safety or environmental protection), it matters, ethically, *how* those decisions are made. Taking proper notice of people's arguments through a deliberative process is not just a way of building in respect but is also a demand of respect.

Virtue ethics

According to virtue ethics, what matters is the character of the actor and, by implication, the motivations of the actor, rather than the act itself or its consequences. Whereas utilitarian and Kantian ethics develop general rules to be applied to circumstances regardless of their specifics, virtue ethics works in the opposite direction. It looks at people's specific responses to specific circumstances and judges the characters these reveal. Like the other approaches, it ends up by making general rather than specific judgments, but inductively rather than deductively. For while people's characters are revealed by their actions, they are not necessarily revealed by individual actions. To judge how ethical a fictional character is, we need to read the whole novel, not just a few pages, and the same is true of real life. We normally judge the virtue of someone not on the basis of a single act, but on the basis of their overall behavior over a period of time (sometimes a whole lifetime) and in a variety of circumstances.

Unlike utilitarianism or Kantian ethics, virtue ethics typically makes no strong theoretical claims. It doesn't seek to derive the virtues from first principles, but generally accepts those that are characteristic of, and recognized within, a particular culture or community. In some versions it serves mainly to systematize or rationalize our established social norms. The first and most famous virtue ethicist, Confucius, argued that the traditional virtues of ancient Chinese society, such as the virtues of loyalty and obedience, should be tempered by the core human virtues of benevolence, justice and human-heartedness. A few generations later, the founder of Western virtue ethics, Aristotle, cast the virtues of ancient Athenian society as the temperate means between intemperate vices. Some modern virtue ethicists have developed lists of virtues that are intended to unify and systematize the various virtues found in different cultures, religions and traditions.

In other versions, virtue ethics is almost anti-theoretical. Most contemporary virtue theorists argue that what is ethical depends critically on the context and specific circumstances, and that there is a limit to how far we can usefully impose general rules on how people should act. On this view, the injunctions developed by normative ethical theories are too rigid, too insensitive to particular circumstances. They can be counterproductive when rigorously applied, constraining people's ethical development and pursuit of a good life rather than advancing it.

One consequence of the emphasis that virtue ethicists place on context and specific circumstances is that the roles people occupy in society are seen as morally significant. A particular role is associated with particular responsibilities and obligations, and so with particular combinations or particular applications of the virtues. Confucius wrote specifically of the virtues appropriate to a scholar or leader (the audience to whom his work was addressed). Aristotle wrote of those appropriate to a free (male) citizen. In contemporary society, we may look for different qualities in a child as compared with a parent, a doctor as compared with a financial trader, a policeman as compared with a chief executive. We do not, however, develop different sets of virtues for each role. Virtues are defined at the level of the wider social community, and in judging the character of the person, we always regard him or her first and foremost as a member of that community.

This is important, because the recognition in virtue ethics of the importance of roles can lead to confusion. We might say, for example, that someone is a "good business negotiator," meaning that he is cold-blooded, ruthless and able to get what he wants, and that these qualities are well suited to effective business negotiating. But that doesn't make him "good" in an ethical sense. What we have to ask is not how a businessman should behave to advance his business interests, but how a virtuous citizen should behave in a business role. If ruthless negotiating is to be justified, it has to be in terms of being a dutiful employee, or something similar, and we would also expect this dutifulness to be weighed against other virtues, like honesty, benevolence, being a dutiful member of society and so on.[21]

In a similar way, if we look at a particular institution or subgroup of society, we do not normally allow it to invent its own virtues. The Mafia has distinctive values that set it apart from the rest of Italian society, but we would judge the ethics of a Mafiosi according to the virtues of Italian society,

---

[21] References to duty can be confusing, especially when Kantian ethics is described, as it often is, as an ethics of duty. In Kant's theory, the categorical imperative imposes absolute duties as a requirement of reason, but when we talk about duties in everyday conversation, or of people as dutiful, we are generally referring to the dutifulness expected of a virtuous character.

not according to the so-called virtues of Mafia society. Suicide bombers are often portrayed by fundamentalist clerics as epitomes of virtue, but we don't have to accept that portrayal.

The list of generally accepted virtues varies in detail from culture to culture, but with a lot of commonality. And although the virtues are typically expressed in terms of the traditions and values of particular cultures, their function is to capture the best and most admirable qualities of human nature generally.

This is most clearly expressed in Confucian ethics, which urges respect for what might be considered the social virtues of loyalty, obedience and conformity with established social duties and rituals (*xiao* and *li*), but advocates that these be tempered and overseen by the fundamental human virtues of justice (*yi*) and, especially, human-heartedness (*ren*), a kind of tempered love or rational benevolence. The Western tradition, similarly, recognizes four cardinal virtues that effectively regulate all others, namely prudence, justice, temperance and fortitude. A similar role is played in Buddhist ethics by the four divine states: loving-kindness, compassion, sympathetic joy and equanimity. Whatever the specific virtues identified by any particular community, a virtuous character is always, in a very general sense, both temperate and benevolent.

As we have already noted, a virtuous person is also sensitive to context: to the particular circumstances, to the particular people involved and so on. Combining these observations, we see that behaving virtuously is not just about acting in accordance with a list of virtues but about balancing those virtues and applying them sensitively to the context. That the dominant virtues might vary from culture to culture is not therefore a problem, at least in principle. We do run into practical difficulties when cultures meet and mix. The virtues of loyalty, compassion and self-reliance, for example, carry very different weights in Chinese, European and American societies, and are applied in very different ways. An American may think that the Chinese take loyalty to extremes, and a Chinese that the Americans take self-reliance to extremes. But a virtuous Chinese is not loyal at all costs, to the exclusion of everything else. There is balance, a "golden mean." And a virtuous American does not insist on self-reliance at all costs, in all circumstances. Again, there has to be a balance, and that balance will vary both according to one's own culture and according to the culture in which one is living or working. The challenge may be greater, but it is not fundamentally different.

In some versions, virtue ethics is closely linked with tradition, and so takes on a conservative flavor. Whereas liberal philosophers (John Rawls, discussed above, would be an example) tend to see communities as the creations of autonomous individuals, communitarian philosophers see people as products of their communities, their identities inseparable from their social context. From this perspective, the idea of an ethical life is meaningless when divorced from the traditions that have shaped a society. There is then a temptation to identify the weakening of moral norms characteristic of modern society, which often seems to take its values more from economic calculations and opinion polls than from any form of ethical reflection, with a fragmentation of community and loss of tradition, and to call for these to be revived.

However, virtue ethics doesn't have to be conservative. Another response to the same problem would be that the old traditions have lost their relevance and that something new is needed in their place. Strong traditions often impose a conformity that is every bit as insensitive to circumstances as Kantian or utilitarian theories, and one of the things virtue ethics can do is to challenge over-rigid norms. That is, indeed, precisely how Confucius used it. It is also worth noting here that virtuous people do not necessarily conform. A virtuous person will generally follow the prevailing social norms, but will also know when to and how to breach them.

Because of its sensitivity to context and its commitment to looking at a situation as a whole rather than abstracting from it, virtue ethics can provide a useful language for exploring the shifts in ethical norms that we are already experiencing – shifts in the norms relating to sexual activity, for example, marriage or familial relationships, as well as in norms relating to business and finance. A key point here is that when we look at the ethics of a particular practice or set of practices, we are often not looking at some completely new phenomenon, but at a change in attitude based on changing priorities and changing perceptions. If we treat sex outside marriage, to take one example, as an act that is either right or wrong, we quickly get locked into a futile dispute. But if we ask instead what a virtuous person would do when faced with a situation in which sex outside marriage is a possibility, we have more room for maneuver. We can perhaps think of characters, in fiction or in real life, who have chosen the option of sex outside marriage, even though traditional norms weighed against it, but who nevertheless seem to be have been virtuous characters. We can ask what it was about the circumstances that made their choice, their weighing of the alternatives, reasonable, and to what extent such circumstances are more widely applicable. We can ask what virtues the tradition was trying to protect and at what cost to other virtues, and we can ask how those virtues might best be represented in the changed circumstances of contemporary society.

Similarly, when we look at the practices of one tradition set within another, as finance is set within contemporary society, or one tradition set against another, as in cross-cultural conflicts, enquiring how a virtuous person would behave gives scope for balancing and negotiating between the different values of the two traditions in a way that asking whether an act is right or wrong does not.

What recommends the virtue approach in cases like these is its combined sensitivity to the social context of community and tradition, the uniqueness of situations and the complexities of real life. This keeps it grounded in reality and focused on the real decisions that real people have to make, rather than on the artificial or abstract decisions of the philosophy text-book. It is not theoretically rigorous, but that is the point. In a complex situation which theories struggle to grasp, it can sometimes help to be evidence-driven rather than theory-driven – or at least to combine the two approaches.

Applying normative ethics

In discussing the various approaches to be used, we have already given some indication of their strengths and weaknesses. However, choosing which approach or approaches to apply to any given problem is often the greatest challenge facing students, and while there are no absolute answers, it may be helpful to set out some general guidelines.

Utilitarianism was first applied to public policy issues and that still may be where it is most useful. It can be applied to the evaluation of a general public policy norm ("people should act in their narrow economic self-interest" would be a relevant current example), to compare regulatory principles or policies (rules versus principles, alternative rules for setting banks' capital ratios), to changes in the law (the repealing of the Glass-Steagall Act) or to corporate policies (governing sales and marketing, for example, or tax avoidance, or facilitating payments).

At the personal level, utilitarianism is normally applied to rules of behavior or general classes of actions rather than to individual acts. We may use straightforward act utilitarianism to analyze specific one-off cases, where the consequences are significant, but we shall not generally use it to provide justifications for breaking general rules in specific cases.

Utilitarianism works best when the consequences are easily identified, predicted and measured. The closer the problem is to one in which the simple economic consequences are what matter, the more straightforward the application. It is much harder to apply when the consequences are hard to identify or measure, when there is a lot of uncertainty or when non-economic factors are important. We need to be especially careful when an action or rule carries significant costs or suffering for minorities (or indeed for small numbers of people generally), or impacts on people's fundamental rights or freedoms.

Kantian ethics is often most effective when utilitarianism is least so. Like utilitarianism, we use it to analyze general rules or principles, but generally where the focus is on personal behavior (personal maxims) and interpersonal relationships rather than corporate or public policy. These relationships don't have to be close. A relationship is established whenever one person's actions affect another person, however remotely. But the focus is on the relationship between one person and another person as an individual person, not just as part of an agglomeration of affected people.

Kantian ethics is especially useful for looking at situations in which a person's action impacts on people differently (giving scope for possible discrimination) or impacts on their fundamental rights and freedoms (possibly neglecting their value as ends), or simply disregards them (again possibly neglecting their value as ends). Indeed, in such cases, we do use it to explore corporate or public policies, though strictly speaking the application is to the people who bring about or implement such policies. It is generally most effective when dealing with big, broad issues and very general principles. It is generally not very effective when dealing with very specific circumstances or with possible exceptions to general rules.

Applications of the Formula of Universal Law are always quite difficult. They are best used for dealing with very general principles, and in using them we generally need to ignore any specific exceptions. Once we narrow down a rule by specifying conditions, by incorporating exceptions or by framing a rule that could only be applied in a limited range of circumstances, it becomes extremely difficult to frame any maxim that could act as a potential universal law.

Applications of the Formula of Humanity are more straightforward, but we need to be careful to focus tightly upon whether an action treats any people who might be affected as ends, and not just ask whether it does them any harm. A Kantian will always try and avoid harming people, but sometimes it is impossible to avoid harm altogether. A classic set of hypothetical problems poses the question as to whether it is sometimes ethical to kill one person to save the lives of many, or in various ways to allow one person to be killed to save the lives of many. Here we can argue over what action would best respect the human beings involved. The answer isn't clear, but the question is a good one and in real-life situations it may be easier to answer. The important thing to bear in mind in a Kantian analysis is that respect for persons is what matters, not the amount of harm done.

In practice, most of the situations we look at do not pose such difficult problems and the Formula of Humanity can be a powerful aid in thinking through many areas of business and finance, in particular their impact on third parties – their externalities, in economic language. Business managers have in general to generate a profit: not to do so would be to treat the primary parties, owners, shareholders or other beneficiaries merely as means to the managers' instrumental objectives. (Delivering a profit might not advance their higher interests, of course, but nor would not delivering a profit and, in the absence of any more powerful considerations, treating people as ends entails respecting their autonomous choices.) In pursuing a profit, they impact, often harmfully, on other people and in an ethical analysis, the interests of one group have to be weighed somehow against those of another. Kantian ethics requires that this be done carefully, thoughtfully and with due respect for all concerned, including all those knowingly affected, whatever their status or voice. To take another example, one of the characteristics of the professions (which would include accountants and, some would claim, financial analysts or consultants) is that the knowledge and expertise of professionals give them an advantage over their clients, and the guiding rule of professional ethics is that this advantage should not be exploited. The clients must be treated as ends in themselves and not as a means of enhancing the professional's reputation or bank balance.

Contractualist and consensus ethics are generally applicable to the same kinds of problems as utilitarianism – to questions of public or corporate policy, regulation and so on. They are useful in those cases in which utilitarianism runs into difficulties: when the consequences are hard to identify or measure, when there are important non-economic consequences or when there is a significant impact on minorities. In applying Rawlsian ethics, we may incorporate utilitarian measures, arguing that people in the original position would wish to maximize overall utility, but subject to distributional constraints that give some protection to the less advantaged. This approach enables us to combine broadly utilitarian objectives with a Kantian-like consideration of people's rights and freedoms.

Consensus ethics is not something we can apply directly in a book or classroom in order to get answers to ethical questions. The whole point of it is that the answers should come from deliberation amongst those who are actually affected. What we can do is point to situations where the process of forming a consensus seems particularly appropriate. These might include, most obviously, cases where those charged with framing a policy or regulation simply don't know how people will be subjectively affected by it and can't find out except through a deliberative process. They may also include cases where there are strong indications that the people framing a policy could have found out how it would impact on people but didn't bother to do so, or relied on culturally biased or prejudiced assumptions, or intentionally distorted the evidence. In some cases we might find that the processes used had obvious flaws or we might know enough ourselves about affected groups to doubt the views attributed to them.

Virtue ethics is applied, like Kantian ethics, to people in their relationships with other people, and not to corporations. But whereas Kantian ethics is applied to general rules and focuses on how people should treat different situations according to the same rules, virtue ethics focuses on the specifics and how people should treat different situations differently.

The application of virtue ethics is more an art than a science. What we don't do is write down a list of virtues and tick them off. Apart from the need to take account of exactly how the virtues are applied in practice and of the balance between them, the approach needs to be reflective. In the language of the social sciences, the methodology is interpretive not hypothetico-deductive. It seeks insights, not demonstrations. A good virtue analyst also needs to be virtuous: sensitive to the situations being analyzed, temperate and even-handed, sympathetic towards the actors and so on.

We noted earlier that virtue ethics can be a good approach to use when looking at situations of cultural change, where it helps us to relate the new circumstances to the old. It is also appropriate to issues of everyday ethics, where the rightness or wrongness of particular acts is not always what really matters. Whether at home or at work, many people's lives are characterized by a need to balance a variety of different responsibilities. Look at any one of the decisions made and you would have no idea whether or not a manager was behaving morally. Look at a series of such decisions and you can begin to judge whether he or she is acting fairly, prioritizing responsibly and so on. Indeed, an evaluation of whether someone's behavior is fair or unfair almost inevitably requires us to look at multiple actions over a period of time and at the balance they achieve.

Virtue ethics can also help us to understand how people might behave ethically in particular roles. Some roles seem on the face of it to license behaviors that would normally be considered unethical. Others impose heightened ethical responsibilities. In practice, different characters are attracted to different roles and we tend to compare bankers with other bankers and priests with other priests, but a careful application of virtue ethics allows us to separate the person from the role and look at the person (citizen, member of the community) in a role. Other approaches cannot achieve this level of subtlety.

I shall give various examples of how the different approaches can be applied in the pages that follow. None are definitive, however, and I expect those interested in the ethics of finance to engage with and challenge the arguments put forward and to develop arguments of their own. That is how philosophy works. In many cases, especially as the book progresses, I shall also leave people to make their own arguments, suggesting what approaches might be taken, but not working through the applications in detail.

4   The financial system

Much of this book will be concerned with the ethical issues that arise in particular financial practices. For each area of finance, we shall ask whether particular practices are ethically acceptable – or even, in some cases, ethically admirable – or whether they give rise to ethical difficulties and, if so, of what kind. As we noted in Chapter 2, however, moral critics of finance are concerned not only with such things as how banks and other financial services companies lend, trade or treat their clients, but also with the way the system as a whole operates. There is a widespread view that the global financial system as a whole is morally bankrupt.

For almost anyone involved in finance, or in business of any kind, such a viewpoint seems on the face of it absurd. Banks and insurance companies, stocks and shares, financial instruments and the markets in which they are traded are a simple fact of modern life. They have evolved to meet economic demands and they are used and taken for granted by almost everybody in the developed world. Some people see them as a positive good, while for others they are just part of the institutional background, with no particular moral connotations one way or the other. But the common underlying assumption is that they are at least utility-enhancing: we would be worse off without them.

These contrasting perspectives on the financial system were brought to the attention of the public in September 2011 by the "Occupy Wall Street" protest movement and the similar protests that followed at financial centers around the world. However, although these generated public awareness, they prompted little reasoned debate. The two sides simply failed to connect with each other. In this chapter we shall first introduce the main components of the contemporary global financial system and then explore some of the ethical arguments that can be made both for and against it.

The global financial system

Broadly speaking, we can think of the financial system as the system of institutions through which monetary funds are transferred and deployed. A list of some of the main organizations involved is given in Table 4.1, and in this section we describe some of their main activities.

Money transfer and exchange

At its most basic level, the financial system includes the system by which payments for goods or services are made and received, and the system by which funds are transferred from one person or account to another person or account, one location to another location, or one form to another form, e.g., from one currency to another currency, or from credit to cash.

To the extent that money is a simple medium of exchange, these basic systems are fairly straightforward. Just listing them makes the point, however, that while for many purposes money can be treated as a simple homogeneous exchange value, it is never quite that simple. Because of the different risks involved, for example, the same amount of money held in account at different banks may not be worth quite the same. Moreover, exchange values between different currencies are continuously changing. So even at this level we encounter markets for the different forms of money, the most significant of which are the foreign exchange (Forex or FX) markets. And as soon as we get markets, we also get speculation. In round numbers, the Forex markets trade about $4 trillion a day, only a small proportion of which arises because people actually need to convert from one currency to another to make a payment for goods or services. The great majority of Forex trading is either speculative – essentially gambling on the exchange rates – or associated with trades in financial instruments (themselves often speculative) denominated in different currencies. Moreover, the majority of Forex trading does not consist in the simple buying and selling of currencies, but in the buying and selling of foreign exchange derivatives (mainly Forex swaps, which involve simultaneously committing to buy on one date and sell on another) as traders either speculate on future exchange rate movements, hedge against such movements so as to remove any exchange rate effects from their profits and losses on other foreign-currency trades, or routinely balance their currency holdings on a daily basis.

Table 4.1. *Some financial organizations*

Description	Examples
Inter-governmental organizations	
International institutions funded by member governments and providing them with emergency or development loans.	International Monetary Fund, World Bank, European Bank for Reconstruction and Development.
Central banks	
State, national or supra-national banks typically responsible for issuing new money, issuing government bonds, setting interest rates, and regulating and acting as lenders of last resort to commercial banks within their jurisdiction.	US Federal Reserve, Bank of England, European Central Bank (covering the Eurozone), Bank of Japan, etc.
Commercial and retail banks	
Banks that are licensed to take deposits and provide loans, and generally provide a full range of banking services. The *universal banks* of France, Germany, Switzerland and other countries have also traditionally engaged in investment banking (see below), but in the UK and the USA (from the 1930s to the 1980s), these were historically separate activities. Today all of the leading commercial banking groups worldwide are conglomerates that include investment banking and other financial services.*	Bank of America, JP Morgan Chase, HSBC, Citigroup, Mitsubishi, Royal Bank of Scotland, ICBC, Wells Fargo, China Construction, Bank of China, Deutsche Bank, BNP Paribas, Barclays, Credit Agricole, UBS, Lloyds, Société Generale, Unicredit, Mitsuho, ING, Santander, Credit Suisse, etc.
Investment banks	
Investment banks issue and underwrite bonds and shares, advise on mergers and acquisitions, manage client assets and trade in a wide variety of securities, both for	JP Morgan, Bank of America Merrill Lynch, Goldman Sachs, Morgan Stanley, Deutsche Bank, Credit Suisse, Barclays Capital, UBS, BNP Paribas, Nomura, etc.

Table 4.1. (*cont.*)

Description	Examples
clients and on their own account (in this capacity they may be described as *broker-dealers*). Most are nowadays part of conglomerate banking groups.*	

Investment or asset managers

| Asset managers invest money on behalf of pension funds, life assurance funds and other institutions, and on behalf of retail customers through mutual funds or unit trusts. Most banking groups have asset management divisions, but there are also a number of specialist firms with substantial assets under management. | Most of the commercial, retail and investment banks listed above, plus BlackRock, Fidelity, Schroders, Prudential, Invesco, M&G, etc. |

Savings and loans / thrifts / building societies

| These specialize in holding savings and mortgaged property lending and have traditionally been structured as mutual societies. Many of the largest UK building societies demutualized in the 1990s and were subsequently taken over by banking groups, while in the 2000s many of the largest US thrifts were also taken over (sometimes rescued) by conglomerate banks. | Washington Mutual (now part of Chase), Cal Fed (now part of Citibank) Nationwide, Cheltenham & Gloucester, Halifax (both now part of Lloyds), etc. |

Hedge funds

| Private investment fund managers serving institutions and very wealthy individuals and specializing in leveraged derivative and arbitrage trading. | Bridgewater, Paulson, DE Shaw, Brevan Howard, MAN, Och-Ziff, Soros, Renaissance Technologies, etc. |

Table 4.1. (*cont.*)

Description	Examples
Exchanges	
Centralized markets for shares, commodities and other securities (energy, emissions, etc.). Exchanges provide regulated environments with registered products and traders and posted prices, in contrast to over-the-counter (OTC) markets, which, while often electronically coordinated, are largely unregulated media for bilateral trading.	Shares: NYSE, NASDAQ, London Stock Exchange, Shanghai Stock Exchange, etc. Commodities: CBOT, CME, NYSE Liffe, LME, etc.
Regulatory agencies	
Governmental or self-regulating organizations that oversee financial companies and markets.	SEC, CFTC (US), FSA (UK: now Financial Conduct Authority), etc.
Ratings agencies	
Private services that provide ratings of bonds and other securities that give an assessment of their riskiness.	Moody's, Standard & Poor's, Fitch.

* In 2013 several countries were exploring the possibility of some kind of enforced separation between commercial/retail and investment banking activities in order to ringfence the former from the risks of proprietary trading (when banks trade on their own account), but the banks were strongly resisting such moves and at the time of writing, no significant changes have been made.

In some ways, the foreign exchange market is the purest of all financial markets. It operates globally and round the clock, and all trading is directly between participants ("over the counter" or OTC), with no centralized exchange. It is highly liquid, with traders able to open a position or close it and withdraw their funds at a moment's notice. It is concerned solely with money and not with material goods in any form. And it is dominated by the banks acting mainly on their own account. It is also characteristic of contemporary finance in that, while it seems far removed from the real world of

Table 4.2. *Foreign exchange markets*

Main transaction types	Approximate daily trading volume (April 2010)*
Spot transactions Buying and selling currencies for immediate (next-day or two-day) settlement.	$1.5 trillion
Forwards Agreements to buy and sell on some future date at an exchange rate agreed in advance.	$0.5 trillion
Swaps Agreements to buy/sell on one date and sell/buy, reversing the transaction, on another.	$1.8 trillion

* Bank of International Settlements, 2010, Triennial Central Bank Survey of Foreign Exchange and Derivative Market Activity. The total daily volume of $4 trillion seems to be about average for the period 2007–12: see Bech 2012.

people and firms, the resultant exchange rates significantly affect this world, both directly and through the government policies needed to cope with them. Forex speculation can seriously damage a country's economy and the level of speculation has been a major source of moral concern. We shall come back to this later in the chapter. In terms of the specific practices, though, we shall have little reason to refer to foreign exchange trading later in the book.

The foreign exchange markets also exemplify recent trends in finance in other ways. Fifty years ago, exchange rates were predominantly fixed within very tight limits and there were very strict controls on the movement of money across borders. Currency transactions were predominantly connected with trade or with the actions of governments trying to address the effects of trade imbalances on their currency reserves. The markets operated through face-to-face transactions for limited hours on weekdays only. And foreign exchange derivatives were unheard of. Today, exchange rates are predominantly variable. Money moves freely across borders. Electronic markets operate round the clock. Trading is dominated by private banks, which now operate globally, rather than by governments. And the market is characterized by speculative and often short-term trading in derivatives. All of these changes are mirrored throughout the world of finance.

Banking, borrowing and lending

Besides simply transferring money, the financial system is also a system for
lending and borrowing. Traditionally this comprises a range of activities. The
core activity of the commercial banks has always been lending, which they do
to individuals, companies, governments and each other, using funds that are
effectively borrowed from their depositors, and making their profit from a
combination of service charges and the differences between the interest rates
charged and paid. A distinctive subset of this activity is mortgage lending.
Traditionally this has been carried out by dedicated mutual organizations –
"savings and loans" or "thrifts" in the USA and "building societies" in the UK –
through which people have saved to buy a property and from which they
have borrowed, using a loan secured on the property, to buy it. In the UK,
however, most building societies have now "demutualized" and become
divisions of commercial banks, while in the USA they have also broadened
their activities and become increasingly tied into the banking system, especially through the securitization of mortgages that ran spectacularly aground
in 2007–8.

Alongside this regular commercial activity, national and local governments routinely borrow to bridge the gap between their expenditures and
tax incomes by issuing bonds. Here the investment banks act as underwriters and intermediaries between the issuing governments and individual and corporate investors. Finally, private companies also use bond issues
to fund their activities, as well as share issues and bank loans. These range
from blue-chip company bonds issued by the most established and secure
corporations to "junk" bonds, also known as high-yield bonds, issued to
finance speculative or risky ventures. Again, the investment banks play a
critical role, both issuing the bonds and maintaining a market in them.
While some corporate bonds are traded on open exchanges, much of the
trade is over the counter, with the banks trading directly with each other at
bilaterally negotiated prices.

Investment and the allocation of resources

Another central function of the financial system is the allocation of financial resources across investment opportunities, typically through the
markets for company shares and corporate bonds. Although the words

Table 4.3. *Loan categories and amounts outstanding*

Category	Approximate global amount outstanding (March 2012)*
Government bonds Issued by governments on a regular basis to finance expenditure.	$43 trillion globally
Corporate bonds (domestic) Issued by companies (the majority by banks, but also by industrials, etc.).	$29 trillion globally
International bonds Typically issued by a company based in one country to raise funds from another country.	$30 trillion globally
	Approximate US amount outstanding (June 2012)
Commercial loans Lending by banks to industrial and commercial companies.	$3.0 trillion (US only)
Personal loans Unsecured lending to individuals.	$1.3 trillion (US only)
Mortgage loans Lending secured on domestic property.	$2.5 trillion (US only)

* For bond figures, see www.bis.org/statistics/secstats.htm.
** For loan figures, see www2.fdic.gov/SDI.

"saving" and "investment" carry very different connotations, the distinction between them is not clear-cut, as any money that is saved through a financial institution (as opposed to being kept in the safe or under a mattress) is effectively made available for lending or investment of one kind or another. The key parts of the investment system, however, are the stock markets, through which productive enterprises attract financial capital (see Table 4.4). All companies need funds to get established and grow, and since their activities are inherently risky, most can only borrow at reasonable rates if they have substantial shareholder capital at risk with which to guarantee their loans should things go wrong.

Table 4.4. *Principal stock exchanges and market capitalization*

Exchange	Approximate capitalization (January 2012)*
NYSE	$12.6 trillion
NASDAQ	$4.2 trillion
Tokyo SE	$3.5 trillion
London SE	$3.4 trillion
Shanghai SE	$2.5 trillion
Honk Kong SE	$2.5 trillion
Toronto SE	$2.0 trillion
BM&F (Brasil)	$1.4 trillion
Deutsche Börse	$1.3 trillion
Australian SE	$1.3 trillion
Bombay SE	$1.2 trillion
National SE of India	$1.2 trillion
Shenzen SE	$1.0 trillion
Total including all others	*$51 trillion*

*Data from the World Federation of Exchanges:
www.world-exchanges.org/statistics/monthly-reports.

Historical contingencies have resulted in very different patterns of share ownership in different countries. Most firms start out as private ventures using capital provided by the founder, often supplemented by friends and family, and across the world, most firms, even the largest, remain privately controlled, though many use share issues to bring in additional capital from outside investors. In the UK and the USA, however, most (though not all) large companies have widely dispersed ownership. The main shareholders are institutional fund managers – often subsidiaries of the large banks – and the funds that they manage are themselves dispersed, with most of the money invested coming from pension funds, from life assurance companies and from mutual funds ("unit trusts" in the UK) through which individual investors effectively delegate the management of their stock market investments to professional fund managers. The result is a system that is thick with financial intermediaries. While I might buy and sell shares on my own account, for example, the bulk of my own financial assets are managed by institutional asset managers who themselves invest in a range of managed funds, which in turn invest in the stock markets and other securities.

Table 4.5. *Pooled investment vehicles*

Category	Approximate assets under management (2010)*
Pension funds	$29.9 trillion
Insurance funds	$24.6 trillion
Mutual funds	$24.7 trillion
Hedge funds	$1.8 trillion
Private equity funds	$2.6 trillion
Exchange traded funds	$1.3 trillion
Sovereign wealth funds	$4.2 trillion
Private wealth funds	$42.7 trillion

*The City UK, 2011, "Fund management 2011," available at http://www.thecityuk.com/research.

The financial system also provides a range of mechanisms for investment in shares that are not publicly listed on exchanges (see Table 4.5). Private equity companies pool the resources of wealthy investors to buy, reorganize and sell whole companies, and in recent years a growing number have sought investments from the public, directly or through asset managers, rather than just through private connections. Venture capital funds specialize in early-stage financing, investing at the point at which a firm's founders can no longer build the company without external investors, but do not yet have a sufficient track record to float shares on the market. They seek to make a profit from an eventual flotation or trade sale of the company, and many also welcome subscriptions from the public. When the time does come for a public flotation (through an initial public offering or IPO), the investment banks again take center stage – and substantial fees.

Insurance

Another distinctive part of the financial system, and one that was until relatively recently quite separate from the parts concerned with savings and investment, is that concerned with insurance. The institution of insurance originated in the late Middle Ages as a means by which merchants could defray the significant risks to ships and their cargoes from storms and piracy. In modern times, it has taken three main forms: property insurance, life insurance and, more recently, health insurance. In all three cases, the underlying idea is that a large number of people contribute regularly to a fund, which pays out to meet their occasional and unexpected losses. The fund might be run either as a mutual fund, owned by its members, or as a commercial business.

In property and health insurance, the business model is straightforward. In any period, the premiums paid and the losses reimbursed are expected to be roughly equal, after allowing for management expenses, profit margin, etc., and while the claims made by any individual subscriber may be quite unpredictable, the average claim over a large number of subscribers is predictable enough to keep the overall risks at a manageable level. As the system has evolved, however, it has been complicated by the rise of reinsurance. The idea here is that in the case of property insurance in particular, the claims on a company may not in fact be stable from one period to another, as extreme weather conditions, for example, may lead to large numbers of concurrent claims. The insurance companies therefore seek to insure their own liabilities, traditionally with insurers of last resort (Lloyd's of London, whose members effectively put up their entire personal wealth as security) and more recently with specialist reinsurance companies, with the risks of each insurer typically being spread across many reinsurers. To complicate matters further, reinsurers may themselves buy insurance from other reinsurers. Different premium rates and different regulatory requirements may lead to arbitrage possibilities and, as in other parts of the financial system, recent decades have seen a massive growth in the number and complexity of contracts, out of all proportion to the amount of risk ultimately insured.

The system of life insurance is more complex still, as here there is a time element. If somebody takes out a life insurance policy, payable on death, he or she will, on average, pay many years of premiums before a claim is made, so the insurance company is not just balancing income and expenditure but is acting as an investment institution as well. Moreover, many life policies today combine life insurance and investment functions, with part of the premium providing immediate life cover and part being invested to be cashed in at a later date or to provide funds to keep paying the premiums after retirement. One consequence of this is that life insurers are major players in the investment markets, with the large firms having their own fund management divisions. Another consequence has been the development of a secondary market in life policies, or life settlements. Since life policies have value, both on account of their investment components and, in some cases, because changes of circumstances make early death more likely, there is a market for them. The benefits of a policy can be sold to a third party, and quantities of such benefits can be bundled together, securitized and sold on in the financial markets.

A further complication, which became significant in the context of the recent financial crisis, has arisen from the spread of insurance beyond its traditional areas, in particular through the rise of CDSs. A CDS is effectively an insurance against default on a loan. An investing institution buying corporate bonds, for example, or high-risk overseas government bonds might hedge its bets by paying a premium to an investment bank or insurance company, which will undertake to reimburse the investor in the event of a default by the borrower. The two main differences from regular insurance are that CDSs do not fall under the regulatory regime of insurance and that they can be bought by anyone, not just the holder of the bonds, and therefore be used as vehicles for speculation or gambling. In the run-up to the financial crisis, bundles of low-quality mortgage loans that had been securitized and sold to the investment community in the form of CDOs were "insured" through CDSs, not only by their purchasers but also by traders speculating on the housing market. At the peak of the market in 2007, over $60 trillion of CDSs were outstanding – about six times the total outstanding US mortgage debt, nearly three times the value of the total US housing stock at the time and nearly four times its 2011 post-bubble value.[1]

Speculation and derivatives

As this brief survey has already made clear, one striking feature of the global financial system is that it is concerned not only with core activities such as lending and borrowing, saving and investment, and insurance, but also, to a very large extent, with speculation, much of which is carried out through derivative contracts, which refer to the price of some underlying asset but don't actually trade that asset.

---

[1] Federal Reserve Board Flow of Funds Account 31.3.11; see www.Freddiemac.com/investors/
pdffiles/investor-presentation.pdf.

Speculation has always been a prominent feature of the financial markets. In early modern Britain, speculators used insurance contracts (much as they today use CDSs) to gamble on the fate of other people's ships, the lives of mercenaries or adventurers, or the outcome of wars.[2] This was banned in 1774 when insurance contracts were legally restricted to those with a direct interest in what was insured, but speculation continued in the equity markets. Speculative stock market bubbles have been commonplace for nearly 300 years and in the 1930s, John Maynard Keynes famously characterized stock market investment as being about predicting what the market would predict that the market would predict.[3] In both London and New York, fixed settlement dates meant that most equity trades were effectively "forward" contracts, enabling speculators to buy or sell with a view to reversing their trade before settlement and capturing any intervening price differences. The development of derivatives, however, was rooted in another part of the financial system that we have not yet mentioned: the commodities markets.

Modern futures contracts were pioneered in the rapidly evolving Chicago markets for grain and other foodstuffs in the mid-nineteenth century, and, like many derivatives, initially acted as a hedging device. Farmers were keen to ensure a buyer for their produce by negotiating sales ahead of the harvest. Wholesalers were keen to secure supplies at a locked-in price, on the basis of which they could plan ahead. There was nothing new about the idea, but in the centralized exchange of the Chicago Board of Trade and the frenzied commercial environment of the time, it didn't take long for traders to recognize the scope for speculative opportunity and to begin buying and selling futures contracts with no intention of physical delivery. Over the years, the practice spread to other commodities markets, from cotton to coffee and from oil and gas to gold, silver and other precious metals; to equity and currency markets; and to other forms of contract such as options (giving the purchaser an option to buy or sell assets in the future, or not) and swaps (combining the purchase of an asset at one moment and its sale at another). In all cases, derivatives markets provide opportunities for hedging and risk management.

Derivatives markets provide opportunities for speculation, especially through options and swaps, which automatically leverage the effects of price movements. By buying only the *right* to buy or sell a security, by

---

[2] See Sandel 2012.   [3] Keynes [1936] 1964, pp. 154–6. This is quoted below in Chapter 6.

Table 4.6. *OTC derivatives: main categories and volumes outstanding*

Underlying securities	Instruments	Contracts outstanding (December 2011)*
Currencies	Forex forwards and swaps	$31 trillion
	Currency swaps	$23 trillion
	Currency options	$10 trillion
Bonds (interest rate derivatives)	Forward rates	$51 trillion
	Interest rate swaps	$403 trillion
	Interest rate options	$51 trillion
Equities	Forwards and swaps	$2 trillion
	Options	$4 trillion
Commodities	Forwards and swaps	$3 trillion
	Options	$1 trillion
Mortgages and loans	Credit default swaps	$29 trillion
Other		$43 trillion
Total		*$648 trillion*

*Data from the Bank for International Settlements: see www.bis.org/statistics/derstats.htm.

combining a purchase and sale in the same contract or by trading in an artificial security modeled on asset prices, a speculator can capture the trading benefits of buying and selling a stock or commodity bundle for only a small fraction of the investment that would be needed to actually buy it. Derivatives also make it much easier to speculate on falling, as well as rising, prices, enabling traders to replicate the effects of selling assets without having to own them first. Of course, in leveraging returns, derivatives also leverage losses. A relatively small price movement in an underlying asset can wipe out a derivative holding completely.

A wide range of simple derivatives can now be traded on exchanges, but the range of tailor-made products traded over the counter, through the investment banks, is staggering and ever-expanding (see Tables 4.6 and 4.7).[4] The market volume is also staggering, with over $600 trillion worth

---

[4] For introductory treatments of derivatives, see, for example, Chisholm 2010 and Durbin 2010.

Table 4.7. *Exchange traded derivatives: main categories and volumes outstanding*

Underlying securities	Instruments	Contracts outstanding (June 2012)*
Bonds (interest rate derivatives)	Futures	$22.4 trillion
	Interest rate options	$33.2 trillion
Equities	Index futures	$1.1 trillion
	Index options	$2.5 trillion

*Data from the Bank for International Settlements: see www.bis.org/statistics/extderiv.htm.

of contracts outstanding at any one time – that is, more than the entire wealth of the entire world.[5] The rise of derivatives has also been accompanied by the rise of a new kind of investment vehicle: the hedge fund. Hedge funds are effectively specialist high-leverage investment funds, specializing in a mix of low-risk arbitrage investment, using computer models to identify and exploit price discrepancies between different markets, and more speculative derivative-based investments.

Enablers and regulators

The financial system as we have described it so far is populated largely by people and companies managing money for commercial gain. There are, however, a range of other important players. There are, for example, the exchanges themselves. Many of these began as membership organizations, rather like private clubs, providing open pits for face-to-face trading, setting criteria for membership and rules and regulations, and developing standard forms of contract and procedures for settlement. Most are now owned by commercial companies and operate fully computerized exchanges with global access. Amazingly, the development of computer trading has meant that location still matters. Contemporary computer trading programs work on timescales measured in micro-seconds, and since they are all trying to compete with each other, there is an advantage, even with

---

[5] As in gambling generally, many of the bets made cancel each other out, so the amount at risk, if all positions were closed, is less than 1 percent of the amount outstanding: just under $4 trillion as of December 2011.

communication at the speed of light, in having your computers a few miles closer to the exchange computers than those of your rivals.

Other key institutions are the ratings agencies, Standard & Poor's, Moody's and Fitch. These assess the risk levels of government and corporate bonds and other securities, and publish their assessments, which impact critically on the value of these securities and the cost of future borrowing by their issuers. As explained in Chapter 1, the agencies are commercial companies whose fees are paid by the institutions whose products they assess. At the end of the day, their ratings are just opinions, and not even independent opinions, but they are immensely influential and are often treated as if they were independent objective measures.

Governmental and inter-governmental institutions are also immensely important. National and regional governments (and the European Union), often acting in part through publicly owned banks, control the money supply, issue bonds, determine fiscal policy and trade in the foreign exchange markets. The International Monetary Fund (IMF) acts as a lender of last resort to governments, while the World Bank, the European Bank for Reconstruction and Development and other institutions fund development projects. Governments also regulate, or attempt to regulate, the activities of the commercial sector.

The regulatory system under which the financial sector operates is immensely complex and constantly changing.[6] It is conventionally seen as comprising two main areas: prudential regulation and the regulation of conduct. Prudential regulation is concerned with maintaining the stability of the financial system as a whole and preventing its failure or collapse. This has traditionally been focused on commercial banks, with particular attention being paid to their capital ratios. The primary aim is to ensure that the system can survive short-term shocks and crises of confidence, in particular a run on the banks when depositors panic and withdraw their money. The regulation of conduct is concerned primarily with customer protection and with the prevention of market abuse. It seeks to curtail mis-selling and other forms of misrepresentation, to ensure the disclosure of price-sensitive information and to prevent the artificial cornering or manipulation of markets.

---

[6] For a recent survey, see Davies and Green 2010.

For a period of about forty years following the Second World War, the finance industry was clearly compartmentalized, at least in the dominant markets of the USA and the UK, and different sectors were subject to different regulatory regimes. Commercial banking almost everywhere was regulated by the central banks (the Federal Reserve in the USA and the Bank of England in the UK), which also acted as lenders of last resort and organs of monetary policy. Their primary concern was with stability, both financial (the stability of the financial system) and monetary (the stability of the domestic economy). The key point of regulation was the specification and enforcement of capital requirements, which placed limits on the scale of the banks' lending and borrowing in the interest of ensuring that they could meet their obligations to depositors in a crisis.

Other financial activities were regulated according to the activity or the security being traded. So there were separate regulatory regimes for mortgage lenders and insurers, while the trading of securities was regulated largely through the exchanges on which they were traded, typically membership organizations that were either self-regulating or self-regulating within some form of governmental oversight (e.g., the Securities and Exchange Commission in the USA or the Economic Ministry of Hesse, regulating the Frankfurt Stock Exchange: in both Germany and the USA, regulation was split between the federal and regional or state levels).

Between the early 1980s and the early 2000s, the traditional compartmentalization of the industry was gradually but almost completely broken down. In 1986, the "Big Bang" deregulation of the London Stock Exchange, which accompanied a shift from open outcry to electronic trading, abolished the traditional separation of stock broking and stock dealing. A number of banks had already built or acquired broking or asset management subsidiaries, and the Big Bang accelerated a process of consolidation. Meanwhile, in the USA, the 1982 Garn-St Germain Act had loosened the terms of the 1933 Glass-Steagall Act, which had enforced a strict separation between commercial and investment banks, by allowing commercial banks and savings and loans to buy corporate bonds. Later in the 1980s, the Federal Reserve loosened the restrictions further by allowing a group of banks to underwrite and trade in government bonds, which until then had been an activity reserved for the investment banks. The Glass-Steagall restrictions were effectively removed completely in 1998, when Travelers, a rapidly growing finance conglomerate that included the investment bank

Salomon, was allowed to merge with retail bank Citicorp, and the Act was formally repealed in 1999. Associated changes in this period included rapid product innovation, especially in derivatives; the development of hedge funds; a massive growth in the investment banking sector, in which the small partnership organizations of the post-war years, employing at most a few hundred people, grew into large multinationals employing tens of thousands of people apiece, most of them now absorbed into banking conglomerates; and a massive growth in inter-bank trading, leading to a much more interconnected financial system.

These developments have posed new challenges for the regulatory authorities, the most significant of which is that systemic risk exposure is no longer limited to the commercial banking sector. The financial crisis of 2008 demonstrated that relatively small derivative trading departments could bring down large banking conglomerates, and that if one bank got into trouble, it automatically exposed the rest of the system to risk.

Different countries have responded to these changes in different ways, but the leading financial centers of the USA and the UK have evolved quite different regulatory systems. In 1997, the UK, which had previously had one of the most complex and disjointed systems in the world, adopted an integrated statutory system with a single regulator, the Financial Services Authority (FSA), responsible for the entire sector. In 2013, the system was changed again and the FSA split into a Prudential Regulation Authority, under the Bank of England, and a Financial Conduct Authority, but with just two clearly defined regulatory authorities, it is both simple and centralized.

The American system, in contrast, remains highly fragmented, with over 100 different regulatory agencies, strong elements of self-regulation and even regulatory competition, with some companies even able to choose their regulatory regime. The regulation of commercial banking, lending and deposit taking is split between fifty state banking regulators, the Federal Reserve, the OCC and the OTS, with some activities also regulated across the sector by the Federal Deposit Insurance Corporation (FDIC). Insurance companies are regulated entirely by state-level Insurance Commissions, with no nationwide regulator. Securities regulation is divided between the SEC, broadly covering equities and bonds and reporting to the Senate Banking Committee, and the Commodities and Futures Trading Commission (CFTC), broadly covering commodities, futures and options and reporting to the Senate Agriculture Committee. Many states also have their own securities regulators. There is also the Financial Industries Regulatory Authority (FINRA), which, despite its name and some legislative foundations, is a self-regulatory organization that in 2007 took over regulatory functions from the New York Stock Exchange and National Association of Securities Dealers. The Public Company Accounting Oversight Board (PCAOB), which regulates the audit function of accounting firms and replaced a self-regulating professional association, is a private sector non-profit corporation with statutory powers.

Taken as a whole, the global financial system is both massive and massively complex. It is also massively powerful. Its origins lie in facilitation and intermediation, in supporting and enabling government, trade and productive enterprise, but over the last half-century – and not forgetting the financial crisis – the institutions of finance have arguably become more powerful than the institutions of government and business they support. And as we shall see in the next section, it is partly this power, and the financial rewards it brings, that attracts the attention of critics.

Finance, investment, wealth creation and self-interest

All businesses, financial or otherwise, are characterized by two contrasting aspects. On the one hand, they create wealth by investing resources in the production of valuable goods and services which people want to buy and which would not otherwise be available. Modern civilization is built upon the institution of business. Without it, our societies would be economically undeveloped and they would almost certainly be poorer, not only in material and financial terms but also in cultural and artistic terms. On the other hand, businesses also siphon off much of the wealth they create for their owners and managers. Indeed, this is why people typically engage in business – to make a profit.

Within contemporary society, these two aspects are reconciled through a political orthodoxy of egoism, commonly associated with the eighteenth-century economist and moral philosopher Adam Smith.[7] The way to maximize wealth creation for society as a whole, it is argued, is precisely by giving free rein, at least in the context of business, to people's self-interest. In a free market environment, businessmen and entrepreneurs, motivated

---

[7] Smith 1776.

by the desire for financial gain, will compete with each other vigorously for custom, and this competition for custom will (through the "invisible hand" of the market) both drive innovation and productivity and direct them toward providing the products and services that are most valued by consumers. There may be arguments about the degree to which markets should be regulated to secure property rights, protect people from unscrupulous fraudsters or protect third parties from the unintended side-effects (pollution, accidents, etc.) of technology-based competition. There are also arguments about the extent to which the distribution of the wealth created should be manipulated by governments, through taxation and welfare, for example, and the extent to which this should be left to economic forces. But there has long been a broad consensus that free market financial capitalism is good for economic growth, that economic growth is good for society and that even if the profits accrue mainly to a wealthy minority, much of the wealth created will trickle down to the rest of the community. Jobs will be created to produce the goods and services on which the wealthy spend their gains, and everyone will benefit from the new technologies and cheaper goods generated by competition.

A key aspect of this consensus (though one that would have Adam Smith, who had no such thoughts, turning in his grave) is that it accepts the finance community's own characterization of financial activity as essentially amoral, as explained in Chapter 2.[8] It is taken for granted that financial actors will seek to maximize their financial returns regardless of the impact or consequences of their actions, and that this is ethically unproblematic.

From the perspective of the finance community, this consensus is unremarkable. Imbued with the ideology and assumptions of orthodox economic theory, financial practitioners and academics take it for granted that people are self-interested anyway, that efficient markets are the most effective way of allocating resources so as to maximize total wealth and that this is what most matters. Critics, however, point to a range of concerns.

From an empirical perspective, it can be questioned whether free *financial* markets are in fact wealth-generating, even if it is accepted that free

---

[8] Although Smith is known today for his reference to the self-interest driving "the butcher, the brewer, or the baker," he took for granted a general moral sympathy between people in a community, and while he assumed that the butcher would advance his own interests, he did not assume that he would be opportunistically self-serving: self-interest was conceived as lying within moral bounds, not as being amoral.

markets more generally are. It can also be questioned whether any wealth created does in fact get distributed beyond its immediate recipients (primarily financial sector practitioners, who take the lion's share of their firms' revenues), or could be so distributed without much more radical governmental and inter-governmental intervention than seems plausible. There is mounting evidence both within and across societies that the rich are getting richer and the poor poorer. Related to this, there is also concern at the exploitation of the financially weak by the financially strong that appears to be an inherent if unintentional part of the system.

There are also more principled concerns. From Socrates onwards, philosophers have argued that we have an ethical duty to ourselves (Kant's Formula of Humanity applies to oneself as well as to others), but critics question whether a system based on pecuniary or material self-interest can ever be ethically acceptable. Some suggest that the maximization of wealth, far from being a route to the maximization of goodness, positively destroys the things that are most valuable in life. They note a tendency of the financial system to bring everything into market relationships, including those that cannot be priced and traded without destroying their inherent moral value. Others focus on the ways in which the financial system diverts resources into essentially non-productive activities, suggesting that it is not so much the heart of the real economy as a cancerous growth or parasite, sucking wealth out of it rather than contributing to its healthy development.

In the following sections we shall look at some of the ethical arguments that can be made against the financial system, but first we need to look more closely at the arguments that can be made in its favor.

The case for the financial system

The core ethical argument in support of the financial system as it operates today is a rule utilitarian one. Total utility is maximized, it is suggested, by the general adherence to two rules:

Rule 1: everybody should always act in all commercial transactions (including employment transactions) in such a way as to maximize their own economic gains.

Rule 2: governments and regulators should always act so as to keep markets of all kinds as free as possible in their operation.

These rules are meant to apply to all commercial transactions and all markets, but the contemporary financial system is justified by their particular application to financial markets. The interpretation of the second rule is open to debate. Some market libertarians argue for the complete absence of regulation. The general consensus, however, is that maintaining free markets requires regulation to protect property rights and enforce contractual obligations, to outlaw fraudulent misrepresentation and to protect third parties from collateral damage. There is also a widespread consensus that human beings and their organs should not be traded, at least without their consent. But, this apart, the rule does not generally allow any limitations on what can or cannot be traded, on who can trade and in what quantity, or on the freedom of those trading to agree a price. The financial system as it currently operates is the product of a political consensus (part of what is sometimes called the "Washington Consensus") to the effect that financial market regulation should be largely restricted to the removal of market imperfections through increased disclosure and transparency, and should not seek to limit capital flows, trading opportunities or product-market innovations.

This is not an area in which we can conduct useful experiments. While advocates of the financial system might make general empirical claims based on the affluence of the West, the argument that these rules maximize overall utility is predominantly a theoretical rather than an empirical one. It requires two steps. First, there is an argument to the effect that this set of rules maximizes total wealth. This rests on economic theory, and in particular on the work of Friedrich Hayek and Milton Friedman. In fact, economists have never been able to agree on the optimal level of government involvement in markets, and while there is a broad consensus in favor of relative freedom from intervention, there is a strong divide between those who focus on the theoretical potential of free markets and those who focus on their practical limitations. Empirically, too, we find a divide between those who focus on the growth of the global economy in recent decades and those who point to the historical dependence of the major economies on tariff protection and government subsidy. The general consensus, however, is that these rules probably are wealth-maximizing, or at least more likely to be so than any possible alternative.[9]

Second, there is an argument to the effect that maximizing economic wealth will also maximize utility on any reasonable definition of utility. This claim is more contentious, but it is supported by some reasonable arguments. There is the trickle-down argument to which we have already referred, suggesting that even if wealth is initially concentrated in relatively few hands, it will eventually work its way through society as they spend it on goods and services. It can also be argued that the efficiency gains from competition and the new products and services created, even if they initially benefit the wealthy, will filter through society. Cars, computers and televisions, which were originally luxury products, are now very widely available and affordable. Since the mechanisms of trickle-down and technology penetration are likely to be most effective in societies that do not correspond to the free market ideals, with redistributive tax and welfare systems, for example, and protected collective wage bargaining, these arguments are not straightforward, but they cannot be dismissed out of hand.

There is also an argument to the effect that since people's ideas of what is good vary considerably, the best we can do in practice is to maximize wealth, which can then be exchanged according to people's wishes. And there is an argument that the richer a society is, no matter how that wealth is distributed, the more likely it is to support and defend the rights and freedoms that contribute to people's non-economic well-being. Empirically, for example, there is evidently a strong correlation between different countries' GDPs and the way in which they treat their citizens.

Overall, a fairly convincing case can be made that the world is a *richer* place for having broadly the kind of global free market system we do. The system may not strictly maximize wealth and in the wake of the financial crisis, there have been numerous calls for greater regulation, but with a view to stabilizing market mechanisms rather than limiting them. It is unlikely that any other kind of system could do much better and the one we have seems better than others that have been tried. Few people today would argue on economic grounds for centrally planned economies or even

---

[9] There is no space here to go into the detailed economic arguments. For a brief and lucid summary, see Turner 2012. For a more substantial but equally lucid critical review, see Chang 2010.

for a return to the levels of regulatory control of the post-war decades. What are more debatable are: (a) whether free *financial* markets, which have particular characteristics not found in industrial markets, are wealth-maximizing; (b) whether the maximization of wealth also serves to maximize total utility, in the broad sense in which we are using the word; and (c) whether maximizing total utility is in this case an appropriate ethical objective.

The peculiarities of financial markets

In a recent review of the state of economics, Adair Turner, Chairman of the UK FSA, concluded that there was no compelling empirical evidence one way or the other in respect of the economic benefits of free *financial* markets. Theoretically, too, he noted arguments both ways. The dominant school of neoclassical economic theory puts a great weight on financial market freedom as ensuring the optimal distribution of financial resources, both directly and through the provision of efficient links, especially through derivative contracts, between all other markets and across different time periods. Critics, however, point to the susceptibility of financial markets to herd effects, leading to frequent asset bubbles and subsequent collapses, often with devastating consequences. Defenders of the system attribute these to residual market imperfections, but critics suggest that they are rooted in human behavior and inherent in financial markets. Since financial markets are largely free of the physical constraints of industrial product markets, they are particularly prone to the radical uncertainty described by Knight and Simon, to irrational psychological biases as described by Tversky and Kahneman, and above all the second-guessing described by Keynes.[10]

Combining these perspectives, it would seem that financial markets potentially have both positive effects, enhancing overall market efficiency, and negative effects, in the form of instability and periodic crises, and, moreover, that these negative effects are not ones that can be easily regulated away. There is no obvious way in which regulators could allow derivatives markets, for example, while preventing the human behaviors

[10] Kahneman *et al.* 1982; Kahneman 2011; Keynes 1920; Knight 1921; Simon 1997; Turner 2012.

associated with them. In terms of overall wealth creation, we simply cannot say, either empirically or theoretically, which of these effects will dominate over time.

Turner's review also makes the point that one thing financial markets do not generally do is add *directly* to the total wealth. Their function is mainly distributive rather than productive, and to the extent that they do contribute to wealth, it is indirectly, through their impact on markets for other products and services. This doesn't in itself make financial services necessarily less valuable, but as the size of the financial sector has grown, far outstripping the growth of the economy as a whole, it raises the question as to whether it might take more wealth out of the productive economy than it puts into it. The same question can be asked of other distributive activities – civil law, for example, or large areas of marketing – but it is particularly pertinent in the case of finance, where the scale of revenues extracted is quite mind-boggling.

To give some idea of this scale, it has been estimated that in the stock market boom of the late 1990s, the financial sector took fees and commission payments of around $1.275 trillion. (Company executives, paid in stock or stock options, took a further $1 trillion out of the system just by cashing these in.) This excludes any profits from derivatives trading on the investment banks' own account (and the costs to the non-financial sector of hedging against the volatility this created) and, of course, profits from bond dealing, mortgages, Forex, etc. By the 2000s, US financial companies accounted for around a third of total US corporate profits, and that was after paying their staff members massively more per capita than in any other sector.[11]

For another indication, look at Goldman Sachs, one of the large investment banks, in an "ordinary" year. In 2009, it had revenues of $45 billion, divided roughly equally between traditional investment banking activities – including mergers and acquisitions advice and other advisory services, underwriting fees in respect of bond and share issues, and investment management – and market-making or trading on its own account. Against this, it had non-personnel operating costs of about $9 billion and compensation costs of about $16 billion divided between about 33,000 staff – roughly

---

[11] Madrick 2011, pp. 25, 332. For data on the growing dominance of the US financial sector up to about 2000, see Krippner 2005.

$500,000 apiece on average.[12] Goldman Sachs is nowadays one of the larger investment banks and does more proprietary trading than most of its competitors, but it is just one player among many. Fee income alone is of the order of $200 billion a year across the industry, while investment management brings revenues of perhaps $1 trillion. Meanwhile, in 2007, the top 25 US hedge fund managers (that is, individuals, not firms) took an average income of over $1 billion each. Of the 400 richest Americans that year, according to Forbes, about 10 percent were hedge fund managers.[13]

These figures prompt several thoughts. First, it seems inherently implausible that the financial sector can be generating wealth on the scale on which it is currently extracting it. Second, it seems quite likely that the scale of rewards is attracting into finance many of the most able people in society, who are not consequently going into the directly wealth-creating sectors of the economy. (The scale of rewards is itself quite understandable: the impact of a financial trader's activity may not be wealth-enhancing, but it is both immediate and measurable, making it rational for financial firms to pay high levels of incentive pay that would not be rational in industry, where outcomes are much longer term and harder to measure.) Third, in markets that are characterized by relatively long periods of growth punctuated by short sharp collapses, the temptation is to treat growth as normal. At any one moment, collapse is less likely than continued growth, so individuals and firms act as if it won't happen. In the good times, they extract profits. In the bad times, their inside knowledge allows them to move quickly to protect themselves and it is left to someone else (clients and taxpayers) to pick up the bill. What we may have here is a kind of "tragedy of the commons," where decisions that are individually rational and short-term wealth-maximizing are collectively and long-term wealth-damaging.[14]

---

[12] Goldman Sachs 2009 Annual Report, at www.goldmansachs.com/investor-relations/financials/archived/annual-reports/2009-annual-report.html.

[13] Madrick 2011, p. 249.

[14] In its original form, the tragedy of the commons focused on the problem of over-fishing. It is always rational for fishermen individually to maximize their catches, even if this has the long-term effect of destroying their livelihood. For applications to finance and related areas, see Frank 2011. For the general effects of distributive markets, see Turner 2012.

Wealth, utility, happiness and welfare

Suppose we set aside these concerns and accept that the financial system is wealth-maximizing. We next have to ask whether it is also utility-maximizing and here we encounter two sets of problems. The most difficult concern questions of distribution and inequality. Before getting to these, however, we first have to define utility.

In economics, the utility of something is reflected in the price you're prepared to pay for it. So, while maximizing utility is equivalent to maximizing satisfaction, utility is defined in purely monetary terms. But utilitarian ethics is rooted in quite different measures, notably the excess of pleasure over pain or, in John Stuart Mill's formulation, happiness.[15] Beginning in the 1990s, a group of economists have been investigating happiness empirically and exploring its relation to income and wealth. They have concluded that, while happiness (or "life-satisfaction," as measured by surveys) seems to be correlated to income at low income levels, the correlation breaks down in wealthier societies and at higher income levels. In these conditions, the link between money and happiness appears to be relatively slight, unpredictable and context-specific.[16]

There are at least two obvious reasons for this. First, many of the things that make rich people happy tend to be limited in supply and devalued by use. Not everyone can have a yacht in Monte Carlo harbor, and the more yachts there are there, the less pleasurable is the experience. This means that the aspirations raised by increased wealth cannot always be met, and of course disappointment brings unhappiness. Second, there is strong evidence that once basic needs are met, happiness is strongly related to relative goods. What people value is having relatively more money and relatively better houses, cars, clothes, etc., than their peers, and if everyone's wealth increases equally, they are consequently no happier as a result.

Another approach to defining what we should maximize can be found in the work of Amartya Sen and Martha Nussbaum on capabilities. The thrust of the argument here is that any measure of what we should be maximizing (generally called "well-being") should include not only economic factors but

---

[15] Mill 1998 (1863).
[16] Turner 2012 gives a useful brief review. For more substantial reviews, see Frank 1985; Frey and Stutzer 2001; and Layard 2005.

also a range of capabilities and freedoms, in particular those associated with human rights, which are seen as valuable in themselves, irrespective of the happiness they produce. These include, for example, the ability to enjoy a full lifespan, good health, a broad and enabling education, physical security, freedom of conscience and association, political enfranchisement and the ability to own property.[17]

The capabilities approach doesn't directly challenge the arguments in favor of the global financial system, as wealth enhancement would seem on the face of it to be capability-enhancing as well, at least in some respects.[18] Once again, however, it raises distributional questions. It is at least plausible that economic growth, while enhancing the capabilities of the rich, might damage the practical capabilities of the poor, both globally and within particular societies, especially if it is associated with high levels of inequality.

In summary, a world with greater economic wealth is not necessarily one with greater happiness or well-being. It may be so, and is perhaps more likely to be so than otherwise, but it will all depend on the details and, in particular, on the way the wealth is distributed.

Questions of distribution

The most frequent criticism of the financial system in the academic literature is that while it may be wealth-maximizing, or at least wealth-enhancing, it also increases inequality, both directly, as wealth is siphoned off by the rich financial sector, and indirectly, through the global flows of capital enabled by the system. Some critics see high levels of inequality as bad in themselves, and we shall look at these objections in the next section. But there is also an argument to the effect that substantial inequalities reduce utility by directly or indirectly damaging people's happiness and well-being, and that this reduction in utility more than compensates for any gains resulting from increases in total wealth.

To explore this issue, we first need to ask whether the system has in fact resulted in increased inequality, and to do this we shall ask first whether

---

[17] Nussbaum 2000; Sen 1985, 1992.

[18] Though not necessarily in all. Emotional capabilities, for example, on which Nussbaum focuses, may be damaged by a wealth-maximizing culture.

inequality has increased over the period in which the financial system has flourished in its current form, and second to what extent any increase can be attributed to the financial system. We then need to ask what consequences can be attributed to this increase. Inequalities of wealth and income exist both within countries and between them, and we shall look first at the case of the USA, which is the country in which the financial system is most fully developed, and then at the global picture.

Inequality in the USA

Inequality has been rising across the developed world for the last thirty or forty years. In the USA, the ratio between the disposable income of the richest 10 percent and the poorest 10 percent has gone up from about 10:1 in the mid-1980s to about 14:1 today, and many developed countries have seen similar proportionate rises.[19] More striking than this, though, is the gap between the very rich, who have been getting much richer, and average or below-average earners, who have not. From the mid-1970s to the mid-2000s, the per-capita GDP of the USA, adjusted for inflation, almost doubled, but the median wage was roughly unchanged. Roughly half of all extra income generated over the period ended up in the top 5 percent of households, and a quarter of it in the top 1 percent. Indeed, for the five years 2002–7, the top 1 percent captured no less than 65 percent of all the extra income generated, and by 2007, including capital gains, they were taking nearly a quarter of the national income. The top 0.01 percent were taking nearly half as much as the bottom 50 percent (and two-thirds as much as the bottom 50 percent of the entire global population).[20] Despite all the extra wealth generated, those below the median wage – which is to say half of all wage-earners – ended up with a *lower* income, after adjusting for inflation, than they had thirty years earlier.

This growing inequality is a product of many different factors. At the bottom end, the main cause seems to have been technological change, which has reduced the demand for unskilled labor, leading to declining real hourly wages and increased part-time working. This is not obviously a product of the financial system. The effect has been exacerbated by the opening up of global markets, with the manufactured products of unskilled and semi-skilled

---

[19] Noah 2012; OECD 2011.   [20] Pogge 2011; Saez and Piketty 2003, 2009.

workers now being imported from the developing world rather than made in the USA, and the global markets that make this possible are themselves made possible by the financial system, but the impact of this is hard to measure. A recent Organisation for Economic Co-operation and Development (OECD) report includes the "surprising" conclusion that globalized manufacturing has not impacted significantly on developed economy inequalities.[21]

At the top end, one factor emphasized by Turner is that increased overall wealth has led to a growing emphasis on relational goods (branded, fashion and luxury goods, speculative investments, etc.), leading to the growth of distributional activities which, as already mentioned, tend to pay high, incentive-based incomes. Finance itself is by far the largest and highest-paying of these, and finance theories of incentives have driven pay levels in the others.[22]

Because of the relational aspect, the growth at the top is also self-fueling. The rewards paid to the elite, whether bankers, sports stars or celebrities, are ramped up as everyone bids for the best (as buyers) and bids to be paid as the best (as sellers). Again, finance is the sector with the highest numbers of very highly paid, and finance also provides the rationale and justification for escalating top-end pay more generally. It is also worth noting here that financial markets themselves can have a significant impact on inequalities among the relatively affluent. The moderately well-off, whose wealth is typically invested through mutual funds, pension funds and life policies, pay much higher fees and have much poorer access to high-return invest-ments than the very wealthy, who have very large amounts to invest. They also seem to suffer disproportionately when markets collapse.

Changes at both the top and the bottom have clearly been affected by a changing political climate and corresponding changes in taxation and wel-fare policies. The rich are now much more lightly taxed than they were and real welfare spending has declined. Spending on public education has also fallen, exacerbating the problems of an unskilled labor force. These changes in turn reflect the political power wielded by both rich individuals and business corporations, but they cannot be attributed specifically to the financial sector.[23]

---

[21] OECD 2011.   [22] Turner 2012.

[23] Political factors are emphasized by Smith 2012 and Stiglitz 2012. For a brief but well-balanced review of the different accounts of American inequality, see Friedman 2012.

Finally, it would seem apparent that the one possible counter to these changes, the trickle-down effect, is not working, or is not working well enough to have much effect. The rich do spend some of their income on goods and services, but they pay relatively little tax (which is the most effective method of redistribution) and rather than finding its way back into the real economy, much of their income is simply reinvested. Again, some of this investment finds its way, through equity markets or private equity, into the real economy. Some of it goes into government bonds, which enable the government to maintain spending in the absence of tax revenues; some of it is given to charitable causes (which is certainly redis-tributive, although extremely slowly – there may be a gap of a generation or more between income and expenditure). But much of it is simply recircu-lated amongst the rich through speculative trading in everything from financial derivatives to works of art.

Overall, it seems fair to say that the financial system is far from being the only cause of growing American inequality, but that it is almost certainly a significant factor at the top end, in the growing gap between the top 1 percent and the rest.

Turning to the consequences of inequality, the most obvious is the one due to declining marginal utility. It seems evident that the utility benefits, however they are measured, of an extra $10,000 a year to someone earning $20,000 a year or even $60,000 a year are much greater than those of an extra $10,000 a year to someone earning $200,000 a year, let alone $2 million a year. Going back to the statistics given above, an increase in total wealth that has left half the population *worse* off must surely have significantly decreased total utility.

There is also substantial evidence that inequality is socially damaging. Kate Pickett and Richard Wilkinson have argued persuasively that across the developed world, levels of inequality are positively correlated with a host of social and welfare problems, including violent crime, illiteracy, mental illness, obesity, teenage pregnancy, low life expectancy and low levels of trust.[24] Whether these problems are actually caused by inequality is contentious, but it seems very plausible that they are more likely to arise in societies which tolerate high levels of inequality and don't seek to redress them. Most of these problems directly damage people's capabilities, as

[24] Pickett and Wilkinson 2010.

defined by Sen and Nussbaum. Many of them are also likely to produce unhappiness.

Finally, we should consider whether extreme inequality contributes directly to unhappiness. This is difficult to assess. People typically compare themselves to their immediate peer groups and may actually gain happiness of a kind from the lives of the celebrity super rich, sharing vicariously in their fortune and dreaming of emulating it. On the other hand, there is clearly resentment in the USA today at the growing gap between the top 1 percent and the rest, with a growing majority feeling left behind or left out.

Global inequality

The literature on the global distribution of wealth is marked by a sharp ideological divide. Some economists maintain that inequality and/or poverty have decreased over the decades of global financial markets, while others claim that they have increased, with each side using the measures and time periods that best suit its case. Some income measures, for example, include only what is commercially traded, so that the crop production of subsistence farmers counts for nothing. Others attempt to measure household income in a way that takes account of home-grown produce. For those concerned primarily with poverty, it seems obvious that the latter measure is more appropriate: if someone moves from being a subsistence smallholder, growing and bartering enough to live on, to being a factory worker earning less than enough to live on, it seems perverse to treat that as a gain in economic output. But for the champions of the global financial system, many of whom believe almost as a matter of faith that wealth creation rests on specialization and the division of labor, the produce of subsistence farmers *should* be ignored.[25] Again, some economists compare the percentage growth in upper- and lower-end incomes, while others compare absolute growth: if the poorest members of society increase their income by 50 percent, from $1 to $1.50 a day, but the gap between them and the rich still grows, some claim this to be reducing inequality, while others say that it increases it. Thus, although the topic has generated a large

---

[25] Reddy and Pogge 2009.

literature, the protagonists generally argue across each other rather than directly taking on each other's arguments.[26]

David Dollar and Aart Kraay represent what might be thought of as the orthodox economic view and contend that the growth enabled by the global financial system has increased wealth without increasing inequality and has been unequivocally good for the poor. While global inequality, measured in terms of the difference between an average income and a median income (the income of an average person), grew steadily throughout the nineteenth and much of the twentieth centuries, they argue, it roughly stabilized around the mid-1970s, following which growth has occurred most rapidly in relatively poorer, developing countries, and especially those that have opened their economies to the global financial system. Even when the inequalities within developing economies have increased, as in China, the poor have gained in absolute terms and the numbers in poverty have decreased. Across all countries, they suggest, the incomes of the poor have grown roughly in proportion to national GDP. In some of these countries, inequalities have increased and in others they have decreased, but these changes are explained most naturally by local policies on taxation, education and welfare, and cannot in themselves be linked to globalization or the global financial system.[27]

Since the conventional economic wisdom is that inequality will tend to rise through the period of early industrialization and then fall again as economies mature, short-term increases of inequality in countries like China and India may not be a matter of concern, though the American data cited above may cast doubt upon that wisdom. What is potentially of very great concern is the impact of financial globalization upon the very poorest countries, many of which appear to have gotten poorer even on Dollar and Kraay's measures, not only relatively to other countries but also in absolute terms. Dollar and Kraay argue that these countries have suffered precisely because they have *not* engaged fully with the global financial system, but this may be too simple an explanation. It would be just as reasonable to say that the system has not engaged with them: that one of the consequences of the rules under which the system operates is that it

---

[26] For introductions to sections of this literature, see, for example, Salverda *et al.* 2009; Stiglitz *et al.* 2009; and Wilkinson and Clapp 2010.

[27] Dollar and Kraay 2002a, 2002b.

excludes the poorest countries, which have little to offer it in terms of profit, from the benefits it confers.

Coming at the subject from a very different perspective, the Nobel Prize-winning economist Joseph Stiglitz has distinguished between the effects of free trade, which he sees as very beneficial, and the effects of free financial markets, which he sees as deeply damaging. Separating these out empirically is virtually impossible, so Stiglitz rests his case mainly on case studies of the damage done by free financial markets. Over the last thirty years, many developing countries have participated in global financial markets, either voluntarily or under pressure from the IMF as a condition of IMF loans. Throughout this period, the IMF was a staunch advocate of free capital markets and of the discipline they imposed on the economic management of debtor countries. In many cases, countries resorted to IMF loans after they had gotten badly burnt by venturing into the global financial markets, only to be required to re-enter these markets. The problem is that developing countries, and even emerging economies, are very poorly equipped to cope with the volatility of these markets. Speculative money flows into the country, giving rise to high debt levels and real-estate bubbles. The bubbles burst and the money flows out again just as fast, taking with it the wealth accumulated in the meantime by the countries' own politically powerful elites and prompting a debt crisis and recession, the costs of which are inevitably borne by the population at large – including the poorest, who in developing countries typically have no welfare protection.[28]

George Soros, the financier and philanthropist, gives a particularly lucid account of what is going on here, and links it explicitly to the intrinsic characteristics of financial markets rather than just to IMF policies. One characteristic of financial markets, he argues, is that they are particularly prone to speculative bubbles. When prices are rising, it makes financial sense to buy, to capture the rise in price. The more people buy, the more prices rise, and the more prices rise, the more people buy. The same is true when prices are falling. Because financial products often have no real underlying use value (their value to the holder is purely a function of what someone else will pay for them), and because the markets are dominated by speculative trading, there are no natural breaks on this process, as

---

[28] Stiglitz 2003 and see also 2010.

there are in ordinary product markets. At some point, the insanity of the situation drives home and the markets go into reverse, but their natural behavior is to swing between far-from-equilibrium extremes, not, as economists tend to assume, to fluctuate closely around equilibrium points. This behavior is exacerbated by the presence of credit and the leverage it provides. Credit is an essential part of the financial system and in contemporary financial markets the degree of leverage is extreme, but credit is what Soros terms a reflexive phenomenon. The ability to borrow, including in our present context the ability of developing countries to borrow, depends on collateral assets (most typically real estate), but the value of these assets depends on what people are prepared to lend against them, so credit accentuates bubbles and busts. To make matters worse, the techniques used by individual traders and institutions to manage their individual risk, through hedging and stop loss control devices, *add* to risk at the systemic level. When prices go steeply down, the institutions cut their losses by selling, sending prices further down, prompting further stop-loss selling, and so on.[29]

The second characteristic of the financial system, according to Soros, is that while it has long been a fully global system, the political and regulatory systems with which it interacts remain national systems. Developing countries, dependent on the global financial system but unable to influence it, are completely at its mercy. Richer countries can influence it, but only through domestic policies that are apt to reflect their domestic interests. Like the risk control mechanisms of the financial institutions, these offer some protection for the countries concerned, but only at the cost of increasing systemic risk and shifting the problems onto other, poorer and less powerful players.

Both Stiglitz and Soros argue that the financial markets are inherently damaging, because of a mismatch between the volatility of their speculative capital flows and the need for a stable financial environment if businesses and governments are to generate real productive growth. Much of the time, their effects may be masked by the positive effects of free trade. But the effects become apparent through the crises they regularly generate and the damage is particularly severe in the case of less developed countries, where it impacts, according to Stiglitz, on both poverty and inequality.

---

[29] Soros 1998.

Another argument along similar lines is made by the philosopher Thomas Pogge, who accepts that free financial markets may be effective engines of wealth creation, but suggests that they suffer, like other competitive systems, from attempts by the most successful and hence most powerful players to manipulate the rules. In the absence of any moral constraint, the regulatory systems under which the most powerful players operate are designed to protect those players and the national interests they represent. There is some incentive for the leading players to bargain amongst themselves, acting in effect as a regulatory cartel, but this acts systematically against the interests of the weaker competitors and in particular those of developing countries.[30]

Stiglitz, Soros and Pogge all offer persuasive arguments, and Stiglitz offers abundant examples of the damaging consequences of free capital flows in and out of developing countries, suggesting strongly that the financial markets are not utility-maximizing. But neither he nor Dollar and Kraay have been able to substantiate their empirical claims well enough to decide the issue. To some extent, globally as well as within countries, wealth flows to the financial sector, and thus to the wealthy, simply through the fees charged. Less developed countries are heavily reliant on richer countries for the provision of financial services, and the net overseas earnings of the UK financial sector alone run at about £45 billion a year,[31] but beyond that, it's hard to come to any clear conclusions. Parts of the financial system are clearly instrumental in enabling many poorer countries to grow, but the periodic crises to which other parts are prone also stunt these countries' growth. The overall long-term impacts on both poverty and inequality, both within and between countries, are still impossible to assess. The impact of these on utility is also incredibly difficult to assess. Growth, when it comes, brings opportunities, capabilities and happiness to some, but the disruptions associated with both economic growth and economic crises are sometimes disabling (as people lose their traditional community support structures) and often distressing.

A full analysis of the utilitarian case for the financial system would require a book itself. The arguments sketched out here, however, suggest

[30] Pogge 2011.
[31] Office for National Statistics, UK Balance of Payments Pink Book, published annually, at www.ons.gov.uk.

that the case is at best unproven. It is hard to separate out the effects of the financial system from those of the larger system in which it fits, and hard to balance the positive against the negative consequences we observe. Much may depend on whether the financial market collapses we have seen in recent years are a temporary phenomenon that can be contained in the future, or whether they prove to be endemic to the system. Even without reaching clear conclusions, however, a utilitarian analysis directs our attention to the kinds of things we might look out for in forming a judgment, and in refining that judgment as the system develops and evidence of its effects grows.

Power and exploitation

So far, we have been looking at the financial system as a means to an end and judging it in terms of that end. But Pogge's argument about the tendency of powerful players to manipulate the regulatory framework to suit their own ends introduces another ethical perspective. Part of his point was that the financial system, as an institution, has certain properties, and that these properties can be judged in terms of criteria such as justice, fairness and respect for persons. The manipulation of competitive systems by their most powerful players not only has adverse consequences but is also ethically objectionable in itself.

We shall come back to the ethics of competition in Chapter 6. In this section we shall focus on two lines of critique of the financial system from the perspectives of Kantian, Rawlsian and consensus ethics.

Sanjay Reddy voices similar concerns to those of Pogge and Stiglitz, but applies the criterion of justice rather than utility. Focusing on the developing country debt crises of the early 1980s and the Asian financial crisis of the late 1990s, he identifies two ways in which global financial markets benefit the rich at the expense of the poor. First, developing countries suffer disproportionately from exchange rate and commodity price volatility due to speculation. The analysis here is essentially the same as those of Stiglitz and Soros discussed above. Second, the domestic monetary policies of the USA and other reserve currency nations, designed naturally enough to serve the interests of those nations, can have dramatic knock-on effects on developing countries. In the

1980s, for example, increases in American real interest rates led to global increases in the cost of borrowing that impacted particularly severely on developing countries, which in any case tend to pay relatively high interest rates, resulting in widespread insolvency. In general, he suggests, adverse changes in interest rates and money supply in the wealthiest countries impact disproportionately on the poorest countries. Their borrowing costs raised, they are left with dramatically reduced funds for non-interest expenditure on infrastructure and industrial development, welfare, etc. Local firms also see borrowing costs raised, economic performance drops, and the impact on the balance of payments and exchange rates raises borrowing costs (often dollar denominated) still further and drives out the foreign capital on which they are particularly dependent, producing a vicious cycle of decline.[32]

As we saw in the last chapter, Rawls's theory of justice combines elements of both utilitarian and Kantian ethics. According to this theory, a society might reasonably be organized so as to maximize utility, but only subject to certain constraints, one of which is expressed in his "difference principle." According to this principle, a just society should be organized so as to be of the greatest benefit to its least advantaged member: inequalities are not in themselves a problem, but the worst off must be better off than they would be in any alternative system.[33] Reddy argues that the global financial system clearly makes the poorest sections of the global community worse off and that it is therefore unethical. From this perspective, compensating benefits elsewhere or calculations of total utility are beside the point. Although Reddy does not make the argument, the same reasoning could clearly be applied in a domestic context. There can be little doubt that the US financial system has been a significant factor in making the poorest sectors of American society worse off, and from a Rawlsian perspective, the fact that the country as a whole may be wealthier is an irrelevance.

Reddy also argues that on *any* perspective that incorporates some concern for, or some recognition of the interests of, the least advantaged members of society, the global financial system is unethical because it disregards those interests. From a Kantian perspective, it does not respect the least advantaged as persons, and from the perspective of consensus ethics, their interests are not represented at top tables of monetary policy

[32] Reddy 2005.   [33] Rawls 1971, 2001.

debate, such as the G8. A broader critique along these lines can be constructed from the writings of David Korten, who focuses on the impact of
multinational corporations on developing countries, but attributes much of
the damage they do to the influence of the financial sector.

Korten documents the social and environmental damage caused by multinationals operating in developing countries through, for example, the
widespread pollution and disruption of communities by oil, mining and
plantation companies; the export of hazardous waste, pesticides and other
products banned in the firms' home countries, without any attempt to
protect or even warn those who may be exposed to them; and the corrupt
manipulation of democratic procedures.[34] Not all multinationals act in
these ways, of course, and many bring positive benefits, but the behaviors
are sufficiently widespread to be considered systemic and are evidently
unethical from Kantian, social contract or consensus perspectives.
Company policies that directly harm people's health and well-being show
no respect for persons and could not conceivably be willed as universal
laws. Policies that harm the poorest sectors of society have no place in a just
society. Policies that take no account of the interests of those affected, and
make no attempt to seek informed consent, clearly fail to meet the requirements of deliberative ethics.

There is no questioning here the harm done, or its wrongness in terms of
these normative theories. The only question is whether the harm can
reasonably be attributed to the financial system as well as to the corporations more directly implicated and, perhaps, the governments that fail to
adequately control these corporations and to protect their citizens.

Korten himself pins much of the blame on the financial system, which he
sees as not merely enabling the exploitation of developing country communities, but as pressurizing the corporations, through the demands of
fund managers, to override any ethical considerations and focus entirely on
short-term financial results. The rise of a financial mindset and the financialization of corporate governance in the 1980s and 1990s served, on this
account, to turn business corporations from largely benevolent institutions
into largely predatory ones, for which exploitation and profiting from the
exploitation of others are second nature. At the time that he was writing,

---

[34] Korten 2001. For well-documented examples and analysis from a business ethics perspective, see Kline 2010.

there was little evidence to back this up, but the imposition of short-term financial models on corporations and the role of the financial sector in bringing this about are now well documented.[35] The financial system is not the only cause of the damage (many firms manage to resist its pressures), but it is almost certainly a contributory cause.

One possible counter-argument to both the Reddy and the Korten arguments goes back to the self-perception of the financial sector as amoral rather than immoral. George Soros, for example, accepts fully that the global financial system causes damage and that this gives rise to serious moral problems. But he is adamant that this is an issue for politicians and regulators, not for financial actors themselves. The challenge in his view is for societies to develop a global political system of collective, ethically focused decision-making that is equal to the task of controlling and directing the financial system, and protecting those who cannot protect themselves. The responsibility of financial actors is simply to make as much money as they can: their speculation may cause harm, but in doing so, it is, he says, a "necessary evil," necessary because of the good to which it contributes. Indeed, he insists that to let morality intrude into a financial system based on free market competition would itself be damaging, since participants with moral scruples would inevitably under-perform compared to those without (eventually being driven out of the market), competition would be weakened and the overall effectiveness of the system as a driver of wealth creation would be reduced.[36]

The part of Soros's argument that finds fault with governments seems uncontroversial. On any theory, governments and administrators have an ethical responsibility to protect the interests of their citizens and it is evident that the governments of many developing countries do not do this, focusing instead on their own private interests. It can also be argued that the most advantaged nations have a duty to help, or at least refrain from harming, the less advantaged. This might not legitimate their interference in another country's affairs, and in economic matters, as arguments over the role of the IMF illustrate, it is not at all obvious where the boundary

---

[35] See, for example, Roberts *et al.* 2006 and Zorn *et al.* 2004.

[36] Soros 1995, p. 83. It is not evident that players with moral scruples will necessarily under-perform in a competitive context, but the fact that the participants in this competition assume they will is probably evidence that they will. For an argument to the effect that competition encourages immoral behavior, see Shleifer 2004.

lies between assistance and interference. (Rawls has argued that interference can only be justified under relatively extreme conditions, as respect for sovereignty effectively trumps an application of the difference principle to nation states, but he was concerned with military, not economic interference.[37]) However, it would seem to impose a duty on the governments of the most advantaged countries to regulate the international activities of companies under their jurisdiction.

What is much more controversial is the part of Soros's argument that seeks to justify the self-interest of the financial system even when it is clearly causing harm. The idea that moral scruples introduce market imperfections and so reduce the efficiency of the market is part of the prevailing economic orthodoxy, but it has no empirical foundation and arguably no basis in theory either. Economic theory assumes self-interest; it does not derive it. The idea that purely self-interested behavior, of the kind assumed here, can be justified in any terms is also contentious. This leads us to a further set of criticisms.

The ethics of self-interest

Most people take the view that self-interested behavior of the kind sanctioned by the financial system, acting without any regard to the impact of one's actions on other people, is simply wrong, and that whether the context is finance or any other human activity is irrelevant. From this point of view, the idea that finance is some kind of amoral competitive game is deeply misleading. Monopoly might be such a game, or chess, or Kinect Adventures or Super Mario Bros, but playing them doesn't risk serious harm to other people. Playing with finance does, and it should be subject to the same moral rules as other real-life activities.

In terms of normative ethics, this is a reasonable criticism. A maxim of acting in one's material self-interest regardless of the impact on other people would clearly not show respect for persons and would fail Kant's universalizability test. A person who was guided by this rule would not generally be considered to be virtuous. From the perspective of indirect utilitarianism, a personal rule of behaving with regard to the impacts of one's actions on others would seem to be a more promising way of

---

[37] Rawls 1999.

maximizing utility than a rule of behaving without such a regard. It would also be more plausible as a social rule under rule utilitarianism.

That much is relatively easy. The more difficult question is whether the general rule should be subject to exceptions. The justification for the financial system is not based on the idea that people should act generally without regard to the impact of their actions on others, but on the idea that the regard for others mandated by the normal rules of society should be suspended in this particular context.

To explore this issue, it is worth switching our attention briefly away from the prescriptions of normative ethics to those of actually prevailing social moralities. Historically, modern societies have almost always had general moral norms mandating some regard for others and condemning aggressive self-interest. But they have also almost always made exceptions, especially in respect of entrepreneurs and financiers. Both groups have been seen as bringing benefits to a society, even though motivated by narrowly conceived self-interest.[38] However, societies have also sought to contain these exceptions in two ways: through regulations designed to protect people from actual harm, and through the maintenance of strong cultural (and sometimes physical) boundaries designed to prevent the values of the entrepreneurs and financiers from polluting the morals of society at large. Financial services, for example, were traditionally provided by immigrant communities, living outside the orbit of mainstream society, and well into the twentieth century, Wall Street remained a relatively closed community. Foreign traders were traditionally confined to the port areas of cities and business corporations were licensed only for specific purposes deemed to be in the public interest. Until relatively recently, large businesses themselves built their organizations on the moral norms of the societies in which they operated, keeping their self-interested pursuit of profit well out of sight.[39]

Over the last forty years, all this has changed. The financial sector has grown far too large to be sealed off from the rest of society. The general

---

[38] These decisions were, of course, made by rulers, who often had their own interests at heart rather than those of society at large. But the legitimating argument is nevertheless a valid one.

[39] For a fuller discussion, see Hendry 2004. A parallel case is that of artists who have been allowed to breach the normal moral rules of decency in the cause of art, but are subject to forms of censorship designed to protect public morals.

business sector has embraced the ideology of finance. And moderate or non-aggressive self-interest has become socially legitimate to an unprecedented degree, not only in business and finance but in social and familial relationships too. Putting one's own interests above those of one's parents or children, for example, is now widely accepted in Western society.

Coming back to normative ethics, none of this affects the Kantian arguments against self-interest. It does, however, affect the utilitarian arguments. The range of rules we can consider as plausible candidates for internalization and routine application changes as our culture and modes of thinking change. And the consequences of applying rules also depend on the culture within which they are applied.

One of the assumptions we made in the rule utilitarian case for the financial system was that encouraging people to follow a rule of self-interest in finance would not have significant spillover effects on their behavior or the behavior of other people in other arenas. Making an exception of finance, in other words, would not reduce the benefits or effectiveness of the general rule against self-interest. So long as the finance community was small and socially contained, this was probably a reasonable assumption, but it seems much less reasonable in the light of recent history. Indeed, it seems evident that the values of the financial system – self-interest and also the prioritizing of monetary value – have already permeated much of society, crowding out moral values, weakening established moral norms and leading us to disregard things we should arguably be cherishing, because no monetary value can be put on them.[40]

From a utilitarian perspective, the main concern here is with the impact of financial norms, through the examples they set and the influence of the financial sector on politicians and the media, and on the norms of people outside finance. However, critics have also expressed concerns as to the impact of financial norms on financiers themselves. The underlying thought here is that people cannot easily separate their lives off in the way that the justification for the financial system assumes, acting out of naked self-interest in one part of their lives and as responsible citizens in another. This takes us into virtue ethics.

It is a common strategy of writers and filmmakers seeking to criticize the financial system to portray its actors as unsavory characters, as selfish and

---

[40] Hendry 2002; Sandel 2012.

> **Box 4.1. The culture of finance? The Enron trading floor and Californian black-outs**
>
> By 2001, Enron's dominance of the unregulated US energy market was such that it could manipulate wholesale electricity prices by removing supply from parts of the grid. Over a six-month period, Enron's traders systematically created artificial shortages in California, leading to 38 "stage 3" emergencies (rolling blackouts across the state), at a time of year when there were ample reserves of generating power in the state and no such emergencies would be expected. (Peak demand in California is in the summer months.) The blackouts were a consequence of removing capacity from the system, part of a manipulation of wholesale prices so that Enron could increase profits, which it did – its wholesale energy division took revenues of nearly $100 billion during the six months. This whole operation could only be effected by coordinated actions across the Enron trading floor. The traders knew exactly what was happening and reportedly rejoiced collectively in the blackouts.
>
> **Source**: McLean and Elkind 2004, McLean *et al.* 2005.

uncaring in their personal lives as in their work. This can take the form of individual character demolitions, such as that of the former Royal Bank of Scotland chief Sir Fred Goodwin by Matthew Hancock and Nadhim Zahawi,[41] or it can be more generic, as in the Enron film *The Smartest Guys in the Room*, which portrays the firm's traders generally as taking positive pleasure from blacking out swathes of California (see Box 4.1). The makers of the 2011 documentary movie *Inside Job* suggest that many bankers, accustomed to getting what they want without having to take account of any moral constraints, are similarly unconstrained outside the office, sleeping around with scant regard for their partners and exhibiting a distinctly warped notion of morality.[42]

How all this reflects on the financial sector is debatable. Filmmakers are typically out to make a point, not to weigh up the evidence, and there is no evidence that finance practitioners behave any less ethically in their personal lives than other people. Nor can we tell whether those who may be unethical have had their values distorted by the financial system or were

---

[41] Hancock and Zahawi 2011.   [42] Ferguson *et al.* 2010.

like that all along: perhaps the financial sector is doing us all a favor by soaking up morally undesirable characters, making them work long hours, channeling their aggression and keeping them out of trouble! Certainly, any barrel as big as the financial sector is going to contain some bad apples.

However, there are some indications of a problem. One commonly acknowledged feature of financial firms, and especially their trading floors, is that they tend to be very masculine, aggressive cultures, and that this often manifests itself in sexist behaviors, both demeaning women and depriving them of any redress.[43] There is no obvious reason why sexists should be particularly attracted to finance, suggesting that this is in part a product of the industry culture.

Again, the most striking scenes of *Inside Job* are the footage of Goldman Sachs investment bankers appearing in congressional hearings and facing the (true) charge that they had promoted to their clients securities they themselves believed would lose value. Asked if they had a duty to their clients, the bankers managed to convey the impression not that they did or didn't have a duty but that they couldn't, as bankers, comprehend the notion of duty. Reporters also asked financial economists who had written papers in support of particular financial institutions why they made no mention of the fact that those institutions had paid for the research. To fail to acknowledge such support in the sciences would be an outrageous breach of professional ethics, but the economists just couldn't see what the fuss was about. The concern here is not about bad apples; it is that the institutional values of finance take no account of the goodness or badness of apples, only their market value.

A more explicit and more reasoned attack on the financial sector from a virtue perspective has been made by the conservative Catholic philosopher Alasdair MacIntyre, a long-standing critic of the idea that any practice could be ethically considered amoral.[44] Lecturing in 2010 on the ongoing financial crisis, MacIntyre portrayed the financial system as being essentially unethical. Of course, an institution is not a person. The financial system cannot be virtuous or otherwise. But it is a social context within which people carry

---

[43] A search of the British or American press at any time will show up a host of recent and ongoing cases. Recent cases (at the time of writing not all proven) have involved Morgan Stanley, UBS, Smith Barney, Merrill Lynch, Credit Suisse, Lehman, HSBC, BNP Paribas, Credit Agiricole, Nomura and many more.

[44] MacIntyre 1981.

out the everyday activities through which their characters are developed. A good character can be developed, according to MacIntyre, in all sorts of social contexts, through all sorts of trades, professions and everyday activities. But some contexts – like the financial system or burglary (organized crime might be a better example) – are simply inimical to the virtues. A practice that takes no account of other people but merely seeks to maximize on one dimension – money – cannot provide a context in which people learn to balance demands. Financial trading provides no opportunities for the exercise and development of the virtues and admits of no golden mean. To be a good trader and to be a good person are fundamentally incompatible.[45]

MacIntyre's version of virtue ethics is a very particular and arguably outdated one. From a contemporary perspective, he seems to have a romanticized notion of work and an idealized view of society, and indeed of the divine, as permeating every aspect of life. We might question whether the financial system, which causes collateral harm, can properly be likened to burglary or institutional crime, which are dedicated to harm. And even while accepting his general characterization of finance and the ideology that informs the financial system, we might question whether the everyday practice is quite as closed to the virtues as he maintains. Financial companies are human organizations, even if much of their work is aimed at eliminating rather than developing the human component. The system as a whole scarcely encourages the development of a virtuous character and may fairly be criticized for that, but it probably doesn't prevent it altogether.

The arguments rehearsed above give a rough sketch of the kind of ethical arguments that can be made in respect of the financial system. They are complex and it is not surprising that opinions are divided, with some strongly for and others strongly against. One theme that runs through the discussion, and one that we have so far kept in the background, is the role of regulation. Free market ideologues call for minimal regulation, while the most outspoken critics of the system contend that things can only be improved by banning certain kinds of speculative trading outright. A middle ground of opinion attributes the problems caused by the financial system to the way in which it has been regulated, and more specifically to

---

[45] Cornwell 2010.

the weakness of its regulatory mechanisms. This is an important topic, but it is one that can only really be treated in the context of specific examples. We shall come back to it at the end of the book, but in the following chapters we shall look at a range of specific issues associated with different aspects of financial practice.

5   Lending and borrowing: where finance meets ordinary people

Introduction: the moral environment

Lending and borrowing are so pervasive in modern life that it is hard to imagine it without them. Everyone who has a bank deposit or savings account is in effect lending money to the bank. Everyone who has an overdraft, a credit card, a mortgage or a personal loan, or has bought a car or electrical appliance on a finance package, is a borrower and debtor. Almost all governments are heavily in debt, relying on bond issues to make ends meet, and so are many companies.

Social attitudes to borrowing and debt are quite complex and shift with the context and with the times. On the one hand, there is a perception that borrowing is often necessary, especially for the poor or for craftsmen, traders and small businesses having to bridge the gap between paying for supplies and being paid, often very belatedly, for their goods and services.[1] When the borrowing is used to finance the development of business or the purchase of a home (especially if the borrower has saved up for a deposit first), it might even be seen as virtuous: a voluntary submission to the discipline of repayment in order to contribute to wealth creation or look after one's family. In recent years this attitude has found expression in the state encouragement of student indebtedness (see Box 5.1) and in the idea, invoked both in the context of microfinance and in debates on mortgage availability, that people have a moral human right to credit and that not lending to people who wish to borrow is a form of discrimination.[2]

---

[1] In eighteenth- and nineteenth-century Britain, those who ended up in debtors' prisons for non-payment were as often viewed as unfortunate victims as they were morally guilty. For an indication of the complexity of attitudes even within a single culture and period, see Finn 2003.

[2] Hudon 2009.

Box 5.1. University education and the language of debt

For most of the post-war period, undergraduate tuition for British students at British universities was paid for through central taxation. With the living costs of students from less well-off families also paid for by the state, the vast majority of students entered their working lives (or postgraduate studies) free of debt. In the 1990s, with a rapid expansion of university education, these subsidies were eroded and in 2010, the British government decided to switch to a system of fees and loans. At the time of writing, most of the public universities in England charge undergraduate fees of £9,000 a year and most students pay these by taking out a government loan, which they will be required to pay back once their incomes reach a certain level.

   This change has created controversies of various kinds, but a point not often examined is why the UK government chose to describe the system in terms of student loans rather than in terms of a graduate tax. It is in fact neither a straightforward student loan system nor a straightforward graduate tax system, but a hybrid which could have been presented either way. The obvious inference is that encouraging – almost requiring – young people to get heavily into debt was considered politically more acceptable than requiring them to shoulder an additional tax burden. It reflects, of course, the language and ideology of a market economy rather than that of a welfare state, but it would not have been possible without a demoralizing of debt and its recasting in terms of the modern virtues of opportunity, enterprise and investment.

On the other hand, virtue might also be attached to staying out of debt:

Neither a borrower or a lender be
For loan oft loses both itself and friend
And borrowing dulls the edge of husbandry

(Shakespeare, *Hamlet*, I.iii, 75–77)

Like the biblical pronouncement with which it is often confused, "the borrower is servant to the lender" (*Proverbs* 22.7), Polonius's famous advice to Laertes is more prudential than moral, but his caution against borrowing also has moral overtones. Going into debt has often been seen as a sign of moral delinquency and an indication that a person lacks the moral virtues of self-reliance and self-control. Borrowers not only relinquish autonomy, it is suggested, but set themselves on a slippery slope, for while there is a clear line between living within your means and borrowing, there is no clear line between borrowing a little and borrowing a lot.[3]

Lending, in itself, carries no such connotations. To lend to someone in need can indeed be seen as an act of kindness. But lending at interest is another matter and has long been considered immoral. In ancient times, lending money at interest, or usury, was prohibited in China and India, severely limited in Jewish law and tightly regulated in Roman law. It was outlawed in Christian countries in the Middle Ages, remaining illegal in England into the seventeenth century, and was tightly controlled in both the UK and the USA well into the twentieth century. Extremely high interest rates are still outlawed in some US states and usury is still prohibited in contemporary Islam.

The definition of "interest" has varied across time and across societies. Sometimes, as in medieval Europe, any charging of interest has been condemned as immoral. More often, the objection has been to excessive or exploitative rates of interest – often defined with reference to a legally specified base rate – rather than to interest as such. Charging additional interest beyond that specified at the outset for late payment of a debt, when the lender has the borrower over a barrel, has also been widely seen as immoral. The core moral objection is thus not to lending, or to the imposition of reasonable charges for the provision of a loan facility, but to lenders making themselves wealthy by exploiting the misfortunes of people who need to borrow.[4]

In the modern world, the prohibition on lending at interest is effectively restricted to unsecured lending in Islamic societies. Secured lending is technically subject to similar rules, but reasonable charges are allowed and in many cases they can effectively be separated out and the loans restructured so as to conform to the rules (see Box 5.2 below). The exploitation of borrowers remains a source of moral concern, however, in all societies, and since borrowers and lenders will tend to have rather different views on

---

[3] There are strong cultural differences in attitudes to borrowing. Americans, for instance, tend to be relatively relaxed about it, whereas Germans and Scandinavians tend to consider it morally doubtful (Americans, for example, hold roughly 50 times as many credit cards per capita as Germans).

[4] Visser and MacIntosh 1998.

what is or is not exploitative – and, more generally, on the place of moral considerations in economic contracts – personal lending continues to raise a raft of ethical issues.

Our main focus in this chapter will be on personal lending and especially the interplay of ethics and economics in personal lending, from payday loans to mortgages and from credit cards to microfinance. We shall also look briefly at the securitization of loans and the issues this has generated, and at the ethics of loan defaults and voluntary bankruptcy. But we shall begin by briefly surveying the different varieties of lending and borrowing, corporate as well as personal, and the kinds of issues to which they give rise.

Varieties of lending

Lending takes many forms, and the ethical issues associated with a payday loan are rather different from those associated with a government bond. In this section we briefly review the main categories of lending and some of the ethical issues associated with them.

One of the most common forms of lending is through regular *bank* (or *building society* or *thrift*) *deposits*. Whenever you place money on deposit, whether in a current or checking account or in a savings account, you are effectively lending it to the bank or other financial institution. The banks don't describe it that way. The impression they want to give is that they are providing you with a service – looking after your money, giving you banking facilities, maybe even a return on your savings – for which you should be grateful, not that they are in your debt. Only when you go into overdraft and you owe them money instead of the other way around does the language of lending get used. But the basic arrangement is that you lend, they borrow, and the services they provide are effectively in lieu of interest – though they might pay that, albeit at a very low rate, as well.

What distinguishes bank deposits from many other kinds of loan is that they are intended to be secure and repayable on demand. Ensuring that they are so in practice, either directly, through government guarantees or indirectly, through access to a lender of last resort, is one of the main tasks of banking regulators, and it also places ethical constraints upon the banks' management. In the amoral world of finance, there may be no moral objection to a bank failing to fulfill a contract with another bank, or even an industrial company; however, as the 2013 rescue of Cypriot banks revealed, for a bank to fail to safeguard its depositors' monies is still generally seen, as it always has been, as a moral as well as an economic failing.

The handling of deposits is where the financial system comes most directly into contact with the general public and is most exposed to the moral norms of society at large. Until relatively recently, bank managers knew many of their customers personally and interacted with them, directly or through the bank tellers, on a regular face-to-face basis. Deposit taking was based on trust, and the reputation of a bank went hand in hand with the reputation of the bank's managers as trusted members of their local communities. In this context, the banks' commitment to safeguarding deposits was understood as a moral commitment and not just an economic one. With urbanization, the introduction of automated teller machines and the rise of telephone and Internet banking, this connection between banks and their communities is now much weaker, and the temptation is for banks to see their depositors as mere customers or consumers. In taking deposits, however, banks still make a promise to safeguard them, and it is still assumed by the depositors and accepted by the banks that this promise is subject to conventional moral demands.

A second feature of bank deposits to give rise to ethical issues is their mobility. Unlike hard cash, bank deposits can be switched from one account to another, from one bank to another and from one country to another instantaneously. And unlike securities, such as stocks, bonds or derivatives, they have no unique identifiers, so that their movements are hard to trace. The consequence is that bank deposits are very suitable vehicles for illegal activities such as tax evasion and money laundering that involve hiding money from view. For banks to assist with such activities is, of course, illegal, but the law is not always well defined and depositors' intentions are not always clear, so in serving their clients, banks may have to take a view on their moral integrity and impose their own constraints especially in respect of international transfers.

As well as depositing money with banks, most people also borrow in one form or another, through overdrafts, personal loans, credit cards, purchase finance agreements and mortgages, or, for the less well-off, through payday loans, title loans and advances from local retailers or loan sharks. Like deposit taking, this *personal lending* puts the financial system in direct contact with ordinary people, in this case with people who may be vulnerable in various ways and who may not fully understand the contracts they are entering into. A core issue here is when the purely economic criteria favored by the financial community are appropriate and when, in what ways and to what extent they should be supplemented by ethical criteria. To what extent should people be held solely responsible for their borrowing decisions and to what extent should lenders be permitted or even required to take over some or all of this responsibility? Subsidiary issues concern loan defaults and the extent to which these should be seen in ethical rather than purely economic terms, and the impact of securitization on lending practices and criteria.

Compared with personal lending, the ethics of ordinary *commercial lending* are relatively straightforward. A bank's commercial customers are characteristically less vulnerable and more knowledgeable than personal customers, and it is widely recognized that in commercial lending, economic, not ethical criteria should normally rule. Where usury laws have continued to operate in a capitalist environment, as in some twentieth-century American state legislation, business lending has often been excluded. Only in the Islamic world does commercial lending remain closely tied to ethical considerations, and even here the focus is on structuring lending so as to conform to the letter of the law rather than on conformance with the spirit of the ethical norm. A key feature of Islamic finance (Box 5.2) is the replacement of what would in the West be loans by sale and re-sale arrangements or lease arrangements.

Rather ironically, these arrangements closely mirror the kind of arrangements used in the West to hide or disguise loans using matched derivative transactions. The transaction structures used in one case to conform to moral norms are used in the other for misleading investors. One practice that was widespread in the late 1990s and came to light after the collapse of Enron in 2001 was the use of prepaid swaps to provide bridging funds, effectively concealed by different accounting treatments for the two parts of the deal (see Box 5.3).[5]

The standard form of short-term company borrowing used by banks and some large corporations today is also structured as a sale and re-sale agreement. Financial institutions lend to each other on a daily basis using *repos*, or repurchase agreements, which as the name suggests use the combined

---

[5] A similar approach is also used in tax avoidance schemes, such as the one that engulfed accounting giant KPMG in 2005. See Box 9.2.

Box 5.2. Islamic banking

The guiding principles of Islamic banking are a prohibition on investing in or funding immoral or un-Islamic activities, a prohibition on speculative or risky trading (*Gharar*) and the avoidance of *riba*, often translated as "interest," but more accurately "excess." The moral prohibition here is on usury or the charging of excess interest, but to ensure conformity, the system that has developed is one in which interest is outlawed completely.

In interpersonal loans and bank deposits, the implication is that while a form of interest may be paid voluntarily, it cannot be demanded. Thus, in order to comply, an interpersonal loan has to be interest free. The borrower may make a goodwill payment to the lender (*Hibah*), but on a purely voluntary basis. Similarly, a bank may choose to pay *Hibah* to its depositors as a form of thanks for entrusting it with their money, but its legal role is simply as a guardian of the monies, providing *Wadiah* or safekeeping.

To conform to Islamic principles, most personal loans are recast as sale and re-sale or leasing arrangements. Thus, instead of giving a personal loan to somebody to buy a house or a car, an Islamic bank will effectively buy the asset in its own name and sell it to the customer at a profit, on terms that are equivalent to a set of loan repayments. The arrangements here (known as *Murabaha*) are more or less the same as those for a conventional secured loan, with the qualification that all payments and charges have to be stipulated in advance, and no additional charges can be made in respect of late payments.

Alternatively, an asset may be financed through a kind of leasing or hire-purchase agreement (*Ijara*). Therefore, while a customer cannot simply borrow money at interest to buy a car, he may buy it through hire purchase, entering into an agreement to lease it from the finance house over a given period and buy it at the end of the period. Again, all the payments are pre-determined so as to give the provider of funds a profit equivalent to the interest that might otherwise be charged. Similar arrangements are also used commercially, for the purchase of plant, machinery and other assets.

Where Islamic finance differs most markedly from mainstream finance is in the provision of general commercial loans, which are typically recast as profit sharing agreements of one kind or another (*Mudarabah* or *Musharakah*). With no identifiable asset, it is much harder here to mimic the effects of a commercial loan, and the bank has to act more like a preferred equity investor than a lender, taking a share of profits (or losses) rather than a fixed return. The payments are much more tightly specified than a shareholder's dividends would be, with the bank taking a fixed, pre-determined proportion of company profits, but the returns still have the variability of an equity investment. Indeed, it is explicitly the risk that, according to Islamic law, justifies the return.

Sources: Choudhury and Malik 1992, Iqbal and Mirakhor 2011.

sale and repurchase (at a higher price) of a security to mimic the effects of a secured loan, the price difference corresponding to the interest charge. With a third-party bank often acting as an intermediary and holding and administering the collateral, repos enable borrowers to utilize liquid securities such as government bonds as an effective source of cash, either on an overnight or on a short-term or rollover basis, without having to cash them in. Repos appeal to lenders because they offer repayment on demand and, unlike a conventional loan, give them legal ownership of the underlying security. As we shall see later, repos can lead to the same kind of problem as with Enron's prepaid swaps if the underlying assets have no clear market price, but for the most part they are uncontentious and just offer a conveniently structured form of short-term lending.

At the other end of the debt timescale are fixed-term *corporate bonds*, which companies use as an alternative source of long-term financing to equity and which investors use, similarly, as an alternative to stocks and shares for investing in the corporate sector. Until the 1980s, the only companies to issue bonds were the largest and most secure ones. The model was government bonds. Since then, however, the range of bonds issued has expanded massively to cover everything from blue-chip to newly created or distressed companies. In many cases, information on the companies concerned and their financial prospects is relatively limited, and issues arise in relation to the accuracy of the information supplied when the bonds are issued. Of particular importance to investors is the risk of default, and this places particular demands on the analytical objectivity of the ratings agencies, which rate the bonds in terms of the risks attached to them.

The risk of default and the judgments of the ratings agencies are also key issues in respect of *government bonds*. It has traditionally been assumed that bonds issued by the governments of developed economies are entirely secure, with effectively zero risk of default, but in the wake of the financial

Box 5.3. When is a loan not a loan? Enron and prepaid swaps

Compared with some of the financial irregularities at Enron, the use of prepaid swaps to keep large loans out of view, artificially inflate asset values and boost the stock price was relatively minor. The amounts concerned appear to have been no more than about $10 billion, and while the accounts were misleading, the transactions themselves were perfectly legal. But even with a company the size of Enron, $10 billion amounts to a significant misrepresentation. The way it worked was this. Enron's bankers, Citigroup or JP Morgan Chase, would set up a pair of matched prepaid swaps, in which an up-front payment was traded for a payment flow based on energy futures. In one of these, the bank, or an energy trading subsidiary set up expressly for this purpose, would pay the cash up-front to Enron. In the other, Enron would pay a slightly higher cash amount up-front, a few months later, in a subsequent accounting period, to the bank, with the payments flows on the two deals being the same. The effect was to lend Enron the money, with the difference in cash prices corresponding to the interest charged, but while Enron got the cash benefits of the loan, the transactions were treated in the accounts as derivatives trades, with the cash appearing as cash from operations and the future liabilities hidden amongst the derivatives contracts that were Enron's stock in trade. Arthur Andersen, the auditors, approved the accounts as a true and fair view of the company, and to the outside world there was no sign of any loan, just a greatly improved cash flow in the first accounting period. (This would of course be wiped out when the reverse deal kicked in, but a new and larger pair of deals could then be set up to cover the next accounting period.) Enron's use of prepaid swaps began in the late 1990s and grew in scale for about three years until the company collapsed in 2001.

Sources: Fox 2003, Chapter 12; Opening Statement of Rick Caplan Before the Senate Permanent Subcommittee on Investigations, July 23, 2002: www.hsgac.senate.gov/download/?id=2bc92434-1465-4085-9506-e419c3c12680.

crisis, that assumption was dramatically called into question. Many countries ran up excessive debt from the mid-2000s, running substantial deficits even at a time when their economies were booming and tax receipts were high, and in the subsequent recession, the idea that a country could not go bankrupt was quickly challenged. At the time of writing, Ireland and Portugal have both received massive assistance from the IMF, Greece is effectively in default, and Italy, Spain and many other countries are forced to pay interest rates on their borrowing that imply a serious risk of default – and that themselves increase the risk of default. As it becomes apparent that countries may be pushed towards default on a scale that cannot be protected against, questions arise as to the ethics of the action. How ethical is it for a government to solve its debt problems by simply defaulting on its loan obligations, and to what extent does it have a responsibility to meet those obligations, even at the cost of extreme austerity? And how should it respond when, in a democratic environment, its people refuse to back the austerity that would be needed? Later in the chapter we shall look at the ethics of default at the personal, corporate and government levels.

Ethics and economics in personal lending

I am lucky enough to be relatively affluent and if I wanted to borrow money, I could do so both easily and cheaply. For low-level, short-term borrowing, through my credit card or the overdraft facility on my current account, the interest rate charged would, by my own terms, be extortionate: at the time of writing, around 7 percent over base rate for an overdraft and 17 percent if I was stupid enough to use my credit card instead. But I would only ever do this for convenience, and the convenience would make up for the charge. For larger amounts or longer-term borrowing, my good credit record, steady income and unencumbered relative wealth mean that I could not only get a loan with minimum difficulty but could also get one with a very low rate of interest: perhaps 1.5–2.5 percent over base rate, depending on what it was for. Most people, even with a sound credit record and a proven ability to repay, have to pay significantly more. Regular mortgages, well secured on the borrower's home and backed by good earnings, currently start at around 4 percent over base rate. An unsecured bank loan with one of the main high street banks might cost anything from 7 to 17 percent over base rate, depending on the details. Rates are generally high for small loans, become lower as the size of loan goes up, but then rise again for larger amounts. Without a good credit record or proven income, the rates increase massively. Payday loans (designed to carry someone through to their next pay check) and title loans (short-term loans secured on a car or other asset) from large and basically reputable finance houses charge interest rates of around 25 percent *a month*. An unsecured loan from a backstreet loan shark, which for someone in poverty might be the only loan available, will charge a higher rate still.

From an economic perspective, this makes perfect sense. The main costs associated with lending are the administrative costs, which are proportionately greater for small loans than large ones, and the cost of delinquency or default, which vary according to the borrower's wealth and ability to repay and the costs of debt-chasing and asset recovery. The wealthier you are and the less you need to borrow, the easier it will be for you to get a loan and the less you'll have to pay for it. The poorer you are and the more you need the loan, the harder it will be to get it and the more you'll have to pay for it.

From a moral perspective, however, this all seems very unfair. Not only do we refuse borrowing facilities to those who most need them, but when we do lend, we impose interest rates that they cannot possibly afford. The economist will argue, quite reasonably, that the interest rates reflect the risk of default, but it can also be argued, equally reasonably, that the risk of default is massively increased by the interest rates charged. There appears to be a vicious circle here, and one that works to the cost of the least advantaged members of society.

The sense of ethical unease this generates is heightened by a perception that banks and other lending institutions often seem more interested in profiting from people's weaknesses than in helping them through their difficulties. The obvious exception to this is microfinance, which is explicitly directed toward lifting people out of poverty, but even this has come in for moral criticism. Is this ethical unease just a kind of moral softness, a sentimental refusal to face up to the economic facts of life? Or are there real ethical concerns here? To address this question, we shall look here at the practices of banks and other lending institutions in four areas of personal lending: payday and title loans; credit cards; subprime mortgages; and microfinance.

Payday loans, title loans and credit cards

The poorer members of society, with no accumulated wealth and limited and often irregular sources of income, have always needed to borrow, whether to tide them over from one payday to the next or to cope with irregular or unexpected costs – the costs of repairs to the tools or transport on which they depend for a living, for example, of items of furniture or clothing, of medical expenses, of funerals and weddings, or of visiting sick relatives. Much of this borrowing has traditionally taken place in the informal economy: housewives buying food "on tick" (deferring payment) or borrowing from the grocer, often without their husbands' knowledge; or, where larger amounts are needed, families borrowing from backstreet loan sharks. Some of these arrangements are relatively benign, others much less so. The loan shark not only charges usurious interest rates but also threatens physical violence in the event of late payment, even if the interest charged means that the debt has actually been repaid many times over. Violence and abuse are also characteristic of bonded labor, today's debt-based equivalent of slavery. The researcher Kevin Bales estimates that there are at least 27 million people in slavery across the world (mainly in developing countries, but including many illegal immigrants in the USA), most of whom are in bonded labor.[6] They or their parents have borrowed from an agent or employer or trafficker to pay the transport or entry costs to get a job, but the wages and deductions imposed are such that they can never repay the debt – they can only keep working or try to run away and risk being beaten or killed.

In comparison with the individuals who use lending to exploit the world's poorest people, the payday and title loan industry is a model of rectitude. Firms operate through branch offices, openly and within the law, and some are quite large. Ace Cash Express Inc. in the USA has been operating for over 40 years and boasts 1,700 branches. Firms typically offer payday loans of up to four weeks only to customers with evidence of future income. Title loans, which typically run for between two and six months, are secured by the lender taking ownership (though not possession) of a car or other asset. There is little regulation of the industry apart from state laws on usury, which sometimes limit the interest that can be charged. If this is set at much less than 25 percent *a month* (around 1,350 percent a year), which is the level at which they feel they can make a good return, the firms simply don't operate in that state.

In economic terms, the high interest charges are needed to cover the high costs of servicing small short-term loans and the risks of default and

[6] Bales 2012.

deception on the part of the borrowers. If mainstream banks were to make these kinds of short-term loans, they would make a loss on them even at these high rates, given their much higher administrative costs. Many payday and title loan firms are very profitable, but they operate in a competitive market. In many cases they also provide a valuable service. If someone depends on an old car or motorbike to earn a living, it breaks down and they have no access to bank lending, 25 percent a month to pay for its repair may not seem such a bad deal.

However, one of the reasons why the firms can charge such rates is that many of their customers are not very numerate and do not fully understand what they are being charged and what they are committing themselves to in signing the deal, especially in the event of failing to meet the repayment schedules. The firms advertise ready money, but even those able to understand it all have to get some way into the fine print to work out what it costs, and many people don't get that far. The paperwork baffles them, but they need the money – typically just to get by – and they sign what they are asked to sign. The result is that many customers take out loans that they have no chance whatsoever of repaying at the rates charged. Sometimes they can't even make the interest payments. Sometimes they may effectively repay the loan several times over in interest payments, but have no chance of repaying the capital and end up losing the asset regardless. And on top of all that, while the debt collectors engaged by the firms (they don't do that unpleasant bit themselves) may stay within the law, they are not exactly friendly.

In the last few years, a lot of payday lending has moved online and the market has grown rapidly. In the UK, loans have roughly doubled in two years, reaching £1.8 billion in 2012. The UK market leader, Wonga, operates entirely online and lends money for up to a month, with a 15-minute turn-around, through smartphone applications.[7] Wonga is completely transparent about its charges – 1 percent a day – but not quite so eager to explain that this works out, if debts are rolled over, at about 4,000 percent a year, or

[7] It also advertises on smartphone apps, and in 2012 was found to be running ads on apps designed for young children. This may have been accidental, but it may not: the public image promoted by the company is very childlike, emphasizing ease of use. See www.guardian.co.uk/money/2012/oct/10/wonga-adverts-talking-ginger-children-game-smartphone.

interest of £40 on every £1 borrowed. It also makes a point of being careful to whom it lends, claiming to reject two-thirds of first-time applications. From the borrower's perspective, however, the effect is to encourage carelessness. An online application is both easier than a written one and in some sense less real. Once a loan has been taken and paid off, subsequent loans are even easier – as easy as borrowing off a friend, but without any of the personal complications. Moreover, once a loan is taken, matters move out of the borrower's control. With a continuous payment authority to the borrower's debit or credit card, the lenders simply roll over debts that aren't repaid on time and keeping collecting the interest.[8]

Many people find the activities of these firms deeply immoral. How ethical can it be, they ask, to entice someone into serial borrowing at extortionate rates, or to sell a vulnerable person a loan that she cannot repay and the consequences of which may be devastating for her life? To answer that question, let us look at the kinds of answers that might be constructed from the utilitarian and Kantian perspectives.

From a rule utilitarian perspective, the firms might reasonably argue that they are just following the rule that says businesses should seek to maximize profits, subject only to staying within the law, and that this rule is endorsed by government and justified as maximizing wealth creation. If society decides that it doesn't want firms to lend in this way, it can very easily legislate against them simply by capping the rates that can be charged. In response to some of the criticisms noted in the last chapter, they might further say that, unlike the big banks, they have no particular political power with which to influence society's rules or prevent legislation: in this case, responsibility for the rule and for restrictions on its application lie clearly with societies and their governments.

If we accept this argument, then within the rule utilitarian framework, the focus shifts to government and the case rests on the validity of the general business rule and the arguments as to whether the payday and title loan industry should be included in this rule or outlawed. We could in principle explore the issue in this way, but we can also cover much the same ground in a more focused way by taking an indirect act utilitarian approach. In this approach we keep the focus on the firms and ask whether

---

[8] www.bbc.co.uk/news/business-20406659.

the practices of the industry (the rules the firms choose to adopt) are utility-enhancing. If they are not, then from an indirect act utilitarian perspective, they are wrong and the firms should desist; from a rule utilitarian perspective, governments should prohibit them.

We now have a straightforward question: do the practices of these firms add utility (ideally maximize it) or do they take it away? Unfortunately, we don't have a straightforward answer to this, as the practices clearly have both beneficial and harmful effects. On the one hand, they bring benefits to many responsible and disciplined people who use them to get out of temporary difficulties and even to improve themselves without having to resort to loan sharks. They may also benefit people who use them in preference to going to loan sharks, even if it lands them in difficulties: had they gone to the loan sharks, the difficulties would probably have been far greater. On the other hand, they bring suffering to a significant number of less responsible or less disciplined people, who might never resort to loan sharks at all but who get sucked into taking on debts they cannot manage. And the interest paid also transfers wealth, straightforwardly, from the firms' customers, who tend to be relatively disadvantaged, to their owners and employees, who tend to be rather better off. In this case, calculating the overall impact, even in simple economic terms, let alone in terms of utility, would require a major research exercise which might well not be conclusive. But whether or not the practices add utility overall, they could surely add more, or take away less, than they do if they were carried out with greater care and attention to the consequences.

While a utilitarian analysis of payday and title lending raises some interesting and important questions, it doesn't take us to the heart of what people object to when they condemn these practices as morally wrong. The social norm that is invoked here is that it is wrong to exploit people. Our notion of exploitation is a little vague and is confused by the fact that we use the same word in an economic context without any moral connotations (exploiting a mineral resource, for example). But it is generally considered wrong to take advantage of the weaknesses and misfortunes of those who are already less fortunate than oneself in order to advance one's own interests. In this case the objection is to profiting from the ignorance and weakness of borrowers by luring them into transactions that are not actually in their interests.

We could address this situation philosophically from various perspectives.[9] Rawls's theory of justice, for example, includes a defense of markets on the basis of their pure procedural justice (i.e., the justice of the procedure of markets independent of their outcomes), but makes this conditional on market exchanges being non-coercive exchanges between free individuals. Within this framework, the fairness of payday lending depends on whether the borrowers are really acting as free rational agents or whether there is some kind of systemic coercion. However, a more straightforward way of addressing the problem is through Kantian ethics.

From a Kantian perspective, the most promising approach would seem to be in terms of the Formula of Humanity. These firms are not pursuing a social mission. Like most businesses, they clearly treat their customers as a means to generate profit. But do they treat them *merely* as a means? This is also a difficult question to answer with confidence, but we can look for evidence in the steps they take, through their advertising and lending processes, to protect the vulnerable from taking loans they cannot afford, and in the way they treat borrowers who default. We cannot reasonably expect them to filter applicants in a way that would completely prevent people from over-stretching themselves; such a strict requirement would rule out not only their own kinds of business but many other kinds as well. Nor can we expect them to take complete responsibility for their customers' decisions. But we can ask whether their advertising and pre-loan processes pay due attention to the risks involved. We can ask what steps they take to ensure that people understand the terms of the loan and the obligations these entail, in the context of a realistic understanding of their own financial circumstances. And we can ask what they do to help people who get into difficulties, prevent them from making matters worse, and treat them with kindness and decency. Treating people with respect in these ways is costly, but if it's not possible within the business model, then on a Kantian view, they shouldn't pursue that business model.

On these criteria, it seems hard to make out any kind of Kantian case for online lenders like Wonga. Their advertising seems designed to make the

---

[9] For a review of some different approaches to the ethics of market exploitation, see Miller 1990, Chapters 7–8.

borrowing seem as easy and painless as possible (as easy as registering for a computer game), to obscure the borrower's risks and to focus attention on very short-term (daily) borrowing costs rather on the potential longer-term costs. Their computerized checking certainly serves their own interests, but it gives them no way of judging whether applicants understand what they are committing to or are, at the moment of application, making sober and sensible judgments. And their debt-collection practices have been frequently and heavily criticized. The case of face-to-face lending is harder to judge. It depends heavily on the attitudes and skills of those making the lending decisions, and the detailed policies to which they work. From what we can tell, it seems most unlikely that these businesses are being conducted ethically, in Kantian terms, but it also seems plausible that, with appropriate policies and staff, they could be.

If payday loans are ethically suspect, what about credit cards, which are in some way their middle-class equivalent? Americans today hold about 700 million credit cards with total debts of about $800 billion. The Japanese hold about 350 million cards and even the British, who are modest users in comparison, hold 61 million cards and owe about $90 billion. Used responsibly, credit cards are a great convenience, giving cardholders one or two months' interest-free credit if they are paid off promptly and enabling them to schedule their payments to match their income flows. In practice, however, people often use multiple credit cards to ramp up and continually roll over debt at high interest rates, with young people especially treating credit as cash and building up debt without any conception that they are actually getting into debt or any plans to pay it off.[10] The issuing banks do nothing to discourage this and their advertising actively encourages it: the message is, quite simply, that if you have a credit card, you can spend more. The interest rates being much lower and the customers much less vulnerable than in the payday loan industry, the ethical issues seem more finely balanced, but the advertising in particular would appear to raise concerns.

---

[10] For the background to this, see Wright 2010. Current data are collected at http://uk. creditcards.com/credit-card-news/uk-britain-credit-debit-card-statistics-international.php.

Subprime mortgages, student loans and securitization[11]

Of all forms of personal lending, traditional mortgage lending was the most conservative. Lending large sums of money over 25 or 30 years, lenders attached great importance to the ability of borrowers to meet repayments. This was partly a question of simple economics. While due diligence might be costly, it was less so than foreclosure, and the cost was very small in comparison with the interest received over the period of the loan. But it also had a moral basis. For the mutual societies that dominated the market, and to a lesser extent for the traditional retail banks, it seemed to be a fair way of rationing the limited funds provided by their savers and a prudent way of safeguarding those savers' funds. When, following the US savings and loan crisis of the 1980s, the source of much American mortgage funding shifted from savings to the government agencies Fannie Mae and Freddie Mac, which bought up and securitized mortgages, strict and conservative underwriting rules continued to be applied. If there was a moral concern, it was that the restrictions were too tight and sometimes discriminatory, depriving people of home ownership who were perfectly capable of taking on the responsibilities involved. Blacks and Hispanics seemed to find it particularly difficult to get a mortgage.

Until the mid-1990s, the subprime mortgage sector was not greatly different. A niche sector accounting for 5–10 percent of mortgage loans, it focused on borrowers who failed to meet the normal criteria imposed by the mainstream lenders, but who failed on technicalities and were at little risk of default or delinquency. Finance houses and brokers, who typically sold the mortgages they originated to commercial banks, looked at each case on its merits and while there were undoubtedly some abuses, underwriting standards were generally maintained.

In the second half of the 1990s, however, consumer groups reported growing evidence of lending abuses, including high-pressure sales tactics, predatory interest rates, high fees and repayment penalties, and the falsification of income and valuation documentation. In the house price boom of

[11] This section is focused mainly on the USA, since that is where the issues are best documented. The discussion of subprime mortgages draws mainly on Financial Crisis Inquiry Commission 2011, Chapters 5 and 7, with data taken from the US Census Bureau, the Bank of England and the OECD.

2004–6, by which time American subprime lending had become big business, running at six times its 1990s level and accounting for well over 20 percent of the entire mortgage market, exploitation was rife; what had once been the dubious practices of small shady operators had become, in effect, standard industry practice.

The key trigger for change appears to have been the growth of private sector loan securitization. At first, the securitizing banks imposed their own underwriting requirements on the mortgage originators, but as demand for new securities grew rapidly, the banks increasingly prioritized volume over quality and the originators responded accordingly.[12]

Two effects of securitization were combining here. One effect was to remove constraints on the supply of funds for mortgage lending. Instead of rationing mortgages as they had in the past, originators were free to create and profit from as many as they could. The other effect was to introduce at least two degrees of separation between loan origination and its consequences. The originator now sold its loans to a bank, which packaged them into securities and sold these on to investors or other institutions. In the run-up to the financial crisis in the mid-2000s, investor demand for seemingly safe investments ("as safe as houses") earning reasonable rates of interest drove even longer chains of transactions. At the end of the chain, the mortgages were no more than anonymous components in a package of fees and interest rates.

In this situation, the mortgage originators, whether independent mortgage brokers, small finance houses, subsidiaries of commercial banks or large specialist companies like New Century and Countrywide, had a choice. They could continue to act cautiously, perhaps easing the traditional requirements so as to make mortgages more available to those who could afford them but who had previously been frozen out, but continuing to make decisions on the same basis as if they had been holding the loans to maturity. Alternatively, they could respond to the demand of the banks and their investors by maximizing their mortgage origination, regardless of traditional underwriting standards. They chose the latter course. Indeed, they stampeded down it, not only lending freely but actually prioritizing poor-quality loans, for which they could charge

[12] For more detail on how securitization worked and on the subprime mortgage market generally, see Chapter 1.

higher fees and interest rates. The aim was to lend as much as possible at rates that were as high as possible. To this end, they pushed borrowers to borrow 100 percent of a home's valuation (whether on an initial purchase or through top-up remortgages) and pressurized appraisers to put in inflated valuations that anticipated rising prices, even when the market had turned and prices were in fact falling. They offered no-doc mortgages to people without any proof of income or creditworthiness and to people whose chances of maintaining repayments were realistically not high. They pushed mortgages with low initial rates, encouraging people to borrow up to what they could service at these low rates, regardless of whether or not they stood a chance of servicing the much higher rates that would kick in after two years. Aggressively pushing the short-term benefits of their products, they not only failed to stress the longer-term risks but also glossed over these, treating their customers' limited appreciation of their significance as a sales opportunity rather than as a cause for concern.

The customers concerned were not the most vulnerable in society, but with home ownership rates in the UK and the USA, roughly average for the developed world, of around 67–68 percent, rising to over 80 percent for married couples and those over 50 (young singles in particular often choose to rent, even if they are in a position to buy), they were people with below-average incomes, many of whom had little comprehension of how much they were borrowing or the implications for repayment.

The ethical arguments here appear to be rather one-sided. In terms of utilitarian consequences, mortgages are generally considered a good thing. They enable people to own their own homes and enjoy the stability and security that this provides, and they encourage them, in effect, to save for their retirement: the mortgage repayments while earning generate rent-free living plus a tradable asset when retired. Therefore, increasing the supply of mortgages might also be considered a good thing, but the benefits generated depend critically on the borrower being able to service the loan, and the consequences of failure, especially when house prices are in decline, are dire. Even if we discount their impact on the purchasers of mortgage-backed securities and the wider consequences of the financial crisis when these collapsed in value, the consequences of American sub-prime mortgage-lending policies and practices in the 2000s were disastrous, and arguably quite predictable.

From a Kantian perspective, these policies also failed to satisfy both the Formula of Universal Law and the Formula of Humanity. A maxim of lending without regard to the ability to repay, for example, would surely lead if universalized to a contradiction of conception, as the normal expectation of repayment (i.e., the expectation of repayment in all but exceptional circumstances) is an essential part of the social practice of lending. If everyone used the conventions of lending to extract fees from unsound loans, the loan market would collapse and they would be unable to extract fees from it. Maxims of aggressively promoting unsuitable products or of seeking to undermine customers' rational judgments would lead to a contradiction of will (you cannot will as universal policies that undermine the will). And while the originators would no doubt protest their innocence, it is hard to imagine a much clearer case of customers, in this case borrowers, being treated merely as a means to profit, with complete disregard for them as people.

From a virtue perspective too, we would expect virtuous loan originators to be balanced and temperate in their actions, matching their offers to the specific circumstances of potential borrowers in such a way as to show kindness and respect towards them as well as earning profits for themselves. We would not expect them to act with the unconstrained greed actually shown.

A counter-argument that is sometimes made here is that the responsibility for borrowing and its consequences should lie with the borrowers and that for the lenders to protect them is to undermine their self-reliance. From this perspective, the traditional underwriting standards, which were not originally there to protect lenders but formed part of the moral framework of a mutual society, inhibited freedom of choice and, rather like welfare systems, prevented people from standing on their own feet. Protecting the vulnerable, on this account, both prevents them from flourishing as autonomous individuals and imposes unacceptable burdens on everyone else, in this case the burdens arising from the shackling of free markets.

In the broader context of welfare politics, this argument has some force. Too much protection of the vulnerable can perhaps do more harm than good, both in terms of its utilitarian consequences and in terms of the example it sets for virtuous behavior. The argument between American conservatives, preaching self-reliance, and European social democrats, calling for care of the vulnerable, can probably not be resolved on purely ethical grounds. In this particular case, however, the lending seems not to have left people to their own judgments, but to have positively exploited their weaknesses, and the consequences for utility seem unambiguously bad.

Given the very widespread nature of the unethical practices here, one question we should ask is how much blame should be attributed to the individual agents and employees who signed people up to a deal and how much to the senior managers of the firms instructing them, or the banks incentivizing them? Representatives of the banks might argue that it was not for them to tell mortgage originators how to do their job, but it seems apparent from their own lack of due diligence that they were both aware of potential failings here and prepared to be complicit in respect of them. The originators might argue that they were only doing what was necessary to keep their jobs and that the pressures from above were too great for them to resist. We can perhaps sympathize with them here. But they were also the ones meeting borrowers face-to-face and were able to assess the damage they were doing. It is hard to avoid the conclusion that agents, employees and managers were all party to the harm being done here and were all ethically at fault.

Mortgages were not the only loans to be securitized in this period. The other main categories were credit card loans, car finance loans and student loans, and of these the category raising the greatest level of concern has been student loans. In 2012 outstanding US student loans topped $1 trillion, with over $100 million of new loans being issued annually. The bulk of this is in the form of various Federal loans, some subsidized, others not, but these are capped and $150 billion of the outstanding amount is made up of private loans, which mimic the structure of unsubsidized Federal loans without their safeguards: they are more expensive and less forgiving.[13]

As in the case of mortgages, student loans used to be given with care, as lenders worked through the intermediaries of universities and colleges. With the rise of securitization and the demand for student loan-backed securities, they began to market directly and to lend indiscriminately. As in the case of mortgages, loans were increasingly given to students unlikely to be able to repay them: students in private for-profit schools, where the proportion of students in debt is much higher than the proportion of students completing, and students with poor credit ratings. Moreover,

---

[13] This section draws mainly on Consumer Financial Protection Bureau 2012. See also Nasser and Norman 2011.

many of these borrowers had not borrowed to their limits within the Federal system and clearly did not appreciate the higher risks and higher costs of private loans. As in the case of mortgages, the result was a very a high level of defaults (and, of course, a collapse in the market for the asset priced securities, which was what ultimately forced a change of practice toward more responsible lending). And as in the case of mortgages, it is hard to find any ethical justification for what was done.

Microfinance

The areas of lending we have considered so far are troubling but arguably exceptional. The bulk of personal lending, through traditional mortgages, bank loans, car finance, hire purchase and credit cards, does not raise ethical concerns of the same order. Microfinance, which we shall consider next, is again exceptional, but it is of interest for the potential good it does, not for its potential harm.

What distinguishes microfinance, or microcredit, from other forms of personal lending is that the primary purpose is, in most cases, to help people lift themselves out of poverty.[14] Most microfinance institutions are charitable or not-for-profit organizations, whose lending is constrained by economic considerations but whose intentions are fundamentally moral. (This is not universally the case: as the sector has matured, a number of for-profit institutions have also evolved. An example is given in Box 5.4 below.) The basic idea, pioneered most notably in Bangladesh by Muhammad Yunus's Grameen Bank, is that relatively small amounts of credit, carefully administered, can make a big and positive difference to the lives of many people in developing countries. Literally billions of people across the world are stuck in poverty, with no access to banking facilities, but amongst these people, it is argued, are many who have the discipline and initiative to help themselves, their families and their communities grow out of the poverty trap if given appropriate financial help.

Estimates of the scale of microfinance vary significantly, but there are probably between 50 million and 150 million loans currently outstanding worldwide, averaging perhaps $200. Loans are offered mainly to women, who are considered to be both socially and financially more responsible

---

[14] This section draws mainly on Argandoña 2010. See also Hudon 2008, 2009 and Sandberg 2012.

than men. They are typically for six to twelve months with weekly or fort-nightly repayments. Instead of the borrower visiting the lender, the lender's representatives visit local communities, and unlike informal loan sharks, who operate behind the scenes, they carry out all their transactions in public. A key element of the system is the application of community and peer pressure to maintain lenders' discipline, and many schemes require the borrowers in a village to take shared responsibility, in public, for each other's repayments. This requirement has become less common as micro-finance has developed, but it remains widespread, and even where it has been discontinued, public peer pressure remains important. Anyone unable to repay an installment must admit to the fact in public.

The purposes to which microcredits can be put vary from lender to lender, but the general principle is that they should be used to create or build small-scale enterprises. They are not intended to be used for consump-tion, to cover exceptional expenses or to bridge income gaps. Indeed, many schemes require the borrowers to build up small amounts of savings during the loan period in order to reduce their vulnerability to such shocks. Of course, the larger the schemes get, the harder it becomes to control the uses to which loans are put, and some money is certainly diverted to purposes other than those intended, but peer pressure again provides a useful con-straint. Lenders may also impose informal conditions designed to secure and leverage the development benefits of the loans. Grameen Bank, for instance, asks its borrowers to make pledges in respect of hygiene and sanitation levels, the proper maintenance of property, the productive use of land, the education of children and the avoidance of traditional practices that support continuing discrimination and burdensome debts.

Interest rates also vary and might be as low as 20 percent and as high as 100 percent or more, but typical rates are around 25–35 percent a year, which seems to be the level at which well-run schemes can eventually become close to self-financing instead of depending predominantly, as most do on inception, on donations, grants and subsidies.

Microfinance has been subject to a lot of criticism from traditional moral perspectives. It has been condemned as un-Islamic, both for charging inter-est and for encouraging women to reject their traditional roles and obliga-tions. Free market critics have condemned its reliance on charitable aid and accused it of passing off welfare as enterprise. From the opposite perspec-tive, others have criticized it for only lending to people who already have a source of income and ignoring the neediest. Charitable microfinance institutions have been accused of charging usurious interest rates and of exploiting the poor by charging high interest rates when they should be helping them by charging low rates. Microfinance institutions that have moved to a commercial for-profit basis have been widely attacked for exploitation. Grameen Bank and other lenders have also been accused of trapping people in debt and using peer pressure disciplines to make some people's lives intolerable, even driving them to suicide.[15]

Few of these criticisms survive much scrutiny. The attacks on Grameen Bank have come mainly from the Bangladeshi government (see Box 5.4) and appear to have been motivated by a mix of politics and traditional moral institutions of discipline that are themselves discriminatory and ethically problematic. The evidence suggests that both the welfare and the enterprise effects of microfinance are strongly positive, and since these are now quite widely achieved with minimal subsidy, a utilitarian assessment would suggest that the policies being applied are ethically admirable.

Some of the practices and impositions of microfinance institutions may appear patronizing and disrespectful from the perspective of the developed world, but in context they seem to show a commendable respect for persons and concern for human rights, and appear to be fully universalizable. The interest charges are generally kept as low as possible and, in stark contrast to payday lending, the costs incurred are largely incurred for the very purpose of ensuring that borrowers do make responsible decisions in the first place and do follow this up with responsible behavior of a kind that will ensure they benefit from the arrangements.[16]

As far as we can tell, the intentions of most of those who create and operate microfinance institutions are also overwhelmingly virtuous, and while the details of practical arrangements can be easily criticized, institutions like Grameen Bank seem to be giving serious thought to finding a judicious balance between competing values.

As some institutions move closer to the world of mainstream finance, their ethical standing becomes more problematic. There is always a risk, when lending at high rates to poor people, of exploitation, and, as illustrated in Box 5.4, finding an appropriate balance between responsible

---

[15] Sandberg 2012.

[16] Sandberg 2012 gives a comprehensive ethical defense of the interest rates charged.

Box 5.4. Two microfinance institutions compared: Grameen Bank and Compartamos Banco

Grameen Bank started out in 1976 as a small-scale university-based project providing credit services to the poor in rural Bangladesh. It was established as an independent bank in 1983. By 2010, it had made cumulative loans of about $8.5 billion and had about 8.5 million customers or members. From very early in its history, the bank was subsidized by the Bangladeshi government, but it has also always encouraged its borrowers to save, and in 2004, deposits overtook loans. Though still subsidized to some extent, it now runs close to breaking even.

Although Grameen Bank and its founder, the economist Muhammad Yunus, received the Nobel Peace Prize in 2006, they are not without their critics. Religious fundamentalists criticize the Bank's activities as un-Islamic, and Yunus has been criticized for governance and accounting irregularities. Established by government statute, structured as a cooperative society and managed until recently by Yunus himself and his close associates, the governance of the Bank and its relationship to Yunus family companies that exploit his folk hero status have always been somewhat obscure, and the published accounts are less than revealing. Following a critical government review, Yunus resigned as chief executive in 2011. However, the criticisms made in the review had more to do with a failure to follow approved procedures than with any substantive wrongdoing and may have been a pretext for a government takeover, steps towards which were taken in 2012. Both for its own achievements and for the inspiration it has afforded other microfinance institutions worldwide, most commentators retain a strongly positive view of Grameen Bank's social achievements.

Originally founded as a non-charitable non-governmental organization (NGO) in 1990, the Mexican bank Compartamos Banco is the largest microfinance institution in South America, with 13,000 employees, over two million customers and outstanding loans of about $1 billion. In its early years it relied heavily on grants, receiving $4.3 billion from donors and development agencies, but in 2006 it converted into a commercial bank, raising about $450 million in an IPO the following year. Its central business remains that of micro-enterprise funding, and while it now provides individual enterprise and home improvement loans as well as insurance services, a large part of its business still uses the mechanism of group lending, where groups of five to fifty borrowers take joint responsibility for each other's debts. It also continues to prioritize lending to women.

Compartamos Banco's distinctive positioning is as "the bank that generates social, economic and human value through an efficient business model." Its commitment is to contributing to social and economic development through enterprise funding for the poorer sectors of society, but in a way that returns a profit to its shareholders, and it has been greatly applauded for pulling off this combination of outcomes. In order to maintain profitability, however, it has to impose much higher interest rates than the non-commercial microfinance institutions. Whereas Grameen Bank's annualized interest rates average about 30 percent, those of Compartamos Banco are over 100 percent, which critics see as extortionate and exploitative.

For the most part, however, these charges appear to be manageable – default rates since flotation have run at around 2 percent, which on such a large and relatively poor customer base is impressive – and they are significantly lower than those charged by title loan finance companies, let alone those charged in the informal economy.

Sources: the account of Grameen Bank draws on the Wikipedia entry http://en.wikipedia.org/wiki/Grameen_Bank), on the Grameen website (www.grameen-info.org) and on various coverage in the media of the 2012 developments: see, for example, Bornstein 2012. The account of Compartamos Banco draws on the company's website (www.compartamos.com) and on the account given in Argandoña 2010.

behavior and commercial viability poses difficult challenges, but it is hard to fault institutions that engage seriously with these challenges and with good intent. We might question those who buy shares in microfinance banks with a view to profit, but so long as the banks themselves retain as their main aim the alleviation of poverty, their recourse to private capital should not affect the treatment of borrowers. From a utilitarian perspective, there will be a trade-off between the much greater number of loans they can finance and the higher interest rates resulting from their higher costs, but this is something that an ethically responsible institution will monitor carefully.

One particularly interesting development has been the entry of mainstream banks into the microfinance market, most controversially that of

Goldman Sachs[17] in 2008, with its 10,000 women global program. This prompted concerns that banks would use microfinance as a publicity stunt rather than engaging seriously with the financing needs of the poor. Goldman's intentions are certainly questionable. It has milked the program for all it's worth in terms of publicity, and while claiming the microfinance label, it has focused on giving loans and training to established entrepreneurs rather than the much earlier-stage financing more commonly associated with microfinance. There seems little doubt that the primary purpose of the program, like many exercises in corporate social responsibility, is to advance the reputation and interests of Goldman Sachs rather than to alleviate poverty. On the other hand, the program has almost certainly done more good than harm, and there are no indications that the borrowers have been exploited. Goldman has used them, but they have also used the opportunity granted them and so far it seems to be a fair exchange.[18]

Default and bankruptcy

Up to this point we have focused on the ethics of lending, but borrowing also raises issues. Traditional moral norms treat borrowing with caution: while borrowing might sometimes be unavoidable or even a good thing to do, people should not take out loans without a moral commitment, and not just a contractual one, to pay them back, and without reasonable expectations of being able to do this. From an ethical perspective, this seems uncontroversial. The norm of responsible borrowing would seem to be a reasonable candidate for maximizing utility either as a social norm (rule utilitarianism) or as a personal one (indirect act utilitarianism), and the consequences of people following the opposite principle, collectively or individually, would seem to be unambiguously bad. In a Kantian view, borrowing without the reasonable expectation of being able to repay would seem to be equivalent to making a false promise: the practice of promising depends on people generally being able to keep their promises,

---

[17] www.goldmansachs.com/citizenship/10000women.
[18] The general question here, which is beyond the scope of this book, is whether and to what extent the good of a charitable gift is undone or undermined by the non-charitable intentions of the donor.

as well as on them generally intending to do so. This does not excuse the lenders discussed in earlier sections any more than the behavior of a weak participant in a crime excuses that of a powerful initiator of that crime. We cannot, as some people have tried to, blame the financial crisis entirely on the irresponsibility of subprime borrowers, but we cannot exonerate the borrowers completely either.

Traditional moral norms also hold that it is wrong to voluntarily default on a loan. To do so is not only to break a promise, which may in exceptional circumstances be allowable; it is also a kind of theft, which is almost never allowable. The issues here are trickier, though. Legally, a default is only a theft if the borrower absconds. Otherwise there is a kind of limbo in which the debt remains active until such point as the lender gives up on it or a court decrees that it should be wiped clean. Moreover, in contemporary Western society, we put more weight on finding a solution that allows people to move on than we do on ensuring full retribution. With over a million personal bankruptcies a year in the USA alone (1,411,000 bankruptcies in total in 2011, of which 1,350,000 were personal),[19] default no long carries anything like the moral stigma it used to, and release from bankruptcy is routinely granted quickly and without anything like full repayment.

The laws relating to bankruptcy vary from country to country and can be highly complex, but they generally seek to achieve two things. One is a balance between the need to wind up a failing company before its debts accumulate too much and the need to ensure that essentially viable companies are not bankrupted because of temporary difficulties. The other is a fair distribution of limited assets amongst a variety of claimants – secured and unsecured lenders, trade creditors, employees, etc. The overall aim is to achieve maximum utility for society as a whole, and most societies take the view that this is most likely to be achieved by taking a relatively forgiving attitude to defaulters, encouraging entrepreneurial risk-taking and enabling all parties to move quickly on. Different regimes embody different views as to the optimal balance between punishment and forgiveness, and the resulting distribution of assets is always contentious. Whatever regime is adopted, somebody will consider it unfair, and whatever procedures are in place, powerful players will seek to turn them to their own

---

[19] See data at www.uscourts.gov/uscourts/Statistics/BankruptcyStatistics/BankruptcyFilings.

advantage. From an ethical perspective, however, there are few clear-cut issues here.[20]

Where bankruptcy becomes ethically contentious is where the procedures are used by people or corporations to default on loans they might well have been able to honor. A prominent feature of American law is the provision, alongside simple bankruptcy under Chapter 7 of the Bankruptcy Code, of bankruptcy protection under Chapter 11 of the Code. This allows the managers of a firm to continue managing it under a receiver's supervision and gives them time both to try and turn it round and to negotiate terms with their creditors. Under Chapter 11, all debts are frozen and can remain frozen for months and sometimes years. Once again, the justification is utilitarian, the aim being to prevent premature bankruptcies and secure a better outcome for all concerned than if firms simply went bankrupt. Whether it works this way, however, remains unclear. Some firms do recover under Chapter 11. In other cases it just delays the inevitable, adding to the losses incurred and both reducing and delaying payments to creditors, while benefiting the managers who got the company into trouble in the first place. It can be particularly hard on small creditors, who have limited negotiating power and for whom a greatly delayed payment may be of little value. Overall, creditors seem to do slightly better out of Chapter 11 than out of Chapter 7 bankruptcies, but against this they have to wait for their money. The utilitarian case is unproven one way or the other.[21]

One of the peculiarities of Chapter 11 is that firms can file, and so freeze their debts and head off any court actions, before they actually go bankrupt, and a number of cases of such strategic liquidations have raised ethical concerns. When the asbestos manufacturer Johns Manville filed for bankruptcy in 1982 in one of the first of such cases, it was a solvent company with net assets of over $1 billion, but was facing legal action for personal injury from asbestosis victims that would certainly have put it out of business. Under the protection of Chapter 11, the legal actions could be determined and the resulting debts set alongside other creditor claims in the liquidation process. This effectively enabled a cap to be placed on the firm's legal liabilities and in 1988 it emerged from bankruptcy with the unpaid compensation written off.[22] Many other companies have since used

---

[20] For a review, see Branch and Taub 2010.   [21] *Ibid.*   [22] Boatright 2008.

bankruptcy protection in similar ways, to enforce settlements of legal claims or to renegotiate agreements with suppliers or collective bargaining agreements with employees and their trade unions. However, while there are frequent claims of unfairness from whichever party loses out, the justification of the general procedure in terms of overall utility seems to stand up.

In the UK, concern has focused more on the practice of firms allowing subsidiary companies to go bankrupt and default on their obligations when these could easily have been borne by the parent company. In other cases wealthy individuals conducting business through wholly owned limited companies have done the same. Legally, this is perfectly allowable. Creditors know that they are dealing with a limited liability company and take risks accordingly. However, when the company is closely associated in the public mind with its wealthy owner, and the unpaid creditors include individuals and small firms that struggle to take the hit, ethical questions are bound to arise. The bankruptcy system as a whole may be justified on utilitarian grounds, but Kantian and virtue considerations would seem to call for treating people with more consideration.[23]

Our attitudes to default seem to vary significantly depending on who or what is defaulting. Within the financial and commercial sphere, default seems to be treated simply as an economic option amongst others. Rational lenders or trade creditors expect a proportion of their debtors to default and take this into account in their contracting. They assume that borrowers will act in their own financial interest, and that in some cases the borrowers will benefit more (or think they will benefit more) from taking the loan money and recklessly spending it than from behaving responsibly and paying it back. They assess the probability of the borrower defaulting, estimate the costs associated with this – the loss of some or all of their capital, the cost of realizing the value of any security or collateral, the cost of court actions and so on – and adjust their rates accordingly. In the case of governments, which cannot be pursued for their debts through the courts and can, effectively, walk away with the money, they also take into account the possibility of voluntary default.

When the lender is an individual, as when one person lends to another or a person is owed money by a delinquent company, default tends to be seen

---

[23] For a fuller discussion and case material, see Sorrell and Hendry 1994, pp. 138–47.

more in moral terms and as generally wrong. Where the borrower is an individual, however, and the lender a large company, the default may be excused on the basis that companies deserve what they get, or that there is no real victim, or some other excuse.

A similar attitude seems prevalent in response to the recent financial crisis in Greece and the possibility that Greece might default on its bonds. Here the money is owed by the Greek people, collectively, who have borrowed well beyond their means and spent unwisely. But the key decisions were taken in government, and the lenders demanding payment are large commercial banks. Many Greek citizens feel that default is the only way forward and they don't feel bad about this – partly because they feel no personal responsibility for the borrowing and spending, and partly because they blame the banks for the crisis. Moreover, many citizens of other countries seem to sympathize with this view.

In cases of default, as in the other topics reviewed in this chapter, we face a situation in which the boundaries between the amoral world of economics and finance and the moral world of personal relationships are unclear. Personal loans and, in a different way, government loans are both part of the financial system and at the same time part of people's personal, social and political lives. When we look at how businesses treat people, who can reasonably expect to be treated ethically, the ethics of the situation seem relatively clear. But when we look at how people treat businesses, which don't necessarily have such expectations, things get complicated. Default is also complicated by the fact that every event is in some sense exceptional. Individuals, company managers and governments all act in different contexts, but none of them have policies on defaulting. It is not something you expect do on a regular basis. Each case is treated as it arises, in the circumstances and under the constraints obtaining at the time.

In looking at the ethics of personal default, this suggests a virtue ethics approach. Novelists have often written of people struggling or unable to pay their debts, partly because as struggling writers they've been in that position themselves,[24] but partly because it is revealing of character: put someone in a hard place and you find out something about what they're made of. This is classic virtue ethics territory, in which we judge people by their responses to specific circumstances and look at such things as how they

---

[24] Finn 2003.

balance their own survival against the claims of others, act with honesty and integrity when it would be easier not to, and avoid the vices associated with destitution. To form a character judgment, we would need to look at a defaulter's responses to a variety of situations, and not just one particularly difficult situation. If we did so, however, we would no doubt find that some defaulters are clearly lacking virtue (and that lack of virtue may have been what got them into default in the first place). In other cases, where people have just been extraordinarily unlucky, for example, we may find a range of more or less virtuous responses, with default in some cases appearing as the least bad option open to people.

We cannot apply virtue ethics to a business or a government, but we can apply it to a business owner or manager, a prime minister or president, charged with steering a path between the interests of creditors and those of employees or citizens. Again, we look for honesty and integrity, respect for all those involved, balanced judgment and temperate and reasonable behavior. When every case is different, it makes sense to ask how someone handles the case facing them rather than to judge in terms of generalities.

6 Trading and speculation: the ethics of financial markets

In Chapter 4 we described the ideology of the financial system in terms of free and unfettered markets, subject to a minimum of regulation. In practice, free markets are an economic abstraction. Any market of any kind is a social institution characterized by a particular structure and particular practices that put limitations of one kind and another (membership, location, technology, etc.) on who can participate and how. In the case of financial markets, we have already noted the existence of two kinds of regulation concerned with how people compete, neither of which are generally considered to impinge adversely on their efficient operation: prudential regulation, designed to prevent the system as a whole from collapsing; and conduct regulation, designed primarily to protect the interests of customers.

Apart from protecting customers, regulations controlling conduct also include various measures to govern and protect the markets themselves: controls whose purpose is to keep the markets free, or at least as free as possible. This sounds paradoxical, but the idea of free market competition is itself paradoxical. It is of the nature of competition that there are winners and losers, and if the competition is truly free and unfettered, there is nothing to prevent the winners from pressing home their advantage to the limit, eliminating their competitors and so destroying the competitive market. Where competitions are run for the sake of competition, as in sport, the effects of winning are generally self-limiting. The winners, to be winners, need worthwhile opponents; you can't run a football league with just one team. In business, though, where the competition is a means to an end rather than an end in itself, the limit of winning is monopoly power, where one player controls the whole market.

In industrial and commercial markets, regulators respond to the problem of monopoly power through antitrust legislation, preventing any corporation from reaching a monopoly position, measured in terms of market share in its industry. Since firms tend to build market share relatively slowly and since market dominance is relatively rare, this kind of regulation can be conducted on a case-by-case basis. A body is given the power to intervene, but does so only when it sees the need. In financial markets, which move much more quickly, there is also a risk of a firm cornering a market and gaining a short-term monopoly. A trader might seek, for example, to buy up all or most of the available stock of a particular security, create a temporary, artificial shortage in that security and sell again at an inflated monopoly price. Since financial securities are artificial constructs with no underlying use value, this will not generally destroy the market. The firm will take its monopoly profit and the market will start functioning again. Within an amoral culture of competitive self-interest, it is also perfectly rational behavior. But it does distort the pricing mechanism on which market efficiency depends, and markets are generally regulated in such a way as to prevent it.

Financial markets also employ a range of controls on the use of information, again on the basis that they distort the price mechanism and so reduce market efficiency. These include controls on collusion (acting in concert or sharing information through cartels), on market manipulation (introducing false or misleading information), on insider trading (acting on private information) and on preferential disclosure (passing company information to some shareholders but not others).

Within the financial system, these controls appear to have a kind of moral force as well as a legal or regulatory force. There is a widespread view, for example, that market manipulation and insider trading are wrong. However, it is not immediately obvious that these practices are ethically wrong in themselves, as opposed to being wrong only in the sense that they are a kind of cheating in the context of the rules of a game. Nor is it entirely obvious why cheating should be wrong in the context of an amoral system in which opportunistic self-interest is taken for granted.

In this chapter we shall focus on the ethics of market manipulation and insider trading. To set these practices in context, however, we first need to understand better the theory and practice of financial markets and to explore the ethics of trading – in particular speculative trading – more generally.

Financial markets in theory and practice

Economics is still a relatively primitive science, and whilst it is quite good at describing static equilibrium states, such as notional efficient markets, it is much less good at dealing with the dynamics of real market operations. The key issue here is information. In simple neoclassical economics, the market is modeled as a completely static equilibrium on the assumption that market participants are not only fully rational and fully competent utility-maximizers with stable preference sets but also have perfect information – about every possible product, about each other's (and, in the case of producers, their competitors') behaviors and preferences, about everything in the world, including everything in the future, that might affect their decisions. Even with these rather extreme simplifications, neoclassical economics can produce powerful results: the basic laws of supply and demand clearly work in practice, for example, even in complex real-life situations that deviate enormously from the theoretical assumptions. But with no time dimension, it cannot model dynamic markets and it has no place for institutions such as firms that evolve over time.

Contemporary financial economics is a product of several generations of attempts by economists to address these limitations, especially through consideration of the costs associated with information – the costs of search, monitoring and so forth. However, while it has made significant progress in some respects, it remains limited in others. In particular, the modeling of financial markets still relies on very artificial assumptions about information. It is assumed, for example, that the impact of information on market price is directly calculable. And it is assumed that, subject to random variations around a mean, all market participants not only share, at any given time, the same information, but also process that information and calculate the price implications in the same way.[1] On these assumptions there is, in an efficient market, an equilibrium price for any security, but there is no mechanism for moving one equilibrium point to another. Allowing random variations in valuation makes room for speculative

---

[1] Recent developments in behavioral finance and, especially, in imperfect knowledge economics have sought to overcome these limitations and have made some small progress, but neither comes close to a predictive account of how markets operate. See Barberis and Huang 2001; Frydman and Goldberg 2007; and Shleifer 2000.

trading, but since all the available relevant information will be captured in the equilibrium price, any attempt to speculate on future movements is doomed to failure.

Real financial markets are different in several respects. Most obviously, they are dynamic not static, and while information may be rapidly absorbed, it is not instantaneously absorbed, so at any moment in time there are information asymmetries. As Friedrich Hayek pointed out in the 1930s and 1940s, what characterizes real markets is the fact that the relevant information is not actually shared but is distributed amongst the market participants. The whole point of the price mechanism is that dispersed information can be brought to bear on prices, allowing efficient resource allocation decisions to be made, without the information itself necessarily being transferred or shared. In a changing world, actors can react rapidly to new information by responding to price signals, without necessarily knowing what lies behind the price changes.[2] On Hayek's model, each investor in a market starts out with a different knowledge base, so each makes different investment decisions; they trade between themselves and the (ever-changing) equilibrium price emerges from this trading.

Another distinctive feature of real financial markets is that the information on which they depend is inherently ambiguous and incomplete. In a world of radical uncertainty, any valuation is going to be as much the product of assumptions and guesses as of any hard data or rational probabilistic analysis. In particular, it will be the product of a mood of optimism or pessimism in respect of various possible eventualities and their combined effects. As is apparent from the recent experience of wildly fluctuating financial markets, these moods are apt to change quickly and unpredictably. In these circumstances the idea of a true value or equilibrium price is still meaningful, but only up to a point. It makes sense to say that a company's stock, for example, has an underlying value corresponding to the net present value of its expected revenue flows, or that there is, in theory, an equilibrium exchange rate between the dollar and the euro based on the expected developments of the American and Eurozone economies. We can often tell when prices are severely distorted by false information or when markets go seriously out of equilibrium in asset bubbles or panics. In

---

[2] Hayek 1937 and 1945.

normal market conditions, however, when price movements are relatively small compared to the uncertainties inherent in valuation, relating these price movements to an underlying value is much more difficult. When it comes to trading on financial markets, the true value of a security is of limited relevance.

Despite all this, some traders do still work on the basis that successful investment is about buying securities that are fundamentally under-valued, according to their own analysis, and selling those that are over-valued. But it is not obviously a rational thing to do and even those who follow the strategy nowadays recognize its limits. It relies not only on the trader's information/analysis being actually better than other people's, but on other people changing their views to recognize this, and on a timescale that is shorter than the timescale on which the information changes significantly anyway. For the vast majority of trading, which is conducted using relatively short time horizons of anything from a few microseconds (in computerized arbitrage trading) to a few months (in traditional equity fund management), underlying value is at most a relatively weak constraint and is often a complete irrelevance.

A more real-life view of how markets operate was given by John Maynard Keynes in *The General Theory of Employment, Interest and Money* of 1936, and is worth quoting at length:

> It might have been supposed that competition between expert professionals, possessing judgement and knowledge beyond that of the average private investor, would correct the vagaries of the ignorant individual investor left to himself. It happens, however, that the energies and skills of the professional investor and speculator are mainly occupied otherwise. For most of these persons are, in fact, largely concerned, not with making superior long-term forecasts of the probable yield of an investment over its whole life, but with foreseeing changes in the conventional basis of valuation a short time ahead of the general public. They are concerned, not with what an investment is really worth for a man who buys it "for keeps," but with what the market will value it at, under the influence of mass psychology, three months or a year hence. Moreover, this behavior is not the outcome of a wrong-headed propensity. It is an inevitable result of an investment market organised along the lines described. [Essentially, this is a market designed with a view to liquidity, but in which information is radically uncertain, i.e., in which possible events cannot be assigned a probability.] For it is not sensible to pay 25 for an

investment of which you believe a prospective yield to justify a value of 30, if
you also believe the market will value it at 20 three months hence.

… [I]t is, so to speak, a game of Snap, of Old Maid, of Musical Chairs … Or,
to change the metaphor slightly, professional investment may be likened to
those newspaper competitions in which the competitors have to pick out the
six prettiest faces from a hundred photographs, the prize being awarded to
the competitor whose choice most nearly corresponds to the average preferences of the competitors as a whole; so that each competitor has to pick,
not which faces he himself finds prettiest, but those which he thinks likeliest
to catch the fancy of the other competitors, all of whom are looking at the
problem from the same point of view. It is not a case of choosing those which,
to the best of one's judgement, are really the prettiest, nor even those which
average opinion genuinely thinks the prettiest. We have reached the third
degree where we devote our intelligences to anticipating what average
opinion expects the average opinion to be. And there are some, I believe, who
practice the fourth, fifth and higher degrees.[3]

Since Keynes's time, the "private investor" has faded from view and investment horizons have become much shorter, but the fundamentals haven't
changed. Most trading takes the form of speculation and it operates much as
he described.

To sum up, we have a theory of financial markets according to which
information is publicly shared and has a clear and unambiguous value, and
we have real-world financial markets in which information is asymmetri-
cally distributed and is of uncertain value. The theory leads naturally to a set
of norms, or rules of the game, designed to ensure that information *is*
publicly shared – no insider dealing, no manipulation, no differential disclosure – but the reality leaves open questions about the relevance of these
rules and their ethical import.

Meanwhile, the one area in which theory and practice are in broad
agreement is the one that is most obviously questionable from a traditional
moral perspective. According to the theory of efficient markets, speculation
is pointless (you can never beat the market), but it is also the only way in
which trading can actually occur. According to the real-world view, trading
is speculation. But according to traditional moral norms, speculation is, to
say the least, dubious.

---

[3] Keynes 1964, pp. 154–6 (Chapter 12, section 5).

The ethics of speculative trading

In Chapters 2 and 4 we touched on three possible objections to financial speculation: (1) that speculation is gambling and gambling is not virtuous; (2) that it causes harm to people indirectly affected, such as the citizens and taxpayers of countries whose currencies are the subject of it; and (3) that it reduces utility by appropriating resources to the financial sector without adding anything of value. Let's consider these in turn.

The first of these objections is rooted in traditional moral values and takes the view that speculation, like gambling generally, is a vice and speculators are immoral from a virtue perspective. They are conceived variously as morally lazy, seeking financial returns for no input of productive effort; as greedy and prone to addiction; and as morally irresponsible. Just as hard work and saving represent the virtues of self-reliance and good husbandry, putting those savings at risk through speculation represents the vices of self-neglect and wastefulness.

This perspective is deeply rooted in nineteenth- and early twentieth-century middle-class respectability, but the rich and the poor have never been that concerned about gambling, and now that most Western governments run state-sponsored national lotteries, it is probably outdated. No-one could reasonably claim that speculation is virtuous, but few would now claim that it is, in itself, a vice, so long as it does not get out of control. Setting aside for the moment the problems of speculating with other people's money (which we shall look at in the next chapter), the criticism from a virtue perspective would not now be of speculators in general, but of those who allow it to upset the balance and temper of their lives. Speculation becomes wrong, on this view, when it becomes uncontrollably addictive, when greed overwhelms reason and speculators abandon responsibility for their own and their dependents' well-being. This clearly happens, but it does not seem to be a particularly common feature of the speculative trading of financial professionals.

The second objection starts from the observation that financial speculation impacts harmfully on the lives of third parties. We noted in Chapter 4 that speculation in the Forex markets and in government bonds can seriously damage developing country economies, harming their citizens and especially the poorest amongst them. We suggested there that a case could be made out to the effect that the principles underlying the global financial system are wrong from a Kantian perspective, using these people merely as means. But what about the individual speculators? If I trade speculatively in the Venezuelan bolìvar, with no thought other than to make money, can I really be said to be harming the Venezuelan people or treating them as merely means? The impact seems too remote and my contribution too uncertain.

One way to explore this is by switching from Kant's Formula of Humanity to his Formula of Universal Law and asking whether the personal maxim of speculative trading can be willed as a universal law. There is no obvious contradiction in conception: a universalized practice of speculative trading does not appear to undermine the general practice of trading, which needs a certain threshold of activity to be viable, or to prevent me from gaining through my own speculations. If I knew that my actions would be harmful or carried a serious risk of being harmful, then to engage in any practice with that knowledge would lead to a contradiction of will, and one could argue that we now have enough evidence about the harmful effects of speculation to make engaging in it unethical from a Kantian perspective. But the great majority of Forex and bond trading is not obviously harmful, so while it might be wrong to jump on a speculative Forex bandwagon once it becomes apparent where it might be going (sending a country into crisis), there seems to be no clear objection to speculative trading in general.

The third objection also goes back to our discussion of the financial system. It starts from the observation that speculative trading is a zero-sum game that serves only to divert wealth from the productive economy into the financial sector, producing a net loss in utility. From this point of view, there may be an ethical case for limiting speculation, perhaps by limiting the derivative securities that can be traded. However, the argument is complicated by two factors. First, contemporary financial markets are the product of rapidly changing information technologies, which have made possible a massive expansion both of the range of securities that can be traded and of the volume of speculative trading that can be conducted. We can point to some harmful recent effects, but we are still in the very early stages of the technology and are still working out how to use it. Many new technologies (industrial, medical, etc.) bring short-term learning costs and from a utilitarian perspective (though not necessarily from any other per-spective), these may be offset by longer-term benefits that would not have arisen without them. Applying the analogy to this case seems a bit of a stretch, but it should at least be considered.

Second, as we have already noted, speculation also has positive economic effects. It ensures that those wishing to use derivatives for hedging purposes can find counterparties, contributes to market liquidity and provides effective price signaling. Without the markets in the assets, underlying derivatives would be less efficient. Up to a point, rules and guidelines that allow speculative trading appear to be utility enhancing. The problem lies only with the current cumulative extent of speculative activity, especially in the derivatives markets, which cannot possibly be justified in this way and must surely be sub-optimal for society at large.

In this situation, the consequences of any individual trader's actions, or of individual guidelines that allow speculative trading, seem impossible to assess. Many otherwise unremarkable activities become harmful, for one reason or another, when carried out to excess or by too many people. The simple act of driving a car, for example, may be utility enhancing when the roads are clear, but as traffic builds up and drivers spend their time queuing, the pollution damage grows disproportionately. However, only those with a very strong environmentalist stance would say that people who drive in traffic jams are wrong, and the same is true here. To the extent that speculative trading may be wrong, we should probably treat it as a matter of inadequate regulation rather than finding fault with traders. In contrast, where the issues to be treated next are concerned, we already have effective regulations. The question is whether they have any ethical basis or are simply rules of a game.

Market manipulation

Market manipulation has a long history. Throughout the nineteenth century and into the 1930s, it was recognized as one of the main ways that people made money in what were then largely unregulated commodity and stock markets. Classic forms of manipulation include wash sales, bear raids, and corners and squeezes.

We now use the term "wash sale" to refer to the practice of realizing tax losses by selling and repurchasing, but it was originally a straightforward form of manipulation. Two equity traders sell to each other in matching trades at a price above or below the current market price. The trades cancel each other out, but providing the identities of the traders can be concealed from view, the impact of the trades on the markets is to artificially raise or lower the share price, allowing the traders to benefit from their long or short positions.

A contemporary version of this is the share-ramping identified in the shares of a London AIM-listed shell company, FEI, in 2003–4. Here an agency stockbroker was used to create artificial trades in the shares (the trades were made between the stockbroker's client accounts, but they were constantly rolled over so that no settlement was required), quadrupling their share price over a period of ten months.[4] The scheme was eventually exposed, the instigator received a hefty fine from the Financial Services Authority, and both he and the market-maker who carried out the trades were banned from the industry.

Another contemporary technique is the use of large-volume trades to support or depress market prices close to daily or option settlement times. In 2007, the London coffee futures trader Andrew Kerr used heavy trading in the one-minute period during which reference prices were set to artificially increase coffee futures prices in the run-up to an option expiry, to the benefit of a client. In this case, no lies were told and there was no collusion, but the rules were broken and the result was again a fine and a trading ban.[5]

In bear raids, traders seek to create an artificial collapse in the price of a security. The aim is to profit both by selling short on the way down and by buying long at the bottom, selling again when the price returns to normal. The price collapse might be engineered by coordinated short selling by a group of traders and/or by the dissemination of false rumors, both of which breach regulations, but these aren't always needed. In 1930, in one of the last "great" bear raids before US legislators acted to control market manipulation, Thomas Howell engineered an artificial collapse in corn prices. Usually bear raiders try and hide their identities, but on this occasion Howell didn't hide the fact that he was aggressively short selling. Other traders, sensing a bear raid, followed his example, driving prices down. Unknown to them, however, he had actually accumulated physical corn stocks and had a net long position. He covered his own shorts, but when

---

[4] www.fsa.gov.uk/pubs/press/background_FEI.pdf; www.fsa.gov.uk/library/communication/pr/2010/084.shtml.

[5] www.fsa.gov.uk/library/communication/pr/2010/088.shtml.

those who had followed him sought to buy corn to cover their own positions, they were stung as prices were driven sharply up again.[6]

At the height of the financial crisis in 2008, there were repeated bear raids on HBOS and other UK and US banks, without any evidence of either explicit collusion or false rumors. In a panicky market, many hedge fund managers saw that aggressive short selling could itself spark off rumors that would push prices further down, and all it took was a few of them to act at the same time, whether by intent, by accident or by something in between, for a raid to be on. The first raid on HBOS seems to have been sparked by a specific rumor, but any rumor, even one intended as a joke, would have done. In this case the authorities couldn't prove that anyone was breaking the rules and had to resort to a temporary ban on the short selling of financial stocks.[7]

In corners and squeezes, traders buy heavily, using futures or other forms of leveraged purchasing to control enough of a security, typically a commodity, where the ultimate demand is for a real product, to create an artificial shortage (cornering the market) or enough of a threat of one to drive up prices (squeezing the market), allowing them to sell at a handsome profit.

Perhaps the most famous example here was the manipulation of the silver market in the 1970s by the multi-billionaire oil magnate brothers Nelson Bunker Hunt and W. Herbert Hunt. Over six years the Hunt brothers, working with a group of rich Saudi investors, repeatedly used the threat of a corner to squeeze the market, lifting the price of silver from $2 to $50 an ounce.[8] More characteristic of contemporary markets are the attempts by Paul Mozer of Salomon Brothers in 1991 to manipulate the market in US Treasury bonds (Box 6.1) by cornering a particular issue and putting a squeeze on rival traders, who had made commitments to deliver bonds from that issue to their clients.

The core of the regulatory objection to market manipulation is that it distorts the price mechanism by introducing false or misleading information, either directly, through false rumors, or indirectly, through trades designed to give false signals. Traders acting in collusion give an impression that the market as a whole is responding to some (as yet unknown)

---

[6] Geisst 2002, pp. 120ff.   [7] Brummer 2009, p. 202; see also Augur 2010.
[8] Geisst 2002, pp. 226ff.

Box 6.1. Salomon Brothers and Treasury Securities

Like all the major investment banks, Salomon Brothers in the early 1990s combined underwriting and advisory services with trading on its own account. However, in Salomon's case the trading was a larger part of the firm. This had arisen from its early emphasis, from its founding in 1910, on US Treasury bonds, new issues of which were sold to a select group of investment banks for re-sale rather than being offered to the public and underwritten as in the case of corporate securities. In return for their privileged access, the primary dealers, as they were called, had to commit to maintaining a market in the securities. In 1991 Salomon was reputedly the largest and most active trader of US government securities, turning over about $20 billion a day. It was also by then the largest player in mortgage-backed securities, and also had a highly successful bond arbitrage group. It was the first of the large investment banks to develop a trading culture and, in the bond arbitrage group, to pay traders large bonuses based on their individual performance. In 1991 both the head of Treasury bond trading, Paul Mozer, and his boss, Vice-Chairman John Meriwether, were alumni of the bond arbitrage unit and fully committed to a trading culture.

The Treasury bond issue process required primary dealers (in 1991 there were about 40 of them) to submit bids on the particular bonds being offered through weekly auctions, specifying both a quantity and a yield: for example, $50 million at 6.46 percent. Bids at the lowest yields were filled first and so on until the issue was placed. Typically the bids would be very closely clustered around two or three basis points and the bulk of the issue might have to be allocated to a number of bidders at the same yield, in proportion to their bid quantities, with each receiving only a percentage of the amount bid for. Dealers could bid both on their own account and on behalf of customers. The system led to all sorts of auction games, including false rumors, bluffs and counter-bluffs, and submissions of bid quantities far in excess of what was actually wanted. In the late 1980s, Salomon in particular often placed very large bids at what it expected to be the "stop price" so as to capture as much of the issue as it could once the bids were scaled down: in 1990, it put in one bid for three times the total issue.

Actual allocations had for some time been limited to 35 percent of the total issue, and to counter Salomon's tactics, the Treasury decided in 1990 to also limit bids to 35 percent of the total issue. Mozer was furious at this restriction on his gaming and in an April 1991 auction, he responded by putting in two bids at 35 percent of the total, one in Salomon's own name and one in the name of a customer – but without the authorization of the supposed customer (Warburg). On receiving the allocations (of roughly half the amounts bid, amounting to 38 percent of the issue in total), his trading desk were instructed to transfer the Warburg notes to Salomon's own account.

Six weeks later, the Federal Reserve noticed that Warburg had also submitted a much smaller bid on its own account and queried the Salomon customer bid. Mozer instructed his deputy to reply that the customer was not in fact Warburg, but one of its operationally separate affiliates. However, the Treasury then decided that the affiliation was too close, retrospectively reduced the combined Warburg bids to 35 percent and notified all parties. Mozer managed to cover things up, but at this point he informed Meriwether of what he had done, and after taking legal advice it was decided that Meriwether, on behalf of Salomon, would have to own up. However, he was not keen and it was not clear how best to do this. Action was deferred.

Meanwhile, Mozer had continued to act aggressively and, using aggressive (low-yield) bids by Salomon and two clients (this time with authorization), had cornered a May issue, taking 100 percent of the issue, putting a squeeze on other banks that had made commitments to their own customers and engineering a nice profit. Since some of the customer allocations were then bought by Salomon, this was of dubious legality and it did not exactly add to Salomon's popularity at the Treasury. More seriously, Mozer had also used Salomon affiliate companies to bid alongside Salomon itself, without declaring the affiliation.

Mozer was soon caught out and was in due course sacked by the company, but by that stage, the fact that they had left him in post after the first transgression and had failed to report this to the authorities put the company itself under threat. Because he had reported the transgression upwards, Meriwether, who had been Mozer's chief defender, escaped official censure, though he soon left the company. The company's Chairman and President were forced to resign and the company was initially barred from Treasury auctions, being rescued only by the intervention of Warren Buffet and Travelers Group, who took it over and pledged to reform its ways.

Meriwether, looking for an environment in which to exploit his bond arbitrage skills without any onerous supervision or regulation, soon set up a hedge fund, Long-Term Capital Management, with the support of Nobel economists Myron Scholes and Robert Merton. This initially made outstanding returns on the basis of sophisticated arbitrage trading, but when the arbitrage opportunities closed down, it resorted to much riskier, directional positions to maintain its growth, taking a series of highly leveraged bets in the equities and currency markets, which lacked the underlying logic of government bond markets. Within five years of its creation, it had to be rescued by its creditors, having amassed losses of $4.5 billion.

Sources: the Salomon case is abstracted from Moreton 1992. For Long-Term Capital Management, see Dunbar 2000 and Lowenstein 2000.

information when there is no such information. Traders acting under others' names conceal crucial information. Generally, the objection is to market manipulators trading in order to try and move the price of a security when there is no outside information that would justify such a price move.

This objection ties in with the theory of financial markets described above. But within a system that is avowedly built on the amoral pursuit of opportunistic interest and in a real world in which information is uncertain and hard to pin down, and in which trading is dominated by people second-guessing each other's moves, it is hard to give it any moral significance. Traders are always trying to exploit price moves and the distinction between coordinated and uncoordinated bear raids, for example, is a fuzzy one. Moreover, while the kinds of market manipulation we have described are in breach of market regulations and are severely punished if discovered, they don't generally breach the criminal law.

How might we address this issue ethically? One approach would be to look at the consequences of people following rules that incorporated restrictions of different kinds. There is some evidence, for example, that when share prices are distorted, this can lead to executives making strategic changes (in response to the share price signals) that harm rather than help the business and its shareholders – though they presumably also help its competitors.[9] Bear raids on a company's stock can also undermine confidence in the company, and where confidence is everything, as in the case of banks, this can have much wider consequences. The main public concern in

[9] Goldstein and Guembel 2008.

respect of the shorting of bank stocks in 2008 was that basically sound banks might be driven to collapse, with severe consequences not only for customers, employees and shareholders but also for society as a whole. Indeed, one well worked-out conspiracy theory blamed the entire collapse of the banking sector during the financial crisis on overseas hedge funds controlled by Russian Mafiosi, seeking to destabilize the American economy.[10] The creation of artificial shortages or artificially high prices in staple commodities can also have widespread consequences, raising the living costs of those least able to afford it.

Separating out these effects from those of the financial system generally will not be easy. Given the nature of the markets, sound companies can go under or commodity prices bubble without any help from manipulators. But a full and careful analysis might show whether or not some of the more extreme practices are unethical from a utilitarian perspective.

From a Kantian perspective, some forms of market manipulation – those that involve the telling of lies, for example – appear to be clearly wrong, but even here some traders would argue that deception is just part of the game and doesn't carry the ethical significance it does in everyday life. And other forms of manipulation, which involve no lying, are much harder to judge. We could perhaps argue that a maxim of trying to manipulate the price mechanism to one's advantage, if universalized, would destroy the price mechanism and so defeat the purpose – except that this is what everybody does, in a small way, all the time, and the markets continue to function. Because the markets are inherently imperfect – price is never a perfect indicator of underlying value – making them a little less perfect doesn't obviously induce a contradiction.

A different approach, given the peculiar nature of financial markets, might be to look at the ethics of games. Since one thing we are clear about is that market manipulation breaks the rules of a practice that is generally seen, by its participants, as a kind of game, we can ask when breaking the rules of a game is unethical and when it is not.

Because social and sporting games are a part of everyday life, our moral senses are more finely attuned to them than they are to an activity like finance, which is remote from most people's experience, and this gives us a useful starting point. According to our social norms, committing a foul in

[10] Freeman 2009.

football, say, is not normally considered immoral, even when it is done intentionally (what we sometimes call a professional foul). At the end of a tight game of basketball, professional fouls are committed quite blatantly as teams weigh up the penalties for a foul against the costs of allowing the opposition to retain possession. The rules of the game not only stipulate breaches but also penalties, and the penalties are sometimes worth taking. In football (or soccer), where punishment is at the referee's discretion, an intentional foul might be punished more harshly than an accidental one, but providing it is not dangerous, there are still occasions when it is considered the right thing to do for the team and its supporters.

Breaking the rules of a game tends to attract moral condemnation in two situations: where there is a danger of serious harm, beyond that inherent in the game itself, and where there is an intention to deceive. The first of these situations arises mainly in physical sports and is probably not relevant here. We can note, however, that intentionally committing dangerous fouls is clearly and straightforwardly unethical, whether from a Kantian, utilitarian or virtue perspective. The second situation arises in all games and is generally described as cheating.

Cheating often involves an element of lying, but it needn't do so. Card players might cheat, for example, by marking cards or passing information between themselves, or athletes by taking performance-enhancing drugs. They might tell lies if challenged and we might well think that this aggravates the offense, but there is a serious moral objection to the action as well as to the lie. Steven Connor, in a rare book on the philosophy of sport, argues that the real moral affront arises because cheats undermine the game by not taking it seriously. What matters is not so much that the cyclist Lance Armstrong took drugs and lied about it, but that, as a result, the competition lost its meaning. The point of a game is to decide who are the best players, and cheating takes this away. It is, in Connor's words, "not an offence in the game but an ontological affront to it."[11]

It would be tempting here to invoke Kant's Formula of Universal Law and suggest that, just as a universalized maxim of lying at will destroys the practice of truth-telling, a universalized maxim of cheating destroys the practice of the game. But the cases are not comparable. Universalized cheating at will would change the nature of the game, but would not lead

---

[11] Connor 2011, quotation at p. 178.

to a contradiction. Indeed, games often evolve to incorporate as legitimate what was once considered to be cheating. Absent the element of lying or actively misleading, the problem with cheating seems to arise from the act, not from its universalization, and to be partly a problem of utility and partly one of virtue. From the perspective of utility, people play and watch or follow games for pleasure, and that pleasure is seriously harmed if the results don't reflect performance or if they find out later that the game was not what they thought. Cheating takes away the pleasure people seek and find from games. From a virtue perspective, cheats are dishonest in intent, whether or not in action. They succumb to the temptation of greed for victory and they lack the courage to compete fairly.

Now, coming back to market manipulation, one thing we might notice is that while finance may be a game, it is not quite like other, everyday games. Although some market manipulators come across as distinctly unpleasant characters, the financial markets are probably too remote from our every-day social context for the concept of virtue to have much hold, and the players are typically playing against "the market" rather than against each other, depersonalizing the impacts and effects of their actions. This game does not seem to have the social, human importance of sports and other games, and undermining the game seems consequently less serious. Market manipulation breaks the rules and it often involves lies and deception, but in such an artificial setting, we are left with significant doubts as to whether it is seriously unethical.

Insider trading

In the winter of 2004–5, TV celebrity Martha Stewart, "goddess of domestic perfection" and author of the USA's favorite cookbooks, served five months in a federal prison as a result of insider trading charges. The country was shocked.

In December 2001, the US Food and Drug Administration (FDA) had announced its rejection of a cancer drug developed by the firm ImClone, leading to a 16 percent fall in the share price. Just before the announce-ment, the firm's CEO, Sam Waksal, sold $5 million of his shares and advised his relatives to sell theirs. His broker then called Martha Stewart, who was another of his clients, to tell her of Sam's sale. She asked him to sell her shares too.

Martha Stewart was not just a domestic superstar, she was also a very successful businesswoman and a one-time securities broker, who had recently been elected to the board of the NYSE. By trading when she did on the information received, she probably saved herself $45,000 – not much considering that she was a billionaire, but seriously embarrassing for a NYSE board member. When the SEC investigated, she and her broker attempted to cover up the use of inside information, giving a variety of explanations, none of which survived scrutiny.

As in the case of Paul Mozer and Salomon Brothers highlighted in the last section, the attempt at a cover-up was considered more serious than the original offense. In the Salomon case it almost destroyed the firm. In Martha Stewart's case it resulted in the prison sentence and two years of post-incarceration monitoring for false statements and obstructing the course of justice. But Stewart was also punished for her insider trading, with a hefty SEC fine and a five-year ban on holding senior office in a public company. The broker was also imprisoned and banned from the securities industry.[12]

Apart from her celebrity status and attempted cover up, Martha Stewart's case was typical of much insider trading, where friends, family and associates trade on information gleaned informally from company directors and consultants ahead of its public announcement. The other major class of offenses involves professional traders who actively solicit and even pay for such information. One of the more famous cases of this kind, involving Ivan Boesky and others, is described in Box 6.2. A more recent case is that of hedge fund manager Raj Rajaratnam, founder of the Galleon Group, who was found guilty in the US courts of conspiracy and securities fraud charges and sentenced to eleven years in prison, the longest sentence yet for insider trading. Thirteen others were also jailed.

It is often said that the main thing you get from studying at a major business school is not the technical knowledge but the personal contacts and access to an alumni network. A Wharton MBA and consummate networker, Rajaratnam made an estimated $68 million trading on information gained from a web of high-ranking corporate executives, including former Wharton classmates. Compared with his overall profits from Galleon, which gave him a wealth estimated in 2009 at $1.8 billion, this was small beer, but it was definitely against the rules and was widely condemned as

---

[12] Jennings 2011, pp. 63–8.

Box 6.2. Insider trading on the grand scale: Boesky, Levine and Milken

One of the great money-spinners of the 1980s was risk arbitrage. This essentially took the form of leveraged investments in corporate takeover targets, or prospective targets, whose share prices did not yet reflect the likely deal price. Having taken a position, well-funded arbitrageurs might also keep buying to push up offer prices or stimulate a bidding war. With the arbitrageurs often working in the same investment banks as advised firms on their acquisition strategies, albeit separated, in theory, by "Chinese walls," the scope for profits from insider trading was considerable. But the most notorious case of the era centered on an aggressive independent trader, Ivan Boesky, often seen as the model for the Gordon Gekko character in the movie *Wall Street*, who was reported by the 1980s to be earning up to $100 million a year.

Obsessively ambitious, Boesky would reportedly ring round everywhere in search of information to give him an edge – analysts, executives, bankers, consultants – but at some point he also started paying for it. In 1986, investigators arrested Dennis Levine, a trader at Drexel Burnham who had been routinely trading on inside information gleaned from his own company and exchanging this with a network of associates elsewhere, to the point where the regulators could not but notice that something was going on. As part of a plea bargain, Levine revealed details of arrangements with Boesky (who was a Drexel client) that included a share of Boesky's profits on any information Levine gave him.

When arrested late that year, Boesky too named names in exchange for leniency and agreed to obtain evidence against them by taping conversations. It eventually transpired that he had paid $700,000 in cash over the past five years to Martin Siegel, a Kidder Peabody banker (who had also ended up at Drexel), who in turn implicated other bankers at Kidder, Goldman Sachs and elsewhere. Boesky also implicated Michael Milken, the Drexel junk bond dealer who was by then the richest person on Wall Street and with whom Boesky had struck up a close working relationship.

Both the SEC and the US Department of Justice were already gunning for Drexel and Milken, whom they suspected of manipulating the markets in junk bonds and in the shares of companies involved in takeover situations, and Boesky's evidence allowed them to act. Drexel was charged with a range of offenses and, after denying any misconduct for over two years, eventually pleaded guilty to six counts of securities, wire and mail fraud. The company paid $650 million in fines and restitution, but was widely considered to have gotten off lightly. It started out with a legal defense budget greater than the total operating budget of the SEC and incurred $100 million in legal costs, and the joke was that the final settlement was "another buyout."

With Drexel admitting to charges in which Milken was personally implicated, he too was eventually indicted on 98 different counts. The focus was on market manipulation, a central charge being that Milken had used Boesky to trade in shares on his or Drexel's behalf, concealing their true ownership. But in the complex dealings of the frenetic take-over market in this period, in which Boesky was trading in the shares of acquisition targets and Milken was launching and trading in high-yield bonds issue by acquirers, the concealment of information and the improper use of that information went hand in hand.

Boesky paid $100 million in fines and Milken paid over $1 billion in fines, restitution and civil lawsuits. Both served about two years in prison.

Sources: Fine *et al.* 2005, Kornbluth 1992, Madrick 2011, Chapter 5, Stewart 1991 and Stone 1990.

---

immoral by regulators and prosecutors. Phone tap evidence collected by investigators included conversations in which well-placed insiders at firms like Goldman Sachs, McKinsey, Moody's, Intel and AMD conveyed critical price-sensitive information, including financial results and acquisition plans, ahead of public announcements.[13]

In society at large, insider trading is not considered especially immoral. If they were lucky enough to own shares in a company and received information that enabled them to make a profit or, especially, avoid a loss, many people would be tempted to act as Martha Stewart did and would see nothing wrong in it. The prison sentence seems to have been more shocking than the initial offense, and Stewart's popularity does not appear to have been dented. Insider trading by members of the financial community may be thought to be more suspect, but that is probably because they are

---

[13] The Wikipedia entry on Rajaratnam is comprehensive and well referenced: http://en.wikipedia.org/wiki/Raj_Rajaratnam; see also www.bbc.co.uk/news/business-13188529.

thought to be more suspect in all their dealings, not because of the insider trading.

Within the financial community, insider trading is known to be against the rules, but it is also thought, within limits, to be part of the game. Well into the post-war period, almost all information was inside information and stockbrokers quite openly made their living by picking up tips and passing them on to their clients. Traders today still look for an information edge. UK equity fund managers, who meet regularly and in private with the senior managers of the companies in which they invest, put a great deal of weight on the information content of those meetings, even though the rules (which are quite rigorously applied) prohibit the disclosure of any price-sensitive information. From their perspective, all inside information is potentially valuable and they get as much of it as they can.[14] Only if money were to change hands would they see it as a serious breach of the rules.

Moreover, whereas market manipulation can be criticized for distorting the price mechanism, insider trading appears to enhance it. Information that clearly is price-sensitive is brought to the market, through the price mechanism, faster than it would otherwise be. This is a breach of the rules, which in this case are very detailed and designed to ensure that, so far as possible, information on traded companies comes to the market through public announcements. In most countries, not only is trading on information obtained from insiders prohibited but there are also very specific limits on trading by corporate executives themselves (forbidding trading in the run-up to announcements, for example, and requiring that directors' trades be publicly registered) and detailed rules as to how company information must be released. However, while the ideal may be instantaneous dissemination of all price-relevant information, the real world just doesn't work like that. Even public announcements have to be interpreted and combined with other information sources for the price implications to become clear. And even more than in the case of market manipulation, the rules appear artificial and divorced from the sphere of ethics. Insider dealing does little if any damage to the market and could quite easily be incorporated into the rules if the authorities so chose.

---

[14] For a detailed analysis of this phenomenon, see Barker *et al.* 2012.

Yet, judging by the punishments handed down, insider trading seems to be considered a much more serious offense, at least in the UK and the USA,[15] than market manipulation, and much, much more serious than some of the blatantly unethical practices that we shall consider in the following chapters.

To explore the ethics of insider trading, it may be helpful to split it into two components: the trading itself and the communication to the trader of company confidential information. When the trading is done by a company employee, these effectively get conflated, but we can still distinguish between the act of trading to make a profit and the use of commercially confidential information to do so. In the case of trading, our focus, from a Kantian or virtue perspective, will be on the relationship with the counter-party to the trade. In the case of the use or communication of confidential information, our focus will be on the relationship with the company and its shareholders. From a utilitarian perspective, of course, we shall need to consider the practice as a whole, because the consequences do not flow from either part on its own.

Almost uniquely amongst financial practices, insider trading has been quite extensively discussed in the applied ethics literature, where there is a clear division of opinion between those who find it ethical on utilitarian grounds and those who find it unethical on Kantian or virtue grounds.[16] We shall begin with the utilitarian case.

Utilitarian approaches follow two main lines of argument in defense of insider trading: that it enhances the efficiency of markets and that it is generally beneficial to all those directly affected. The first line of argument starts out from the assumption that the system of efficient financial markets is utility-maximizing and demonstrates that insider trading enhances efficiency by bringing information to the market faster than would otherwise be the case, by bringing to the market tacit information that cannot effectively be captured by public announcements and by generally enhancing liquidity.[17] As discussed in Chapter 4, the initial assumption might be contested, but given that assumption, the argument seems straightforward and convincing, especially as empirical studies find no evidence to suggest

---

[15] Some other countries, like France and Japan, appear to adopt a much more relaxed attitude, with fewer restrictions that are less ardently enforced.

[16] For a recent review, see Engelen and Van Liederkerke 2010.

[17] Engelen and Van Liederkerke 2007; Moore 1990.

that insider trading damages efficiency by undermining investor confidence in the market, a major concern of the regulators.[18]

The second line of argument seeks to show that while insider traders might benefit from their deals, others do not suffer. In particular, it is claimed, allowing corporate executives whose pay is linked to share performance to trade on inside information will enhance shareholder value, while a ban on insider trading benefits market professionals at the expense of shareholders. The insider traders' counterparties may also benefit. To go back to the Martha Stewart example, whoever bought her ImClone shares paid significantly more than they would have after a public announcement, but less than they would have if there had been no insider sellers in the market and, as is likely, they were bidding at best price.[19] It is a big step from considerations like these to estimates of the impact of insider trading on overall utility, but they do suggest that the opposite argument, that insider trading is utility damaging, is going to be very hard to sustain.

Ethical objections to insider trading mainly argue either that it is unfair on the counterparty or that it entails a breach of fiduciary duty or misappropriation of property rights between employee and firm.[20] The arguments from fairness typically liken it either to playing with marked cards, or some other kind of cheating in a game, or to selling someone a pup. On this latter view, the shares sold by Martha Stewart were like a second-hand car with a cracked head gasket: they came with a major defect that the seller knew about but failed to communicate and that the buyer had no means of knowing about.

We suggested in the last section that the analogy with cheating in a game had limited force even in the case of market manipulation, and it seems to have even less force here. Yes, insider traders break the rules, but they don't appear to ruin the game for everyone else, which is the main problem with cheats.

The suggestion that insider traders knowingly harm their counterparties and are therefore unethical on Kantian grounds is also problematic. For one thing, as we have already noted, the harmful impact can be disputed. For

---

[18] Bainbridge 2000; Young 1985.

[19] In any particular case, counterparties may benefit or suffer from insider trading, depending on the details of their instructions to their brokers, but in general they would seem more likely to benefit. For a more detailed discussion of the arguments in this paragraph, see Engelen and Van Liederkerke 2010.

[20] See, for example, Werhane 1989 and 1991.

another, the analogy is unclear. Some critics appear to rely on a claim that any trade in which one party has an informational advantage is unfair, but in reality a buyer and a seller almost always have asymmetric information, and this is not generally considered a problem.[21] If I undertake a lot of research before buying something, I am not normally expected to share all this research with a seller, for example.

At some point, a failure on the seller's part to disclose relevant information does become an ethical problem, but where that point comes depends on the specifics of the market context. If I were selling a car in a private sale to someone who knew nothing about cars and who had been personally introduced, I would feel an obligation to reveal everything I knew about its faults. If I were selling to the trade, I might be less forthcoming, though I would answer any questions honestly. If I were selling under the explicit condition that all items were bought as seen, I would be more reticent still. In the case of the stock markets, the implicit assumption is that shares are bought as seen, and people generally trade on that basis and accept the risks entailed. It can certainly be argued that insider traders act selfishly and without due regard to the impact of their dealing on other people, treating them as merely means, but even this objection lacks force: in the depersonalized context of financial markets, they don't really "treat other people" at all.

The most we can probably say here is that the selfishness and greed that motivate insider traders is not very virtuous – and we may not find agreement even on that. Much will depend, in a virtue analysis, on the environment and circumstances. Many people trade on inside information under pressures of one kind or another, or without knowing quite what they are doing. Given her knowledge, experience and position as a public role model, Martha Stewart should surely have shown better judgment, and the fact that she didn't, and that she subsequently panicked and attempted to cover her tracks, says something about her character. But we would need to understand her much better to know exactly what it says. Even Raj Rajaratnam, a philanthropist whose values have been shaped by Sri Lankan as well as American culture, comes across as a very complex and in many respects quite virtuous, if seriously flawed, character.

---

[21] Moore 1990.

The arguments against the *providers* of inside information – the CEO and broker in the Martha Stewart case, Dennis Levine and Martin Siegel, or the various suppliers of information to Raj Rajaratnam – seem rather stronger. In most firms it is quite clear that information relating to the firm is confidential and that a condition of employment or of the engagement of professional advisors is that this information is not communicated to outsiders or used for personal gain without explicit permission. Some writers have criticized these arrangements. It has been argued, for example, that it would be in shareholders' interests to allow a firm's employees to trade on company information. However, the fact is that they do not. Moreover, it is generally agreed that property rights to commercially sensitive information held within a firm lie with the firm and its shareholders, and not with individual employees. Regardless of any consequences, for an employee or agent to use that information for personal benefit without the company's permission (and, in a CEO's case, the shareholders' or board's permission) is consequently a misuse of company property.

In terms of the normative ethical theories we have been using, the main issues here are breaches of trust and of contract, which fail the test of Kant's Formula of Universal Law through a contradiction of conception. Universalized breaches of trust would destroy the institution of trust on which the employee or agent depends in order to be able to profit from the breach. The same applies to breaches of contract. There may also be a question of theft if the private use of the information detracts from its value to the company. If we attribute value generally to possession of the *sole* use of information, we might even say that there is always theft here, even if the firm suffers no economic loss.[22]

Virtue considerations may also be salient here. The relationships with which we are concerned are not the impersonal ones of financial markets, but personal ones between people who have engaged with each other on the basis of trust and reputation. The relative emphasis on informal trust relationships and formal contracts varies considerably from society to society, but trustworthiness in one form or another is always a fundamental virtue. We would need to look in any particular case at why trust was broken and at what pressures the individual was under, but the initial impression here is one of clearly unethical behavior.

---

[22] Moore 1990 makes this argument.

Whether from a Kantian or a virtue perspective, the case against the providers of inside information seems to be strengthened when the information is not merely misappropriated or misused, as by Martha Stewart's broker, but sold for cash, as it was by Boesky's informants. From the Kantian perspective, there seems to be a clear case of theft: if information is sold, the proceeds belong to its owner, the company, and not to the individuals who sold it. From a virtue perspective, we just add to the lack of trustworthiness an element of greed and extra deceitfulness. People who sell things that don't belong to them are generally characterized as tricksters or fraudsters, lacking not just in particular virtues but also in a basic conception of what virtue might entail.

We have finished this chapter by suggesting that some aspects of insider trading appear clearly unethical, but overall we have found it quite hard to find ethical fault with the behaviors of financial market traders, even when they break the rules on market manipulation and insider trading. We have not looked at the related issue of preferential disclosure of some kinds of information to large shareholders, but this too seems likely to be unproblematic once we take account of how markets operate, and the forms information takes, in reality as opposed to theory. One assumption we have made throughout the chapter, however, is that the traders are trading on their own account. In fact, many are playing with other people's money and this raises a different set of issues, which we shall consider in the next chapter.

7   Agency and accountability: managing other people's money

A common joke on Wall Street and in the City of London is that once investment banks started significant trading on their own account in the wake of the Big Bang, they no longer had any need for clients – except to dump their loss-making deals on when things went wrong. In fact, banks are very careful to keep their proprietary and client trading activities separate (indeed, they have to by law), but the joke highlights the fact that traders are not generally trading with their own money and it reflects a general perception that they might behave differently depending on whose money it is. Most financial traders are employees, trading with and risking other people's money rather than their own. In some cases this is their firms' money. In many cases it is their clients' money. This raises a range of ethical issues, some of which we shall consider in this chapter. To set the context, we begin with some reflections on the relationships involved, from both economic and ethical perspectives.

Agency and accountability in economics and ethics

In the world of finance it is common to think of relationships in terms of economic agency theory. Agency problems arise when one party, the principal, engages another, the agent, to act on their behalf, and the interests of the agent differ from those of the principal.[1] Agency relationships of this kind are ubiquitous. They arise not only whenever someone is formally

---

[1] Note that the words "agent" and "agency" carry rather different connotations in economics and philosophy. In both cases an agent is someone endowed with the ability to make choices and act on them, but in economics this is set in the context of a principal–agent relationship so that an agent is someone who acts on another's behalf (as in an "estate agent" or "advertising agent") and the freedom to choose is cast as a problem, not an asset.

employed, but also whenever one party becomes dependent on the behavior of another and whenever people undertake joint projects (in which case each is agent to the other as principal).

The economic theory of agency addresses agency relationships from the viewpoint of the principal and focuses on what principals can do to maximize their returns. It assumes that all parties are opportunistically self-interested and that agents will shirk, lie or feather their own nests whenever they can get away with it. It also assumes that principles and agents are both perfectly competent, the former in expressing their wishes and the latter in acting on their self-interest. As so often in economics, these simplifying assumptions are there to enable the theory to generate plausible predictions rather than because that is how people necessarily behave.[2] They sometimes capture real behavior, sometimes not. The assumption of opportunistic self-seeking also carries, in the economic context, no moral connotations. The term used to describe the risk to the principal of an agent's self-seeking behavior is "moral hazard," but this is in effect a technical term: the theory imputes no moral blame, it just assumes that that's the way people are.

As with the economics of free markets discussed in the last chapter, the assumptions of economic agency theory are often carried over into the way people think about finance in practice. In particular, there is a tendency to focus on relationships from the principal's perspective and to assume that when agents fail to perform, it is due to self-seeking, not incompetence. There is also a tendency to treat agents as if they were accountable to only one principal. Agency theorists recognize that one agent might in practice be accountable to multiple principals, but such situations are difficult to model and so tend to be ignored.

From a broader, social perspective, the relationships described by agency theory are of course much richer and more complex. In the real world, people work within social and political settings that place a variety of pressures upon them. They are rarely completely competent. They have complex motivations and multiple and often conflicting accountabilities, many of which are morally loaded. Consider, for example, a trader working in an investment bank and investing client monies. Figure 7.1 illustrates

---

[2] For an analysis of the assumptions of agency theory and their possible broadening, see Hendry 2002.

Figure 7.1   The multiple accountabilities of a trader

just some of the relationships through which such a trader is accountable to others. We might note here that there is nothing very special about this figure. The figure for a footballer, for example, would look quite similar, but with supporters replacing clients. It does, however, raise some interesting questions.

Institutionally, the trader has an accountability to management, and through them to shareholders, and an accountability through the client management team to the clients whose funds are being traded. There is also an accountability, through the compliance unit and senior management, to the regulators. At a more personal level, there may be an accountability to colleagues on the same desk or in the same department, whose performance will be measured collectively as well as individually and who are also social colleagues. There will probably be an accountability to family members or others who depend on the trader's income and emotional support. And in juggling all these, the traders will also need to take account of their self-interest, both economically and in other respects (psychological wellbeing, growth and development, etc.).

The nature and extent of these accountabilities and the ways in which people are held accountable all vary. Accountability may be exercised through form-filling, reports or face-to-face accounts, for example, and routinely or only on demand. We saw in the last chapter that accountabilities to regulators, through the observance of regulations, are often treated in this context as a technical matter rather than a moral one. Accountabilities to families and colleagues, on the other hand, and some accountabilities to oneself clearly take the form of moral obligations. Accountabilities to clients and shareholders tend to be treated in the amoral terms of economic agency theory, but also appear, when seen from a social perspective, to carry moral responsibilities. The degree to which a trader's different accountabilities impose consistent and mutually reinforcing requirements and the degree to which they pull in conflicting directions also vary with the kinds of behavior concerned, the agent, the setting and the incentive structures in place. The perceived salience of the accountabilities, both individually and in comparison with each other, similarly vary with the person of the agent, the incentive pay structure and the social settings in which they live and work.

Given this complexity, the ethical situations in which traders find themselves are necessarily quite specific. There are, however, a number of general concerns raised by commentators and critics of finance that can usefully be addressed by situating them in this context. This is partly because they relate to potentially conflicting accountabilities and partly because the social context appears to be a salient factor. In this chapter we shall look at the phenomenon of over-trading or noise trading, at the phenomenon of rogue traders and at bankers' bonuses.

Churning and noise trading

There is a general consensus that the volumes of trading on financial markets are much higher than can be explained by simple profit-seeking. In financial economics, this trading over and above the level needed to adjust prices to new information and take profits from known price discrepancies is referred to as noise trading – noise in acoustics referring to the sounds that mask rather than contribute to a signal, in this case the signaling of the price mechanism. This excess trading is purely speculative and is a zero-sum game: overall, there are no gains or losses in terms of security values. There are, however, costs involved in carrying out the trades, so the net effect is that traders make a loss overall. On the face of it, noise trading is therefore against the interests of the party whose money is being managed, whether this is the shareholders of a bank trading on its own account or the clients of an asset manager. In the context of traditional fund management, where the securities being traded are typically equities and bonds rather than derivatives, we talk of churning. Equity fund managers repeatedly buy and sell in search of short-term gains, incurring costs at each stage, when holding securities for a longer period would be more beneficial to the client. This is especially problematic when, as is traditionally the case, the trading costs are charged to the client rather than being incorporated in a fixed management fee.

Financial economists have come up with various explanations of this and sociologists observing markets in action have suggested various other explanations,[3] but we can safely make a couple of observations. The first is that traders cannot develop their skills and succeed as traders without trading. Part of this is learning and part is building networks and reputations. In OTC markets especially, where there is no single exchange-quoted price, nothing can happen without people requesting and delivering prices. This process is only meaningful if people follow through with trades and there is consequently a conventional expectation that they will do so. You cannot follow the market without engaging in it. For a bank trading on its own account, a modest amount of noise trading may be a perfectly acceptable, even necessary, cost when seen as part of the education and development of its traders. Even when trading with client monies, a case could be made. Of course, every client expects its trading to be handled by experienced traders and not by novices. And, of course, banks will tend to put their best and most experienced traders on their proprietary desks. But in this industry as in any other, people have to learn and the fact of the excess trading that results may be less important than whether it is properly supervised and controlled so as to protect the client's interests.

The second, more problematic observation is quite simply that traders love to trade. Some may be addicted to it, others just enjoy it, but most traders get a terrific buzz from trading. Self-interest pulls them to over-trade, even when this is neither in their firm's nor its clients' interests, nor in their own narrowly economic interests (because the poor performance resulting from their high trading costs will be reflected in their bonus packages). This pull is strengthened, moreover, by the social environments

---

[3] Both sides are reviewed in Willman *et al.* 2006.

in which they work. It is very hard to sit at your desk in an aggressively competitive trading room and *not* trade.

When banks are trading on their own account, the incentive systems under which traders and their managers work are lined up to serve the general interests of the bank and there is no significant ethical problem. The way things work might benefit the bank's staff over its shareholders, but no-one is being cheated or misled. When client monies are at stake, however, things get more complicated. In particular, since the client is carrying the cost, the bank's managers have less incentive to control it.

In this situation, it may be instructive to compare the different normative theories and see what they tell us collectively. There is no obvious problem with excess trading from a Kantian perspective. The practice appears to be universalizable without contradiction (it is indeed pretty universal) and while the client monies are used as a means to the traders' enjoyment, it would be a stretch to argue that the traders are using the people ultimately affected – the ultimate beneficiaries of pension funds or endowments, for example – as merely means. The causal chain connecting them is a relatively long one and the primary accountability to the beneficiaries lies here with the various intermediaries (pension or endowment fund trustees) rather than with the traders. The traders do not even consider the ultimate beneficiaries because that is somebody else's job. There may be ethical issues around the way the fund management service is presented to clients, and we shall look at these in the next chapter, but it is hard to see over-active traders as doing anything seriously wrong from a Kantian perspective.

From a utilitarian perspective, on the other hand, something would seem to be wrong here. What seems to be happening, in effect, is a transfer of wealth from the clients (or rather their ultimate beneficiaries) to the owners and operators of the financial system (the stock exchanges which benefit from the trading costs), accompanied by an increase in pleasure for the traders and a decrease in pleasure on the client side (as they see their investments consistently under-perform on expectations). So there is a transfer of wealth from ordinary people to the financial system and those ordinary people are also paying simply for the traders to enjoy themselves. The loss of utility is difficult to assess systematically, let alone in respect of the policies and practices of an individual trader, but a loss of some kind seems very likely.

According to virtue ethics, much will depend on the situation. On the face of it, excess trading is intemperate almost by definition: it is indulging in excess. It is also making free with other people's property and without their permission, which is generally considered thoughtless and irresponsible. We might think of children who play in someone else's garden and kick up the lawn or the flowerbeds in the process, not doing intentional harm but still leaving their mark. On the other hand, we have to take account of the culture and environment in which the traders work, the pressures they are under and so on. The position of experienced traders cynically enjoying themselves at other people's expense may be very different from that of youngsters striving to build a career and fit in by doing what is expected of them, or of traders who honestly believe, as many clearly do, that their frequent trading is productive. Like all gamblers, and indeed like anybody else, traders tend to be optimistic in judging their performance, measuring it in terms of its peaks or potentials rather than its average.[4]

Putting these three perspectives together, we probably won't reach any black and white conclusions, but we will get a good overall picture of the ethical situation. There is something ethically wrong with over-trading, but it's not egregious and a fair assessment will have to take account of the individuals concerned and the situations in which they find themselves.

Rogue traders

Few people outside the world of asset management are aware of the problem of noise trading. Almost everyone is aware of the problem of rogue traders. In February 1995 Nick Leeson, employed by Barings Bank to trade Far Eastern stock market index futures from its Singapore offices, sent a note to his boss saying "I'm sorry" and fled the country (see Box 7.1 for an account of what he had done). The losses on his trading amounted to over £800 million – more than enough to bust the bank, which went into administration within days and was eventually bought by ING for £1.

At the time, the Leeson affair was seen as a one-off: a cautionary tale of what could happen when an old-fashioned investment bank dabbled in derivatives trading that it didn't understand, but something that was unlikely to be repeated elsewhere. The Barings back-office controls may

---

[4] See Kahneman *et al.* 1982 and Kahneman 2011.

Box 7.1. Nick Leeson, rogue trader

Founded as an international trading company in the mid-eighteenth century, Barings Bank was an old-fashioned English merchant bank that had built its reputation on commercial credit, acting as an agent for government procurement and supply, and issuing and underwriting government debt and other international securities. Having almost gone out of business following over-exposure to South American government debt in 1890 – it was rescued with the help of the Bank of England – Barings became known in the twentieth century for its cautious restraint and close ties to the monarchy and the state. However, when investment banks generally started to make large profits from derivatives trading in the late 1980s and early 1990s, Barings followed suit.

On leaving high school, Nick Leeson had joined Coutts Bank in a junior clerical role in the settlements department. After a brief spell at Morgan Stanley, he was recruited by Barings, aged twenty-two, as a settlement clerk in its derivatives department. After about three years, having performed well, he was sent over to a new Singapore office that had been established to trade derivatives on the Singapore International Monetary Exchange (SIMEX). Leeson's original assignment was to manage the settlements office. However, he also applied for a broker's license and in due course began arbitrage trading on Barings' own account on the SIMEX pit floor. In theory this should have relatively low risk, as the essence of the trade was arbitrage between NIKKEI stock index future prices quoted on the Singapore and Osaka exchanges, buying on one and selling on the other. The amounts traded might be massive, but the price differences were miniscule. Leeson, though, started to speculate on index future price movements by delaying one half of the trade. Sometimes this was successful, sometimes not, but in control of the back office, he could control what appeared in the accounts. When the trading was successful, he booked the profits (though without indicating how they were earned – the trading accounts had to be doctored). When it was not successful, he hid the losses in an error account.

As far as the head office of Barings could see, Leeson was a successful trader. He showed good profits (in tens of millions of pounds) and was rewarded with good bonuses. There was some concern at the size of his positions and in 1994 position limits were imposed. There was also concern that one person was acting on both the trading and the settlements side, which should have been a complete no-no, but given the profits, no-one was concerned enough to do anything about it. There is evidence that derivatives arbitrage was a complete mystery to senior figures at the bank and Leeson himself suggested that nobody asked any questions because they were afraid of looking stupid.

The whole thing came tumbling down in early 1995. By this stage, both SIMEX and Barings' auditors were on Leeson's trail, but the critical event was the steep fall in the NIKKEI after the Kobe earthquake. Leeson bet heavily on a rapid recovery, but it didn't happen and two days before his twenty-eighth birthday, he fled the country, leaving Barings with losses of £827 million, far more than it could sustain.

Source: there are many accounts of this story, but the fullest and most reliable is Fay 1996. See also Leeson and Whitley 1996.

have been inadequate to cope with a determined rogue trader, but other banks were more sophisticated. Besides, once alerted by the Leeson case, they were unlikely to repeat the mistake. It couldn't happen again. But it did happen again … and again and again. Table 7.1 summarizes some of the most notable examples. The most recent case, at the time of writing, was that of Kweku Adoboli, a thirty-one-year-old graduate who was also engaged in speculative trading on index futures, this time at Swiss bank UBS's London offices. UBS by this time was hardly a newcomer to derivatives trading and its risks, and had in place what senior managers believed were robust control systems, but by September 2011, Adoboli had racked up losses of over $2 billion from unauthorized trading, which he had successfully concealed from his employers. Finally admitting that his losses were unrecoverable, he owned up and was arrested. He was trading on the firm's own account and, with annual profits of around $6 billion, UBS could survive the loss, but it meant a significant hit for shareholders and forced the resignation of the firm's CEO, Oswald Grübel, as well as of Adoboli's division heads.

The biggest rogue trader incident to date involved a relatively junior derivatives trader at the French bank Société Générale, Jérôme Kerviel, and again involved index futures. Kerviel held a Masters in Finance and had joined Société Générale after graduation in 2000, starting on the compliance side and moving into trading in 2005. In the course of 2007 and January 2008, he appears to have engaged in a growing volume of unauthorized trades eventually totaling nearly €50 billion, and up until

Table 7.1. *Some rogue traders*

Trader	Date	Amount lost	Bank	Securities traded
Nick Leeson	1995	£827 million leading to bank failure	Barings Bank	Stock index futures
Toshihide Iguchi	1995	$1.1 billion	Resona Holdings	US Treasury bonds
Yasuo Hamanaka	1996	$2.6 billion	Sumitomo Corporation	Copper
John Rusnak	2002	$691 million	Allied Irish Bank	Foreign exchange options
Chen Jiulin	2005	$550 million	China Aviation Oil	Jet fuel futures
Jérôme Kerviel	2008	€4.9 billion	Société Générale	Stock index futures
Kweku Adoboli	2011	$2.3 billion	UBS	Stock index futures

Source: http://en.wikipedia.org/wiki/Rogue_trader.

mid-January to have shown (or rather to have concealed) a healthy profit, estimated by some sources at €1.4 billion. In the second half of January, however, the equity markets turned and Kerviel's positions moved rapidly into negative territory. By the time they were discovered and closed out by the bank, it had lost nearly €5 billion. In this case, bank executives stuck to the line that the bank was a victim of a rogue trader's fraud for which they were not responsible. Both they and the bank survived, but apart from the trading losses themselves, the incident also hit confidence in the bank. Its debt ratings were lowered, increasing its borrowing costs, and the total cost to shareholders must have been far more than the €5 billion trading loss.

An interesting aspect of the rogue trader phenomenon is that while the banks blame the traders, as individuals, most people seem to put the blame mainly on the banks and their management. This points us toward two features of the map of a trader's accountabilities shown in Figure 7.1 that we have not yet considered.

First, when one person, A, is accountable to another person, B, this may place moral obligations upon B as well as upon A. While trainees are accountable to their supervisors, for example, the supervisors are also accountable to others *for* the behavior of their trainees. Moreover, the moral obligation here may actually be greater on the supervisor, who has the benefit of knowledge and experience, than on the trainee. In accountancy and other professions, qualified professionals explicitly accept moral responsibility for the actions of unqualified staff under their supervision. More generally, managers are normally held accountable, and to some extent morally responsible, for the behavior of their staff.

Second, the system of accountabilities serves not only to allocate responsibility but also to allocate, and in particular to deflect, blame. Blame is a complex phenomenon. It is a form of moral judgment that both judges a character (we blame somebody) and focuses on an action (we blame them for something) in situations where both may be questionable. Somebody may be blamed without necessarily being blameworthy or might be blameworthy without necessarily being blamed. We might blame someone for doing something obviously wrong, but we might also blame them for something that is less obviously wrong or less obviously their own doing, or we might exempt them from blame for something they clearly did. ("It wasn't really his fault," we say.) It acts as a medium for expressing moral consensus, yet we can also agree to apportion it differently without differing too significantly in our moral perspectives. I might blame young Jack for trampling over a neighbor's garden while you blame his mother, but we both agree: (a) that he shouldn't do it; and (b) that he should be brought up not to do it.

Philosophers disagree as to exactly what blame is, what emotions are or are not essential to it (anger, sorrow, resentment or none of these) and under what conditions it is appropriate. Fortunately, this need not concern us here.[5] What is relevant in this context is how it works socially, and from this point of view a key feature of systems of accountability is that they are often designed to deflect blame from one party towards another, typically from those at the top of an organization or in control of a regulatory system to those at the bottom or those being regulated. When a firm requires employees to sign up to an ethical code of conduct, for example, this is done partly to promote good conduct, but partly to absolve the management from blame when someone breaks the code. More generally, when

[5] For different accounts, see Gibbard 1990; Owens 2012; and Scanlon 2008.

something goes wrong in a society or an organization, people will seek a scapegoat to take the blame and relieve them of the burden of responsibility.[6]

Coming back to rogue traders, the phrase used to describe them carries two significant connotations. First, the trader is classified as a rogue. Rogues are immoral individuals who take advantage of innocent victims. Second, there is a specific reference to rogue elephants. Elephants are powerful but normally docile animals that are generally no threat to humans and are widely used in India as domesticated working animals. Occasionally, however, without warning, an elephant goes rogue and causes widespread damage, rampaging through villages and causing serious harm to property and to any individuals that get in its way. The rogue trader, by analogy, is seen as something that cannot be predicted or prevented, but just has to be taken out before it does too much damage. The very use of the term "rogue trader" is an attempt to deflect blame away from those to whom the trader was accountable and plant it firmly on the trader himself.[7]

When we look at what we know about rogue traders, neither the rogue nor the rogue elephant analogy seems very apt. All the well-known rogue traders acted in ways that were expressly forbidden by their employers and they all lied about it. They all acted intemperately and showed a certain weakness of character, allowing themselves to be carried away and deceiving themselves as well as others. But they were not all rogues in the usual sense. There are indications that Leeson was always less than honest: it was reported that there were several legal actions against him for unpaid personal debts before he left London, and even that he was denied a UK broker's license due to false information on the application. His subsequent behavior, capitalizing on his fame and even seeming to take pride in his wrongdoings, is not exactly suggestive of a virtuous character.[8] But Kerviel seems to have been something of a computer and finance nerd who got carried

---

[6] The classic cases of scapegoating are the myth of Oedipus, who in Sophocles's tragedy is appropriately blamed (from a societal perspective) without being blameworthy (from an individual perspective), and the Salem witch trials, in which the problems of a damaged society were loaded onto innocent girls and young women. On the scapegoat in general, see Douglas 2000; and Girard 2004.

[7] It's not entirely clear when the term was first used in this sense, but it appears to have been by Barings executives in describing Nick Leeson.

[8] See his website at www.nickleeson.com.

away and mistook the rules of the game.[9] Adoboli had been head boy at his Quaker high school in the UK and was widely regarded as a virtuous character, but he was an outsider in the City and seems to have been sucked into unauthorized trading by his desire to be accepted and succeed. At his trial for fraud and false accounting in 2012, he portrayed himself as devoted to UBS (which he called his "family") and motivated only by the desire to make profits for the firm.[10]

Adoboli's pleading may not have been genuine, of course, but it highlights two important aspects of the rogue trader cases. First, none of them set out to steal from their companies. On the contrary, they worked within the banks' incentive structures, and insofar as they sought personal profit, it was entirely through the profits they could create for the banks. Second, with the exception of Leeson, they worked within a context that was driven not only by these incentive structures but also by a particular culture and environment.

The bank trading rooms in which most traders operate have their own organizational dynamics. Traders are in competition not only on behalf of their employers, with "the market" or with traders from rival firms, but also within the firm, with rival teams and even with colleagues in their own team. Trading rooms are aggressive, macho environments that combine high levels of rivalry and aggression with rituals of bonding. They generate a pack mentality, which raises the psychological temperature, increases levels of risk-taking and generally encourages collective behaviors that as individuals the traders might well consider immoral. In this context, Adoboli's reference to "family" is reminiscent of the Italian Mafia and even of the accounts of professional cyclists that emerged, also in 2012, with revelations of extensive, almost universal, blood-doping in the 2000s. Endurance cycling is an aggressive team sport in which the teams are built around a dominant individual and it is clear that many professional cyclists, the support members of the team, were cajoled and bullied into taking drugs as a condition of "family" membership. Everyone was doing it, so it wasn't cheating to take advantage, just part of pulling their weight in the team.[11]

---

[9] See http://en.wikipedia.org/wiki/Jérôme_Kerviel for extensive references to press coverage of the Kerviel case.

[10] www.guardian.co.uk/business/2012/oct/26/ubs-trader-kweku-adoboli-trial.

[11] Hamilton and Coyle 2012.

On top of these social pressures, the computer-based nature of contemporary financial trading also gives it an air of unreality, which again encourages risk-taking. The immediate trading experience is not dissimilar from that of playing a computer game, and traders are drawn into acting as if they were merely computer gaming (Kerviel admitted at his trial that he had lost all sense of reality).[12] If you get wiped out in a computer game, you just press re-start, and it is tempting to behave as if that were the case in financial trading too, especially when you get in too deeply to have any realistic chance of recovering your position.

In all the cases reported, it was when the traders got in too deeply that the worst of their deceits arose. But in racking up massive losses through double-or-quits attempts to recover the situation, they behaved much as humans always behave in such situations, struggling instinctively to recover their losses.[13] No gambler likes cutting his losses, and finding themselves in a position in which absolutely anything bar a complete recovery would mean the end of their careers, the traders naturally gambled, whatever the odds, on a complete recovery. They forgot, of course, that it was other people's money they were gambling with and that for those people it made an enormous difference whether they lost $1 million or $1 billion. But that was partly because, like all addicted gamblers, they believed deeply that they could win in the end and partly because, as mainly young and relatively inexperienced traders, the sums involved became unreal.

Set in this context, the ethical position of the rogue traders appears much less clear-cut than their employers would like to claim. Since the main effect of their practices was just to redistribute wealth across the financial system, they arguably did little or nothing wrong from a utilitarian perspective. Their own companies' losses (and those of their employees, shareholders, etc.) were by and large other companies' gains. From a Kantian perspective, they were lying and deceitful, but most of them didn't set out to be so; they didn't have a maxim of lying, they just resorted to lies when their guiding maxims – of trading to make a profit, matching or exceeding their colleague's results, etc. – got them into a mess. They broke the rules, but

[12] www.huffingtonpost.com/2012/11/05/jerome-kerviel-most-debt-in-the-world_n_2077219.html.
[13] Kahneman *et al*. 1982; Kahneman 2011.

not in a way that led to any logical contradictions. Indeed, in several cases, there were suggestions that the firms knowingly allowed the rules to be broken. From a virtue perspective, the variations in specific circumstances and our lack of detailed knowledge of those circumstances make judgments difficult.

If the context partially exonerates the traders, however, it also raises questions about their managers. The senior managers of a bank are accountable to shareholders for profit and to depositors (in the case of a deposit-taking bank) for security. The nature of the accountability to shareholders is contentious, and we shall come back to it in Chapter 9, but let us assume for now that it entails some element of moral responsibility. The accountability to depositors certainly does so. Managers are also responsible for the culture of the organization and its units; for the systems of settlement and compliance; for the incentive systems under which traders operate; and for the recruitment, training and monitoring of traders and other employees. All these influence the ways in which individuals behave and it seems reasonable to suppose that managers have some moral obligations to exert their influence in a way that controls unethical behavior. When it comes to managing staff, for example, most people would say that managers have an ethical duty to understand their reports, recognizing their weaknesses as well as their strengths and taking appropriate management precautions. We expect a sports coach in charge of a group of testosterone-fueled intensely competitive adolescents or young men to manage them rather differently from how they might manage a group of middle-aged mothers.

Banks knowingly recruit for their trading desks people who like to gamble, to compete aggressively and to take risks. They then openly encourage them, through bonus schemes and through the creation of highly competitive cultures, to act in self-interest and to take risks. And they put them to work in environments where risk control is inherently difficult. Derivatives trading is not only very risky but also hard to track and document. In particular, with very short timescales, the settlement and even the formal documentation may lag well behind the trading. In the Adoboli case, the formal documentation of the class of trades in which he was engaged wasn't even issued until after settlement of the trades (i.e., payment) was made. This creates a sizable window during which a trader can book a deal on his company's system and use any monies due for further deals, before actually settling on the original trade, or alternatively not settling and effectively erasing it. Non-settlement, or fail-to-deliver, is quite common – it averages $200 billion a day in US markets – and is not always recorded.

It is the conventional wisdom in investment banking that risks are what bring rewards, so setting up the organization to take risks is fair enough, but in setting up the situation, managers also have an obligation to keep it under control. Investment banks are not heavily loaded with people-management skills; it's not what they're good at. So, in limiting the risks from unauthorized trading, and indeed from authorized trading, they have to rely heavily on their compliance systems.

Unfortunately, that doesn't seem to be what they're good at either. Compliance is not where their brightest and best are put to work or, given the incentive systems, where they would want to work. It was argued in UBS's defense that its internal control team was focused on the fixed income area, which had been making massive losses. Compared with losses of nearly $40 billion on authorized trading in mortgage-backed securities, Adoboli's losses were indeed small, but failure in one area is a lame excuse for laxity in another. In a House of Lords debate on the Barings fiasco, Lord Bruce made the blunt point that, given their lack of financial controls, Barings shouldn't have had a banking license in the first place: this seems a fair comment.[14]

The banks also instruct their traders, of course, to stay within the rules. But it is a well-known fact that the major banks repeatedly break the rules and have to be taken to task by the regulators, and that in many contexts their employees are not merely allowed but are actively encouraged to break the rules. Kerviel insisted that his employers Société Générale must have been perfectly aware of what he was doing and tacitly condoned it as long as it was profitable. Many commentators reached the same conclusion. In the Adoboli case, too, expert commentators argued that there must have been some complicity, or else extreme neglect. An FSA investigation, which resulted in a £30 million fine for UBS, noted that the bank had not questioned the profits returned by Adoboli's desk, even though these could not have been achieved without breaking trading limits.[15] Within days of the Adoboli scandal breaking, UBS was also fined $12 million by US regulators for systematically *allowing* its traders and some of its clients to break the

---

[14] *Lords Hansard*, 21 July 1995.
[15] www.fsa.gov.uk/library/communication/pr/2012/105.shtml.

rules on short selling. This was followed by a further fine of $8 million a few weeks later. Earlier in the year it had faced $11 million of fines and restitutions for mis-selling to clients. In February 2009 it had been fined $780 million for helping its depositors evade US taxes.

Banks repeatedly bend or break the rules and take any ensuing fines in their stride. They take the view that it is up to regulators not only to make the rules but also to enforce them. When client monies are lost, they will defend their traders, even if the rules were broken, and blame the losses on exceptional market conditions. Writing about the Adoboli case, the financial journalist Moshe Silver suggested that while "losing the bank $2 billion is called fraud," "losing a client $2 billion is called a streak of bad luck."[16] However, when it comes to their own employees acting in ways that lose the firm money, they put the blame entirely on the employee. Some would say that it's a bit like keeping lions in an enclosure with an inadequate fence and then putting the blame entirely on the lions for the carnage that ensues (unless, of course, the public are hurt, in which case it's just a terrible accident).

From an ethical point of view, the issue here would hinge on the responsibility of the keeper to find out what kind of fence was needed and make sure that it was in place. The banks might argue that in this case complete protection, like complete protection from rogue elephants, was impossible and that the controls in place were proportionate. The argument here would be similar to one that a mining company would use in respect of pit safety – that mining runs risks and, however uncomfortable it might be, that there has to be a trade-off between the costs of safety and the costs of lives lost. In a trading pit it is the livelihoods of the shareholders that are at stake rather than the lives of the employees, but the cases are similar to the extent that most safety system errors are, in the end, human errors. However, if the managers of a mining company took the same approach to its safety regime as the managers of banks do to their control systems, they would be morally condemned and legally prosecuted. We would need much more information to prove any of the rogue trader cases either way, but there must be a strong suspicion of willful neglect.

---

[16] http://finance.fortune.cnn.com/2011/09/27/the-fine-line-between-bad-luck-and-rogue-trades.

Bankers' bonuses

If the constraints put upon traders' risk-taking are not always adequate, the rewards of such risk-taking appear to be ample, and a major source of public concern about the financial sector is the level of bonuses paid to bankers, and especially to traders. Some of this can be put down simply to envy, but the figures suggest that there is a case to answer. From 2000 to 2007, the top five US investment banks paid out a total of $190 billion in bonuses, on top of salaries, before declaring profits of $76 billion. In 2008 they declared *losses* of $25 billion, but still paid $26 billion in bonuses. At its peak in 2006, the average pay per person including bonuses at Goldman Sachs (which employs over 30,000 people worldwide) was over $600,000 – and that includes the secretaries and reception staff. Over 100 of the firm's employees earned more than $20 million each. These figures are now much reduced, with the very top earners getting around half of what they once did, but much of this reduction seems to have been achieved by a greater use of share options, which aren't fully reflected in the figures, and average pay is still about $500,000.

The most common criticism of bankers' bonuses is that the pay levels are simply unfair. It is thought unfair that people whose work contributes little or nothing to society get paid, on average, several times as much as qualified doctors, and many times as much as teachers or nurses. It is thought especially unfair, in the wake of the financial crisis, that while the mass of the population are suffering from high unemployment, reduced pay and the erosion of savings, the people held to have caused that crisis are still taking home millions in bonuses.

But what is fair? Fairness is associated in philosophy with justice and the distribution of benefits, but there are many ways of assessing it. Some philosophers argue that benefits should be distributed equally, others that they should be distributed according to need, and others that they should be distributed according to merit, which itself can be understood in various ways.[17]

Whichever notion of fairness we choose, it can also be applied in different ways. Bankers' bonuses are the products of employment contracts between banks and their employees, which may or may not be fair. But

---

[17] See Lamont and Favor 2012.

they are also the products of particular societies, with laws, policies and cultures that may or may not be fair and that allow or encourage these contracts and modify their effects to a greater or lesser extent through redistributive taxation. Most of the public concern with bankers' bonuses seems to relate to fairness in this wider social context, but we can start our analysis with the bankers and work outwards.

The philosopher Robert Nozick argues, from a consideration of property rights, that the rewards people receive are justified or fair if they are the product of a just process.[18] The setting of traders' salaries and bonuses is a legal and open process, carried out freely and without coercion or duress, within an agreed contractual framework. So long as we restrict ourselves to the relationship between banker and bank, there is nothing obviously unjust about it. Nozick's is a particular, and quite extreme, free market perspective and we might well argue that it is inappropriate in some situations. Many people would consider it wrong, for example, to take such a pay packet from a charity or the public purse. But in this context it seems appropriate. We might think that the bankers don't deserve their pay, but within a society like ours, there is no apparent ground on which one might say that they don't have a legitimate right to it. And while some people might feel guilty receiving such a pay packet and choose to give part of it away to good causes, few people would have any qualms themselves about taking it from a bank.

The problem then, so far as there is one, would appear to lie somewhere between society and the bank rather than with the trader. There might be something wrong with a bank offering such pay packets and there might be something wrong with a society that allows them to do so. Even Nozick's theory allows the state to override private property rights in order to prevent a "catastrophic moral horror," though he seems to have had in mind something much more immediate and dramatic than the effects of bankers' bonuses.[19]

The arguments in respect of society are largely the same as those we rehearsed in Chapter 4, when looking at the ethics of the financial system as a whole. From a Rawlsian perspective, for example, the key criterion is that society should be arranged so as to be to the greatest benefit to its least well-off members. We suggested in Chapter 4 that the financial system as a

---

[18] Nozick 1974.   [19] Ibid., p. 30.

whole probably fails on this criterion, but what part bankers' bonuses play in the failure is impossible to say. They seem to be more a symptom of the problem than a cause.

From a utilitarian perspective, the question is whether a society that allows the bonuses is utility-maximizing and this breaks down into: (a) whether the financial system as a whole is utility-maximizing; (b) whether within that system, as a system of wealth creation, the bonuses are wealth-maximizing; and (c) whether the level of bonuses has any particular consequences for utility besides those arising from their contribution to the system. We have already addressed (a) and shall come back to (b) shortly. In the case of (c), one obvious concern, given the level of public debate, is that allowing these bonuses might cause harm by setting a bad example, with repercussions beyond the financial sector. Much of what goes on in finance goes on behind closed doors, but bonuses are very public and allowing them to continue at such a high level, especially in the wake of the financial crisis, gives a potentially damaging message, namely that it is not only fine to do things with harmful consequences, but that it is fine to be massively rewarded for it.

Another perspective that might be relevant here is that from deliberative ethics, which focuses on the fairness of the political process rather than the outcomes. Societies like the UK and the USA are open democracies, with robust mechanisms for public deliberation and debate. They are not perfect. We may question, for example, whether some minorities are adequately heard. But in this context, that is not an issue. The opponents of bankers' bonuses have a voice and they use it. There is indeed wide agreement, not only amongst the public but also amongst government politicians, that bankers' bonuses are excessive and unfair, and that banks should be made to do something about it. At the same time, however, there is no sign of any real attempt to do anything about this. Something seems to be going wrong here.

Part of the issue here may lie in the complexity of our social structures, which means that problems cannot easily be treated in isolation and that a consensus on what is wrong is not necessarily reflected in a consensus on what to do about it. Many people would probably agree that our society would be fairer if incomes were tilted to reflect the social contributions of people's jobs a bit more and economic markets a bit less. But that doesn't mean they would agree to the taxation policies that might be needed to achieve that redistribution. Even if people might agree that the pay of bankers should be capped in some way, they might not agree to the general principle of capping pay – indeed, they might well see it as an unfair infringement of people's liberty. So it may be that the deliberative process is ethical, but that it just gets mired in the complexities and practical problems of implementation.

Part of the issue, however, may be that political influence is disproportionately and unfairly weighted towards the banks. Everybody has a voice in the debate, but once the debate is over, some people continue to have a voice and effectively block any action. The deliberative process appears to be ethical, but is unethically subverted by powerful interests. There can be little doubt, in fact, that both political discourse and, especially, political action in these societies are very heavily influenced by the financial sector, through lobbying, political payments and privileged access to politicians and government. Many government politicians share the public concerns about bonuses. They are also concerned about the moral examples set and make a point of stressing that the current level of bonuses is not morally acceptable. They also play political games, of course, the party in opposition blaming the situation on the party in power and the party in power deflecting that blame onto the banks, but in many cases their concerns seem genuine. However, it appears that the banks are powerful enough, one way or another, to have their way, regardless of what people or politicians may think.

The power of the banks in this case, and the fact that the bonuses evidently serve their own self-interest, suggests that we should look rather carefully at the arguments they give for paying such high bonuses. The bonuses are justified on two main grounds. The first is that they are needed to recruit and retain the best people, and that in such an intensely competitive arena, having the best people is critical: in a zero-sum game with a limited number of players, there is no point in being average. There is an open global market for traders, the pay packets are a reflection of market price, and in order to fulfill their duties to their own shareholders by competing effectively in the industry, banks have to pay that price.[20] The second ground is that the bonuses are needed as incentive mechanisms to

---

[20] The banks would not openly describe it as a zero-sum game, of course, but that is the reasoning.

motivate the traders to perform in the best interests of the bank and its shareholders.

Whether traders' pay packages really reflect a market price is unclear. At the top end, they probably do. In an extremely competitive game, not everyone can be a winner, and just as there is a global market for the very best footballers, so there is for the very best traders. Supply is short, demand is high and the prices are high – and economically justifiable in terms of the returns they bring.[21] Lower down the scale, it is less clear that the laws of supply and demand are in effective operation. For every trading position in a major investment bank, there are thousands of quite plausible applicants – often tens of thousands. Hundreds of these may well be as good as the person selected, as far as can be objectively determined, and many would take the job for little or nothing, given the chance. Yet the starting pay is significantly higher than any of those applicants could conceivably earn elsewhere. Banks pay the salaries and bonuses they deem necessary to retain people, but they rarely if ever put this to the test. There is no evidence that if bonuses were reduced, staff would leave and go elsewhere. It is part of the creed of the financial sector that markets are generally efficient, and in most cases they probably are, but seen from the outside, the market for traders doesn't look that way.

A more obvious explanation of the bonus levels is that the banks have become so profitable that they can afford to spread it around, and to keep spreading it around even in the odd bad year. When the investment banks were run as partnerships, this was the partners' prerogative. The firm was like an immensely well-endowed private club, where membership was very tightly controlled but the benefits were great and shared. The senior members felt more comfortable being surrounded by people who were themselves very well paid. Now that they are limited companies responsible to shareholders, this attitude may not be appropriate, but old habits die hard.

The incentive justification of bonuses is also open to critique. According to financial theory, incentive pay is a response to agency problems. If traders were just paid a salary, so the argument goes, their opportunistic

---

[21] This is not to say that every trader is worth his pay: banks, like football clubs, sometimes get it wrong. Nor could this argument necessarily be applied in other situations, where the competition is less intense and performance less easily measurable. But it seems to work here.

self-seeking would lead them to shirk, to do what they could get away with rather than to do their best, or to trade for their own pleasure rather than for the bank's benefit. Incentive pay overcomes this problem by aligning their self-interest with the interests of the firm.

The most common applications of the agency theory of incentive pay are to blue-collar work, where it is relatively straightforward (the incentive pay takes the form of piece rates), and to CEO pay, which is much more complex. Financial economists have been arguing for incentive pay for CEOs, to align their interests with those of shareholders, for over twenty years, and as understanding of the problem has grown, their prescriptions have changed significantly. Whereas incentive pay initially took the form of bonuses, it was quite quickly recognized that these reflected short-term results and did not provide a match to shareholder interests. The focus moved to stock and stock options, which now dominate in practice as well as theory. However, even these have problems. Apart from detailed questions of pricing and timing, they have no downside: there is a carrot but no stick. In the last few years, things have consequently moved on again. Current theories require that CEOs hold a significant part of their wealth in company stock, so that they lose from any fall in share prices as well as gain from any rises, and practice is beginning to follow this prescription.

Given that the theory of incentive pay is a core part of financial economics and that the financial sector is taking the lead in calling for more sophisticated applications of the theory to executive pay in commercial and industrial firms, one might have thought that the sector's own applications would be reasonably robust. Not so. Though the banks' top managers are increasingly rewarded by shares and share options, trading incentives are still dominated by bonuses and traders' bonuses (and the bonuses of their managers, which reflect those of their reports) are still based on short-term results and reward the upside without penalizing the downside. Moreover, as shown in Box 7.2, using mark-to-market and mark-to-model accounting, they can even reward trading losses.

Given that senior investment banking positions are populated by people who are in general both highly intelligent and financially literate, and who admit themselves to being driven entirely by self-interest, it is quite hard for an intelligent outsider to take seriously their argument that trading bonuses are a rational response to questions of motivation and shareholder value. It does look much more as though they are simply taking the rest of society for a ride.

Box 7.2. Bankers' bonuses and mark-to-market accounting

Consider the performance of two investments held across an accounting period end:

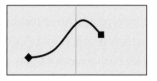 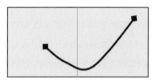

Here the vertical dimension represents the price, the horizontal dimension represents time and the vertical line indicates the period end. Both investments make reasonable profits overall, but using mark-to-market accounting, they are valued for both financial reporting and bonus calculations as if closed and reopened at the period end. Each makes a loss in one year and a big profit in the other. Once aggregated with many other trades, the accounting may not affect the traders' bonus significantly. This will reflect a paper loss in one period and a paper profit in the other, but over the two periods combined, the accounting effect will be removed. If the performances reflect broader trends, however, the bonuses will be inflated in both cases. In one period trading profits are exaggerated and bonuses are exaggerated accordingly. In the other period losses are exaggerated, but if the trader is operating at a loss overall, that makes no difference to the bonus, which is zero – or more likely some "guaranteed" base level – in either case.

Consider a third example:

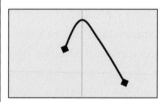

In this case the investment is a disaster, but the trader might still earn a substantial bonus on the basis of the first-period paper profit.

For many OTC derivatives, there is no market price, so instead of mark-to-market, the banks use mark-to-model accounting, where the value of the investment is calculated according to a mathematical model of what it should be worth based on whatever assumptions they choose to use. For some curious reason, mark-to-model accounting almost never shows losses!

Our focus in this chapter has been on traders, but in each of the three examples we have discussed, we have concluded that the problems lie more with the cultures of the banks in which the traders work than with the traders themselves. This suggests that we also need to look at the accountabilities of the banks' senior managers, and especially their CEOs, and we shall do this in Chapter 9. Before that, we shall pick up on another set of issues raised by this chapter concerning the ethical responsibilities of banks and other financial institutions with regard to their clients. We have already looked in Chapter 5 at the responsibilities to personal borrowers, and in this chapter at the issues raised by excessive trading of client monies. In the next chapter we shall look at the broader question of the marketing and promotion of investment products.

8 Products, promotion and client relationships

One of the suggestions raised in the last chapter was that, providing banks and other financial institutions get their fees, they are not overly concerned what happens to their clients. This may be unfair, but it resonates with the public. Time and again, the financial sector is charged and found guilty by its regulators of promoting and selling dodgy products and services of one kind or another. The list is so long that we cannot feasibly analyze each case individually, but the cases also differ in significant ways, so we cannot just analyze them as a class. We shall begin by running through some of the main areas of concern, highlighting the concerns that have been voiced and using boxes to describe a particular case of each kind in more detail. We shall then review some of the ethical issues raised, passing quickly through those that lend themselves to a relatively straightforward application of normative ethics, but looking more closely at factors that make some of these cases much more difficult to decide. We shall focus in particular on the issue of negligence, in respect of either the product or the welfare of the client, and on the issue of misrepresentation, where this falls short of outright lies.

Picking up on the questions raised in the last chapter around over-trading, we shall begin our survey with the promotion of fund management services. We shall then look at the promotion of retail financial products, the selling of complex derivatives to the corporate sector and two features of the promotion of common stocks: sell-side research and IPOs. We shall finish with the promotion of potentially illegal or unethical products, such as shares in fraudulent ventures, and avowedly ethical products.

Active fund management

Suppose you wish to invest in shares quoted on the London or New York Stock Exchange. Apart from making trading decisions yourself, you have two main options: you can invest in an index tracker fund, which trades only periodically and in an automated way to keep the balance of shares in line with their index weightings; or you can invest in one or more mutual funds (in the UK, unit trusts), whose fund managers actively trade individual stocks according to declared "investment strategies." If you are investing as a trustee of a substantial endowment or pension fund, you have a larger but essentially similar range of options: from index tracker funds through quant funds, which use sophisticated computer models to try and beat the index but revert to it, to more or less active fund managers. (There are also asset managers who will invest your money in a fund of funds, trying to pick fund managers just as the fund managers try to pick stocks.) There are numerous competing active fund managers, ranging from those who will aggressively stock-pick on your behalf to those who will operate within fixed percentage points of the index weightings. Each of the asset management houses has its own investment strategy or ploy to try and outperform the market.

Fund management has come in for a variety of criticisms over the years, not least for bundled brokerage and soft dollar or soft commission arrangements. Here brokers provide various services to institutional fund managers (anything from research reports to entire computer systems, with plenty of hospitality thrown in) in return for an inflated brokerage commission, which is then passed on to the fund managers' clients as dealing costs.[1] The core issue, though, is what active fund managers are providing for their fees.

It is a matter of simple arithmetic that not everyone can beat the market and that, after taking account of their higher dealing costs and adding in their generous fees, active fund managers will on average under-perform. Indeed, since conventional equity funds have an inbuilt disadvantage compared to long-short hedge funds (they cannot short sell stock they don't own, which hedge funds using derivatives effectively can), it is to be

---

[1] Since these practices were highlighted by the UK Myners Report on institutional investment in 2001, both the UK and the US regulators have tried to limit them and, where this is not feasible, make them more transparent, so that clients are at least told what they are paying for. Their attempts have been met with very mixed responses, some in the industry welcoming the clarification and transparency and others strongly resisting it. See archive.treasury.gov.uk/docs/2001/myners_report0602.html; www.fsa.gov.uk/pubs/cp/cp05_05.pdf.

expected that this under-performance will be quite significant. Some, of course, will do better than others, but increasingly sophisticated statistical analyses have found no evidence of fund managers being able to sustain out-performance with respect to the index over multiple accounting periods.[2] And this is before you add in their fees.

Why, then, do the trustees of pension funds and similar institutions engage active fund managers? It is hard to know for sure and there has been no systematic research. Part of the answer is probably a good measure of optimism and self-delusion all round. Part, however, seems to be that this is what the trustees are advised to do by specialist pension fund advisors, who take a fee for themselves and are very much part of the financial system. And part of it is that the fund management houses present themselves to clients and prospective clients as being able to out-perform the market by more than enough to justify their management fees and trading costs. Whatever the mix of factors at play here (negligence, misrepresentation, delusion), the financial sector benefits and the pensioners pay.

Box 8.1 summarizes one of the few cases in which active fund management has hit the front pages: when Unilever sued Merrill Lynch. The focus of the court case was on the care and competence of the fund managers, but what also stands out is the deal itself, by which, quite typically, the fund managers agreed a benchmark they were very unlikely to achieve but could not, they assumed, be held to.

Personal finance

The promotion of financial products to consumers has long been a source of complaints and concerns. Going back at least to the 1840s, there have always been promoters out to make a profit by selling dubious investments to innocent investors. The main concern in recent decades, however, has been with the products and promotions of the largest and most respectable institutions. Every few years, a new class of product is aggressively promoted and enthusiastically taken up. Some years down the line, it turns out not to have been such a good thing after all, at least as far as the customers were concerned. Complaints mount and the regulatory authorities

---

[2] Berk and Green 2004; Blake and Timmermann 2003; Cuthbertson *et al.* 2008; French 2008; Kosowski *et al.* 2006.

Box 8.1. Unilever versus Merrill Lynch

In 1997, Mercury Asset Management (MAM) were re-appointed by the trustees of Unilever Pension Fund as fund managers for their UK equities portfolio, then valued at about £1.4 billion. MAM, who had about £200 billion of assets under management in total, were at the active end of the active fund manager spectrum, giving their individual fund managers more license than most to stock-pick, both within and across sectors. The firm's senior managers believed strongly that this aggressive approach was the way to generate investor returns and they were scathing of their counterparts in the insurance sector, who tended to track the FTSE 100 Index, and of rival asset management houses described as "closet-indexers," where managers deviated from the weightings of the FTSE 100 Index only by small margins. However, they did not release figures on their own performance and there is no evidence that they beat the market. Already clients of the firm, the Unilever trustees presumably favored this approach, but in the 1997 investment management agreement, they tried to place some limits upon the risks entailed. The objective of the fund managers was set at a return of 1 percent a year in excess of the index benchmark, but with a caveat that under normal circumstances they wouldn't be expected to drop below the benchmark by more than 3 percent over any twelve-month period.

In 1997–8, during which time MAM was taken over by investment bankers Merrill Lynch (but kept the same management team), the Unilever fund performance fell well short of the lower boundary agreed. After getting a cumulative return of 10.5 percent *below* the benchmark over five quarters, the trustees terminated the agreement and subsequently took Merrill Lynch MAM to court, claiming both breach of contract and negligence and demanding damages of £130 million.

During the period in question, the portfolio had actually grown in value, but it was a period in which the big growth was in the largest stocks, and especially in the financial and technology sectors. The Unilever portfolio was invested heavily in medium-sized companies and in other sectors: not only did these under-perform, but their performance was under-reflected in the index.

The two parties eventually settled for about £70 million, so the case was never tested in court. Had it been so, the key issues would have been whether the fund manager responsible for the portfolio showed reasonable care and skill, whether he was subject to proper oversight and supervision, and whether MAM was negligent in failing to take sufficient regard of the instructions in the agreement. It was not contractually bound to the lower limit, but it was bound to take it into account in its own risk management.

> **Source:** this case was widely reported in the press. See, for example, www.business week.com/1999/99_44/b3653221.htm. It was also the subject of a Harvard Business School case: Perold *et al.* 2002.

eventually act, lambasting the financial institutions for mis-selling and requiring them to compensate customers who have lost money.

This can be seen most clearly in the UK, which combines an aggressive financial sector with a unified regulator of conduct. Since the late 1980s, there have been four major scandals involving endowment mortgages, personal pension plans, payment protection insurance and split-cap investment trusts.

Endowment mortgages were promoted by life insurance companies, which persuaded homebuyers that, instead of repaying their loan capital in the normal way, they should instead invest in the firm's stock market funds, using the proceeds of that investment to pay off the loan at the end of the period. This was great for the institution, which took hefty fees from the investment as well as the loan, and in bull markets it worked for the homebuyer too. But when stock markets collapsed, so did the investments. Borrowers, left carrying large losses and unable to repay their mortgages, complained that the risks had not been properly explained.

The same companies were also behind the aggressive promotion of personal pension plans, based on investment in their in-house stock market funds and sold by offering very high commissions to independent financial advisors (IFAs). Again, this was good business for the provider firms and for the IFAs, most of whom in this period offered their services for "free" and made their money from heavily frontloaded commissions, which typically ate up most of the first few years' pension contributions. But the fees and commissions combined meant that the products offered very poor returns, especially for the thousands of people who were persuaded to exit their subsidized and much better-value company pension schemes and buy these new products instead.

Payment protection insurance is sold by retail banks alongside loan products and is designed to insure the borrowers in the event of their being unable to meet repayments. For a decade or more, the UK banks aggressively promoted these insurance products, or just bundled them in with the loans, with minimal explanation. They were highly profitable for the banks, with premiums often exceeding interest charges, and in some cases they were also appropriate for the customers. But for many they were inappropriate, unnecessary or could have been purchased much more cheaply elsewhere. Many customers didn't even know they had taken out the insurance and many found that when they came to claim, their cases weren't covered.

The fourth case, split-caps, is covered in Box 8.2. In all these cases, the products offered were initially welcomed and problems only arose later, in particular when market conditions turned. In each case, sections of the press accused the financial institutions of gross immorality, misrepresenting their products to customers, failing to take proper account of the customers' interests and failing to think through the implications for products and customers under different market conditions. This press coverage pushed the regulators to action, but while industry insiders accepted that they should perhaps have been more careful, there was little sense that this lack of care amounted to any unethical wrongdoing. The underlying logic of finance is that to get returns, you take risks, and the feeling is that however much you tell this to consumers, you can't always make them listen.

Corporate finance and the promotion of derivatives

Many of the concerns around banks' promotions of products to the corporate sector have been related to the sale of interest rate swaps. The first cases to come to public notice involved two local authorities: the London Borough of Hammersmith and Fulham in the UK, which built a derivatives portfolio of £6 billion on the back of an annual operating budget of just £85 million and lost £1 billion; and Orange County, California in the USA, which lost a similar amount, $1.7 billion. In both cases, the organizations, encouraged by their banks, were trying to stretch their limited budgets by trading in fixed-floating interest rate swaps and came to grief when interest rates shot up in 1994.[3]

---

[3] Geisst 2002, pp. 260–3, 315–25.

Box 8.2. Split-cap investment trusts

Split-cap investment trusts are effectively stock market investment funds of fixed duration (five to ten years) with different classes of shares designed to appeal to different customers. For example, zeros, or zero-dividend preference shares, pay out a fixed amount at the fund's expiry – providing that the fund is solvent. Income shares offer a varying proportion of dividends, combined with varying degrees of capital protection. Capital shares offer no income but a residual share of the capital on expiry. These products were devised in the 1990s, in the expectation of steadily rising share prices, but following the stock market collapse of 2000–1, many ran into difficulties and faced the prospect of having to default even on the zeros, never mind returning capital to the income or capital shareholders. In a desperate attempt to get through the problems, funds started taking on debt and gearing up, which made the losses far worse, issuing new shares and investing in each other. By the end of 2001, a significant number of split-cap investment funds were invested primarily in other split-cap investment funds. The UK regulator, the FSA, was initially concerned primarily with this last point, but customers were concerned that the zeros, which had been marketed as ultra-safe, very low-risk investments, were not safe at all and often worthless. Eventually the FSA took this on board and negotiated with the firms some measure of compensation, but it was widely perceived as too little, too late. Many of the investors in zeros had been saving for a particular event, by then long past. Many, indeed, were dead by the time the compensation schemes were implemented.

Split-caps are still being promoted, less aggressively and under somewhat more careful regulatory oversight. The underlying idea appears sound and the reluctance of the FSA to get involved despite press condemnation of the firms involved suggests that in this case they thought that the initial promotion was not seriously misleading. But where do you draw the line?

Sources: this was well covered in the press. For informative articles, see, for example, http://news.bbc.co.uk/1/hi/business/4465039.stm; www.independent.co.uk/news/business/analysis-and-features/investment-trusts-torn-apart-by-the-split-capital-crisis-656430.html.

Interest rate swaps are also at the center of a scandal unfolding in the UK at the time of writing. In this case, the clients are small businesses: shops, farms, hotels and care homes. Borrowing from their banks in the mid-2000s, they had been sold what looked like fixed-rate loans but were actually combinations of standard variable-rate loans with interest rate swaps. These were presented as protecting the client from rising interest rates, but proved very costly when rates fell and stayed low. In practice, a fixed-rate loan would have had much the same result, but with the cost appearing in the form of high locked-in interest charges rather than derivative losses. But in some cases, the banks, which made significant profits from the derivative transactions, seem to have made them a condition of the loan, to have persuaded companies to take on extra risk and to have failed to fully explain either the product or its downside risk, and the FSA has highlighted about 40,000 cases of apparent mis-selling.[4] As in the other cases we have looked at, we find public accusations of negligence and misrepresentation, but these accusations are strongly contested by the banks.

The swaps involved in this case are standard products, bought by the banks for re-sale to their customers. However, the situation is reminiscent of an earlier case in which one bank, Bankers Trust, created such products for its customers on a customized basis, acting as both seller and counterparty (see Box 8.3). Similar issues arose here, but in an exaggerated form. The clients were much larger companies and they should not have been easily misled. But the deals they were offered were also much more questionable.

The same bank acting as seller and counterparty is also a key feature of one of the most interesting cases to have emerged from the financial crisis: the promotion by Goldman Sachs of the Abacus brand of synthetic CDOs. As we shall see, this poses some particularly interesting ethical questions and it is described in detail in Box 8.4.

Sell-side research

The reports and recommendations issued by sell-side (brokerage) research analysts are supposedly independent and objective, part of the service that

---

[4] See, for example, www.telegraph.co.uk/finance/newsbysector/banksandfinance/9135 986/Bank-mis-selling-victims-from-the-chippy-to-the-small-hotel.html; www.telegraph. co.uk/finance/rate-swap-scandal/9576563/FSA-lifts-estimate-of-mis-sold-swaps.html.

Box 8.3. Bankers Trust, Gibson Greetings and Proctor & Gamble

In 1991 the large American company Gibson Greetings raised $50 million through an issue of 9.33 percent fixed-rate bonds. Interest rates almost immediately came down and, looking to cut its borrowing costs, it used plain vanilla interest rate swaps to convert the bulk of the loan to variable-rate debt. When these terminated, in 1992, Bankers Trust Securities Corp (BTS), the broker-dealer arm of the commercial bank Bankers Trust, aggressively run by the former trader Charles Sanford, offered more complex derivatives to achieve the same end, and through the first nine months of 1993, Gibson engaged, on BTS's recommendation, in an ever-more complex series of derivatives transactions, including highly leveraged Treasury-Linked Swaps (cash-settled put options based on spreads between short- and long-term Treasury bond rates) and Knock-Out Call Options.

The initial deals were profitable, but the more complex deals were loss-making, and as each one expired, Gibson was advised to roll over into a new one. With the leverage, Gibson's exposure reached $150 million and when the positions were finally closed out in 1994, it had lost heavily. Bankers Trust, meanwhile, as counterparty to the derivatives transactions, had profited and had also taken over $13 million in fees. Because the derivatives were customized, they had no open market value and the value at any time could only be determined through BTS's own computer model. A feature of the case that particularly concerned the SEC was that BTS did not actually use its model valuations when reporting to Gibson, but instead gave it figures that greatly under-stated its losses, the true size of which became apparent only when Gibson sought to close off the options and was quoted the model valuation. One consequence of this was that Gibson's financial statements were materially wrong. Of much greater concern to Gibson was that, with neither the expertise nor the computer models to conduct its own valuations, it had been seriously misled.

It soon transpired that Gibson Greetings was not the only company to make significant losses from the interest rate derivatives offered by BTS at this time. Proctor & Gamble (P&G) made the largest losses, eventually taking after-tax losses of over $100 million and suing Bankers Trust for $195 million. In the course of its legal action, however, P&G obtained the release of 6,500 audio tapes of Bankers Trust telephone conversations (banks routinely record all telephone calls, mainly to settle trading disputes), which showed a dozen clients suffering from essentially the same process as was reported in the Gibson case, one of which, Sandoz, was reported to have lost nearly $80 million.

The tapes secured by P&G laid bare the BTS business model, which was essentially to sell clients derivatives while: (a) acting as the counterparty; (b) pricing them to favor themselves; and (c) taking a healthy commission, apparently known as the rip-off-factor (ROF), which instead of being clearly stated was hidden in the bid-offer spreads – not always revealed to the clients – on the prices at which the derivatives were traded. Among the items recorded were a discussion between two bank employees on misrepresenting a client's loss on a trade and a reflection on the firm's "funny business": "lure people into that calm and then just totally f——'em." In another conversation, bank employees satisfied themselves that P&G "would never be able to know how much money was taken out" in commission.

> **Sources:** for the P&G case and the content of the tapes, see *Business Week*, 16 October 1995, www.businessweek.com/1995/42/b34461.htm. For the Gibson case, see SEC releases 33-7124 / 34-35136 (22 December 1994), 34-36357 (11 October 1995) and 33-7269 / 34-36906 (29 February 1996).

brokers provide to their clients. By the mid-1990s, however, by which time the main brokers had been taken over by investment banks, this wasn't generally the case. Many analysts had their pay tied to the investment banking business derived from the companies they researched, and "buy" recommendations had become the almost-universal norm. As veteran analyst Ronald Glantz testified to Congress in 2001:

> Now the job of analysts is to bring in investment banking clients, not provide good investment advice ... In 1997 a major investment banking firm offered to triple my pay. They had no interest in the quality of my recommendations. I was shown a list with 15 names and asked, "How quickly can you issue buy recommendations on these potential clients?" ... It is an open secret that "strong buy" now means "buy," "buy" means "hold," "hold" means that the company isn't an investment banking client, and "sell" means that the company is no longer an investment client.[5]

---

[5] Mills 2003, pp. 122–3; also quoted in Madrick 2011, pp. 321–2.

Box 8.4. The Goldman Sachs Abacus deals

Between 2004 and 2007, Goldman Sachs, which was already a major issuer of both mortgage securitizations and ordinary CDOs, created and sold 47 synthetic CDOs under the Abacus brand, with a total value of $66 billion. To explain how they were structured, we shall look at the first of these, Abacus 2004-1, valued at about $2 billion. Like other synthetic CDOs, Abacus 2004-1 looked like an ordinary CDO, in that it had a number of tranches with different risk-return properties, and these were defined so as to mimic the performance of a notional pool of real mortgage-backed securities (see Chapter 1 for a typical CDO structure). But since it didn't own these securities, it had a rather different structure. As with other synthetic CDOs, there were three groups of parties to the deal.

Funded investors bought the equity and mezzanine tranches of the deal, in this case valued at £195 million, paying Abacus 2004-1 the capital and receiving the stream of payments they would have received from the reference securities if they had been owned. They also took liability for any losses they would have made on the reference securities in a real CDO, which was achieved here by their selling CDSs on these securities to Abacus 2004-1.

Unfunded investors took the part of the buyers of the senior tranches of a regular CDO, but since there were no underlying securities, Abacus 2004-1 had not had to pay anything to buy such securities and, given their supposed safety, there was consequently no need for the unfunded investors to put money up-front. Instead, they received premiums from Abacus 2004-1 modeled on the difference between the interest they would have earned from the reference securities in a real CDO and the interest they would have had to pay on a loan to buy them. They also took liability, just as the senior tranche-holders would in a real CDO, for any losses that would have been made on the reference securities beyond those covered by the mezzanine tranche-holders.

Short investors bought CDSs on the reference securities from Abacus 2004-1, the premiums received by Abacus 2004-1 effectively paying for the CDSs it bought from the funded investors and for the premiums it paid to the unfunded investors.

The end result was that if the assets performed, the funded and unfunded investors would get the same returns as from a real CDO, with the short investors paying the bill. If they failed, then the funded investors initially, and the unfunded investors if things went really badly, would be liable, just as in a real CDO, with the payments going to the short investors. Either way, Goldman Sachs took a fee. Since the primary purpose of the synthetic CDO was to meet and make money from the demand for mezzanine tranches, Goldman Sachs originally retained a $1.8 billion super-senior tranche as the main unfunded investor and also acted as the short investor for the entire deal. It then sold senior tranches to two other unfunded investors, both asset management firms. The funded investors were two banks and the same asset management firms.

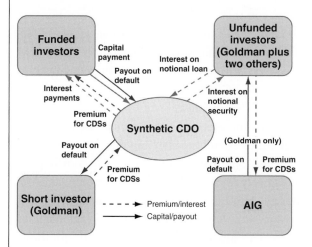

Had this been a real CDO, involving a $2 billion-plus outlay of capital to buy the reference securities, Goldman Sachs as holder of the super-senior tranche would normally have hedged its position by buying CDSs on those securities. In this case its short position was already larger than its long position, so it had no exposure to hedge, but after about a year, it nevertheless bought CDSs on the entire package of reference securities from AIG for a premium of $2.2 million a year – a premium of about 0.1 percent, which gives an indication of how safe mortgages were reckoned to be, but was to Goldman Sachs, which had growing doubts about the mortgage market, irresistibly cheap. In the end, the assets failed, the funded investors lost almost all their money, the unfunded investors also lost money, and in addition to its fees Goldman made profits of about $930 million from its CDSs, $806 million of it from AIG (or rather from

American taxpayers, once the government had taken over a bankrupt AIG) and the rest from the investors.

Goldman Sachs under attack

The structure of Abacus 2004-1 meant that from the beginning Goldman Sachs was selling securities to clients while at the same betting on their failure, but that is what people do when they trade derivatives. It wasn't going out to the investors and saying "we think these investments are going to perform for you." It was saying to other sophisticated financial institutions: "you want investments with these characteristics, we'll structure a deal that gives you that, effectively by taking the other side of the trade." Once it bought the CDSs from AIG, however, it was effectively betting against the investors and, having taken a proprietary view that the mortgage market was at risk, it continued to aggressively market mortgage-backed securities, CDOs and synthetic CDOs. And with Abacus 2007-AC1, it arguably went further.

By 2007, the synthetic CDO market had become quite sophisticated, with a number of hedge funds simultaneously buying senior tranches and shorting junior tranches. Goldman Sachs was heavily shorting the mortgage market in its entirety (in that respect, its judgment was probably the best in the industry), but it was still promoting mortgage-backed securities and their derivatives, and indeed pushing the ratings agencies to give them high ratings. This already raised some difficult questions about its responsibilities to clients, but two things particularly incensed people when they came to public light later. One was that in internal emails, Goldman Sachs staff members described some of the securities they were promoting as "junk," "shit," or "crappy." The other was the way it put together and promoted Abacus 2007-AC1.

One of the tricky issues in creating a synthetic CDO is what mortgage securities you reference to. The promotional literature for Abacus 2007-AC1 stated that the underlying assets had been picked by ACA Management, an independent CDO manager. However, it turned out that, unbeknownst to the investors, ACA had worked at Goldman's request with Paulson & Co, a hedge fund that had been set up specifically to short mezzanine CDO tranches and that was to be the main short investor, alongside Goldman, on Abacus 2007-AC1. Paulson and Goldman argued later that the reference asset pool was disclosed to all investors, as was Goldman's own short position, and that the purpose of putting the pool together was not to bias the performance one way or another, which would be counterproductive, but to build a pool that both long and short investors (all of which were financial institutions, so sophisticated investors who should not need any special protection) could agree on. ACA, however, seems to have been unaware of Paulson's position, believing that he was going to take both long and short positions, and emails later published suggest that it was puzzled by some of his views on the reference portfolio, in particular the exclusion of subprime mortgages that it thought to be relatively sound.

The SEC action against Goldman Sachs charged it with fraud for telling investors that the asset pool was "selected by ACA" when in fact Paulson, whose interests were opposed to those of the investors being targeted, had played a significant role in the process. For the public, the abiding images come from TV footage of Goldman Sachs executives appearing before a Senate panel, insisting they had done nothing wrong, suggesting that the main problem with the emails was that the views were recorded, and unable to answer straight questions about what responsibilities to their clients meant to them.

Source: this case draws on Financial Crisis Inquiry Commission 2011 and a range of news articles, including Phillips 2010 and Sorkin 2010. Footage of Goldman executives before the panel is included in Ferguson *et al.* 2010.

Had the "open secret" been truly open, there would have been little risk of deception, but for individual investors especially, these reports were all they had to go on, and while they might note their generally optimistic tone, it didn't occur to them that they were anything other than what they seemed.

When New York Attorney General Elliott Spitzer started investigating this, together with other fraudulent practices, he soon found evidence of widespread malpractice. With various regulatory agencies eventually getting involved too, the banks investigated ended up paying fines totaling $1.4 billion. For the most part, the analysts were seen to have been responding to pressure from their employers and were not personally charged, but several were given substantial fines and were barred from the industry for life. Box 8.5 describes the case of one of these, Jack Grubman of Salomon Smith Barney,

Box 8.5. Jack Grubman: objectivity acquires a new meaning

Jack Grubman built his reputation as a sell-side telecoms analyst at Paine Webber and then at Salomon Smith Barney in the 1990s. Sell-side analysts produce research reports accompanied by buy/hold/sell recommendations that stockbrokers provide as a service to their clients and that are presented as independent and objective. Where a brokerage is owned by the same firm as an investment bank, as at Salomon Smith Barney (which itself became part of Citigroup), the two are supposed to operate independently so that the brokers' reports are not distorted by the fact that some of the companies analyzed may be investment banking clients, or potential clients, while others are not. Grubman, however, worked closely with Salomon's clients, advising their CEOs and, in the case of one client, Global Crossing, getting actively involved in its flotation and sitting in on board meetings. With another client, WorldCom, he was actively involved in its growth by acquisition, advising on its takeover of MCI Communications. At the same time, in his capacity of analyst, he strongly promoted shares in these companies.

When challenged in an interview for a *Business Week* article as to the potential conflicts of interest, Grubman responded to the effect that the more an analyst knew about the companies he reported on, the better and more "objective" his analysis would be:

> What used to be a conflict has now become synergy. Someone like me who is banking-intensive would have been looked at disdainfully by the buy side 15 years ago. Now they know that I'm in the flow of what's going on. That helps me help them think about the industry. The notion that keeping your distance makes you more objective is absurd. Objective? The other word for it is uninformed.

Citigroup Chairman Sandy Weill concurred:

> Jack probably knows more about the business than anybody I've ever met. The more knowledge and understanding an analyst has, the better job they can do in analysis.

Despite his inside knowledge and supposed objectivity, Grubman kept touting both Global Crossing and WorldCom to within months of the points at which each went bankrupt. His reward was a $20 million salary plus perks – quite high for an analyst. At one point, for example, Sandy Weill arranged for a $1 million donation to a top nursery school in which Grubman wanted to place his children, apparently in return (though this was never definitively proven) for an upgrading of his recommendation of a company whose CEO's support Weill needed in a boardroom battle.

Source: Elstrom 2000.

and is striking for the denial, by both Grubman and his bank's CEO, Sandy Weill, of any misrepresentation.

Initial public offerings

One form of stock promotion in which proprietary analysis inevitably plays a key role is IPOs, when a growing firm first launches its shares on a stock exchange. In boom times, some IPOs are little different from the old-fashioned stock promotions of the nineteenth century. In the dot-com boom of the late 1990s, for example, thousands of new companies were launched onto the market on the back of glowing prospectuses and at inflated prices, generating fees of about 7 percent for the issuing and under-writing banks, but proving worthless in the long run for those who bought them. Whatever the circumstances, however, IPOs require difficult judg-ments and lead to complex conflicts of interest.

In an IPO, the issuing bank researches the company and prepares a preliminary prospectus, giving basic information on the firm, an assess-ment of its prospects and an indication of the size, timing and pricing of the proposed issue. It will then typically line up a consortium of banks which between them will underwrite the issue and distribute it through their brokerage arms. Shortly before the issue date, a revised prospectus is issued with fuller and updated information and an offer price. The aim is normally to price the issue so that it is fully subscribed by the banks' institutional investor clients. This will inevitably leave some unsa-tisfied demand, so that when the shares start trading, they move to a premium on the offer price. However, if the issue has been well priced and nothing dramatic has happened between the pricing and the launch, the premium should be relatively small, perhaps 10–15 percent for a company that can be easily valued. In the case of rapidly growing technology and Internet companies, it is much harder to set a market price, and the issuers and underwriters normally aim for a more conservative offer price and a higher initial premium in order to ensure that the issue is a success.

The aim of an IPO is to raise capital for the company and, in many cases, to provide early-stage private investors with an opportunity to cash in some of their gains by selling some of their own shares. It is also an opportunity to allocate shares to employees and, more controversially, to other insiders, and this is where some of the problems begin. Because the bank is paid a percentage of the issue price, there is an inbuilt incentive to price as high as the market will bear, and this puts pressure on the writers of the prospectus, who have to protect themselves legally by incorporating every caveat they can, but who are also trying to sell a product and present it in the best possible light. Meanwhile, because the bank has control over the distribution of shares, it also has an incentive to under-price. Apart from removing any underwriting risk (which the high fees are supposed to compensate for), this allows insiders and associates to receive allocations at well below the market price. These can either be held or immediately sold at a more or less guaranteed profit.

An extreme example of a banker using large post-IPO premiums to reward friends and associates and secure favors – and in this case kickbacks – in return is given in Box 8.6. Much more common, indeed quite commonplace, is the practice by which associates and favored clients of the underwriting banks routinely pick up modest allocations of new issues as a courtesy or favor, it being conveniently forgotten that someone, somewhere, is paying for these.

As the more recent case of the 2012 Facebook IPO shows (see Box 8.7), issues do not arise only when there are anticipated large premiums. With very high public interest, the issue price can also be set higher than a sober financial analysis would suggest, the well-informed underwriters in this case taking their fees and using the demand from much less well-informed investors (who may not even have read the prospectus) to offload the shares before the bubble of expectations bursts and the price drops down to a more sustainable level.

Box 8.6. Frank Quattrone and the IPO

In the dot-com boom of the 1990s, Frank Quattrone became known as the King of the IPOs. Working first for Morgan Stanley, then Deutsche Bank, then Credit Suisse First Boston (CSFB), he brought a string of new companies to market, including Netscape, Linux and Amazon. With the issuing bank taking fees of around 7 percent, these issues made Quattrone's employers hundreds of millions, if not billions of dollars, and at the height of the boom, he himself was reported to be earning $100 million a year. But the issues offered other sources of income beyond the fee. With IPO shares in high demand and often trading at a substantial premium of the offer price (gains of 100–300 percent were commonplace; the Linux issue, which was priced at $30 a share, closed its first day's trading at nearly $240), the issuing bank's ability to allocate shares was priceless. Quattrone would allocate shares to senior executives of his bank's client companies, or of potential clients, which they could quickly cash in at a profit. One accusation was that he deliberately under-priced offers to guarantee these profits, depriving the companies he was launching of the funds they would have raised were the price higher, but in the environment of the late 1990s, this probably wasn't necessary.

In return for Quattrone's favors, it was made clear that the recipients, typically fund managers, would be expected to push trading business through the bank's broker-dealing arm at greatly inflated commission rates. What the executives gained in a personal capacity, their investors lost in extra commissions. The ensuing SEC investigation detailed heavy and blatantly spurious dealing by share recipients in the days following an IPO at commissions up to 30 times the norm. In one email subpoenaed by the SEC, a CSFB employee wrote to a recipient of Quattrone's largesse:

> OK we got another screaming deal and I weaseled you guys some stock we've yet to see any leverage out of you guys for the free dough-re-me does it make sense for me to continue to feed your guys with deal stock or should I take the stock to someone who will pay us direct for the allocation.

> **Source:** www.sec.gov/litigation/complaints/complr17327.htm, summarized in Madrick 2011, pp. 329–32, quotation from p. 331.

Box 8.7. The Facebook IPO

When Facebook shares were launched on the NASDAQ exchange in May 2012, the underwriters were faced with a difficult pricing problem. Despite the size of the Facebook community (then about one billion active users worldwide), the financial attractiveness of the company lay in its potential rather than its actual revenues and analysts were divided as to the viability of its earning model, especially in relation to smartphone use. Valuations ranged from $25 to $46 a share. Having indicated a likely range of $28–35 just a fortnight before the launch, the underwriters eventually agreed on a price of $38, valuing the company at over $100 billion.

The first day's trading was marked by confusion as technical glitches with NASDAQ's systems left orders unfulfilled, but the shares ended the day roughly where they had started. In the ensuing days, the share price dropped below $30 and at one point in the summer was down to $20.

In retrospect, the issue had been priced too aggressively, but given the uncertainties, the popular interest (including interest from many people who felt they had lost out on the earlier and very successful flotation of Google) and the volatility of the markets at the time, this was perhaps understandable. What was harder to understand was that the under-writing banks, while setting a price at the top end of their own earlier estimates, all appear to have cut their earnings forecasts for Facebook just days before the launch, but communicated this only to their main institutional clients. By early 2013, the full details had still to emerge, but the impression was that the banks knew or suspected, perhaps from a Facebook source, that they had over-stated the firm's financial prospects and over-priced the issue, but had decided to keep up appearances knowing that the shares would sell, in the first few days of trading, to an uncritical and uninformed public.

Sources: http://en.wikipedia.org/wiki/Facebook_IPO includes copious references to the press coverage; www.businessinsider.com/exclusive-heres-the-inside-story-of-what-happened-on-the-facebook-ipo-2012-5?op=1 gives additional background.

Illegal and ethically questionable products

A recurring problem in the finance industry is the promotion of what are claimed to be investment products but are actually fraudulent ventures of one kind or another. These are typically small-scale affairs in which a crooked promoter persuades innocent people to invest in a fund that doesn't exist, but occasionally something larger turns up. By the time he was arrested in 2008, NASDAQ veteran Bernie Madoff's investment fund, which was in reality a simple Ponzi scheme, was over-stating its client accounts by $65 billion and had lost its investors $18 billion.

Madoff's scheme was quite clearly both illegal and unethical – he lied and he stole. But what about the feeder funds that invested in it? These funds took client monies and invested them in the Madoff fund, apparently without realizing anything was wrong, but without carrying out any checks, even though there were clear signs of irregularities. In 2009 the principal of one of the feeder funds, who had put $450 billion of client monies into Madoff as well as several million of his own, responded to a journalist: "Doubt Bernie Madoff? Doubt Bernie? No. You doubt God. You can doubt God, but you don't doubt Bernie. He had that aura about him." In retrospect this looks severely negligent, but is that a fair charge, given Madoff's impeccable reputation and standing in the industry? In Box 8.8 we describe the Madoff fraud and the evidence that might have raised suspicions.

As well as occasionally promoting products that are fraudulent and illegal, the financial sector also promotes many products that are ethically questionable, as well as many that are explicitly labeled as "ethical." The main focus of debate here has been upon the morality of industry sectors such as tobacco, alcohol, armaments and gambling. Beginning in the 1970s, so-called ethical investment funds invested in the stock market like any other mutual funds, but excluded investment in firms whose practices were seen as unethical – cigarette manufacturers, armaments manufacturers, alcoholic beverages companies and so on. Over the 1990s and 2000s, the term "responsible investment" came to cover a wide range of practices embracing multiple combinations of ethical investment as originally understood, social shareholder activism oriented towards corporate social responsibility, investment on the basis of criteria that combined financial, social and environmental measures, and investment on the basis of long-term and sustainable shareholder value rather than short-term returns.

Responsible investment now accounts for about 10 percent of funds invested in the USA and 20 percent in Europe, but the more mainstream it

Box 8.8. Investing in Bernie Madoff

Bernard Madoff's Madoff Securities, founded in 1960, was one of the pioneers of off-exchange electronic share trading and a major player in the growth of the NASDAQ electronic stock market. By the early 1990s, Madoff Securities was executing $740 million of trades a day, equivalent to 9 percent of the total New York Stock Exchange turnover. Throughout the 1990s and 2000s, it was one of the largest traders on Wall Street, and Madoff himself served as Chairman of the National Association of Securities Dealers (NASD).

Alongside the dealing business, Madoff also ran an investment management division, effectively a hedge fund, purportedly based on a split-strike conversion strategy around SP100 stocks. His investment clients were mainly large charitable institutions, together with some very rich individuals and a number of feeder funds. He sold his funds, on the basis of his dealing reputation and society connections, as being very exclusive and hard to get into. Most of the investors were either unlikely to take much money out (in the case of the large charities) or reluctant to do so in case they couldn't get back in.

Though the details were always kept notoriously secret, the Madoff funds reported steady gains, significantly above those that would be achieved by normal stock market investments and much steadier, gaining in declining as well as rising markets, but generally not so high as to raise suspicion. In reality, though, it was all a sham, and the money used to pay out was just money that investors had put in. A few large investors who chose to cash in on the claimed performance made considerable fortunes: the estate of one investor, Jeffrey Picower, eventually settled claims of $7 billion. However, none of the money entrusted to Madoff appears to have been invested, at least (on Madoff's own admission) from the mid-1990s onwards and quite possibly from the beginning. It was either diverted overseas to his own accounts (much of the money has never been located) or just stored in a bank account used to make repayments. When clients took money out, he would create a fake back history. When the fund was wound up following Madoff's arrest in late 2008, the client accounts were found to be over-stated by $65 billion, with actual losses to investors of $18 billion. The financial crisis had finally created a situation where there were more redemption requests than Madoff could satisfy.

If the overall gains reported by Madoff were not suspicious, their regularity was, and a number of people raised questions over the years. From 1999 to 2005, one financial analyst repeatedly sent evidence to the SEC that the returns cited by one of the Madoff feeder funds were mathematically impossible: the numbers simply didn't add up. In the early 2000s, several financial journalists also questioned the consistency of Madoff's performance, and one large hedge fund withdrew its monies, suspicious both of the steady returns and of the fact that the level of options trading that would have been needed to support the claimed strategy wasn't visible in the markets. However, although an SEC report on one of the feeder funds had already noted its "curiously steady" returns, the SEC appears not to have been interested.

The fact that the auditor of the supposedly massive fund was a local one-man accounting firm might also have given rise to suspicions, but while one hedge fund advised its clients to steer clear on this basis in 2007, this wasn't widely commented on until after the collapse. In general, the view seems to have been that if anything unethical was going on, it was probably happening through the trading arm, with Madoff trading on behalf of his own fund ahead of trades carried out for other parties. The SEC did conduct several investigations of this side of the business, but never found anything wrong – which in retrospect is not surprising.

What prompted Madoff to run his fraud remains unclear. The other side of his business was extraordinarily successful and appears to have been quite legal and above board.

Source: the Wikipedia articles on the Madoff case are extensive and well referenced: http://en.wikipedia.org/wiki/Madoff_investment_scandal; http://en.wikipedia.org/wiki/Bernard_Madoff. See also Lewis 2012.

has become, the more the ethical and financial elements have been conflated. Terms like "responsible investing" and "sustainable investing" are increasingly used to describe financial strategies that are responsible and sustainable in the sense that they are relatively long term, but with no necessary connection to social responsibility or environmental sustainability. An "ethical" fund today might justify its position by only investing in the "most ethical" cigarette and arms manufacturers, but still be fully weighted in those sectors, which may raise questions of representation.

The ethics of ethical investment have more to do with general business ethics than with finance ethics and are inherently difficult to resolve. Endowment trustees, for example, may have to balance a mandate to invest ethically with a mandate to maximize returns, and the appropriate balance will depend on the purposes of the endowment and its financial standing amongst other things. From the perspective of the fund manager providing an investment service, the onus is probably more to be clear about what is and is not being invested in than to take decisions of principle that should really be taken by the client.

Issues and analysis

One thing most of the examples in this chapter have in common is that they are not ethically black and white. Quattrone was corrupt, and the IPO process generally is open to corruption, but even the Facebook underwriters seem as likely to have been guilty of negligence or poor judgment as of a conscious attempt to deceive. Indeed, there are a few instances of outright lies or deception. The people at Bankers Trust appear to have lied to their clients about the values of their derivative holdings and to have intentionally misled them on other key issues. Goldman Sachs's failure to mention in its Abacus prospectus that Paulson had had a hand in selecting the asset pool was tantamount to a lie, an omission of key information that any investor would have expected to be included. Some people were almost certainly told that they needed to take out a bank's payment protection insurance when they didn't, and Jack Grubman must surely have lied knowingly about the prospects of the firms he promoted, albeit under the guise of "opinions." In most cases, however, we are instead looking at incomplete information or potentially misleading representations of information, exaggerating some things and glossing over others, combined with persuasive marketing tactics. The customers were not actually lied to, but nor were they always given the information needed to make informed rational choices.

The ability of customers to make informed rational choices matters ethically in a marketing context because of the utilitarian consequences. Efficient markets, which are central to the utilitarian case for financial and industrial capitalism, rely on it. Because economic theory assumes opportunistic self-interest, this is not immediately obvious. It seems natural to argue that in efficient markets self-interested actors will do whatever deals they can and that the principle of *caveat emptor* (buyer beware) will apply. But the theory also assumes full competence and completely shared (or in more sophisticated versions easily purchasable) information. Even more realistic theories of markets, such as the Hayekian version discussed in Chapter 6, assume that relevant information can be effectively disseminated through price signals so that the true value of a product like payment protection insurance will be apparent from its market price. In practice, the situations described in this chapter all show strong and persistent information asymmetries between buyers and sellers, corresponding to highly inefficient markets.

Informed rational choice is also important from other ethical perspectives. Somebody who sells a product to a buyer knowing that that buyer is poorly informed or otherwise incapable of rational choice, and that the product will harm him or her in some way, is acting unethically from a Kantian perspective, using the buyer merely as a means, and from a virtue perspective, lacking in benevolence, human-heartedness and other core human virtues. In looking at questions of marketing and promotion, we normally invoke these lines of argument when the buyers are vulnerable in some way and their ability to choose is restricted by rational incapacity or inexperience – in the case of children, for example, or the simple-minded, or some of the buyers of payday loans discussed in Chapter 5. But they are also applicable when, as here, the products being offered are complex and hard to understand, and the buyers are hampered by limited information.

The difficulty with the cases discussed here is that while it is surely wrong to willfully misrepresent a product, expecting that it might do harm, each of the words "willfully," "misrepresent" and "expecting" is problematic. It is unclear in many cases either what the sellers expected or what they should, if acting diligently, have expected their products to deliver. It is unclear whether and to what extent they were misrepresenting their products, what level of understanding they might reasonably have assumed on the part of the buyers and what level of information provision would have been adequate, in this context, to render the buyers reasonably informed. And it is unclear to what extent any misrepresentation may have been intentional or accidental, knowing or neglectful.

Institutional fund managers, selling a relatively straightforward service to relatively informed clients, appear to believe that they can deliver what they claim and work hard to do so. But as people who pride themselves on their analytical skills, they should surely be able to take a more realistic, evidence-based view. So should the pension fund advisors who recommend them, and there is an argument in both cases that "can" here implies "should." Of course, both are getting good fees for enjoyable work and the clients (whose reliance on consultants satisfies their own perceived obligations as trustees) are generally not complaining. There is no incentive to be more careful. But we may reasonably ask whether ethical fund managers would need such an incentive. When Unilever did complain about Merrill Lynch, the fund managers were shocked, but appear to have been shocked more by the idea that anyone might complain and spoil the party than by the thought that they might have been negligent. They had never thought about their obligations in that way.

The clients of the Madoff feeder funds didn't complain either until the fraudulent nature of Madoff's business was exposed, but in this case, the fact that the customers were happy does not appear to excuse the feeder fund managers from duties of care and due diligence. Representing the product as you see it is not enough if you are not looking hard enough at it. The evidence that something fishy was going on was clearly there, but the fund managers, seduced by the consistently high returns, simply trusted Madoff's reputation rather than questioning the basis of those returns or doing any due diligence. In their defense, one of the functions of the institution of trust in a society is to save on search and monitoring costs. What they did in investing their own money was not unreasonable. But unless they made it quite clear to their clients on what basis they were investing, they should surely have done more to protect their interests.

In neither of these cases did the fund managers set out to deceive. They seem to have been guilty more of a lazy negligence than anything, and the same might be said of the promoters of personal finance products. The promoters of endowment mortgages and personal pension plans expected the stock markets to keep rising fast enough to generate profits all round: a good return for their customers and large fees for themselves. At the time, this was probably a reasonable expectation, at least for the foreseeable future. But the products had lifetimes well beyond what was foreseeable. Mortgage endowments might be twenty-five-year investments and pension plans even longer. It is not clear whether anybody looked at the possibility of markets not performing as the "illustrative forecasts" provided to customers, which were based on returns that now seem quite ridiculous, suggested. If they did, they dismissed it as unlikely enough to warrant no more than a stock warning, "the value of investments may go down as well as up," which could then be dismissed by the salesman or independent financial advisor: "we have to say that, of course." There are no indications that anybody thought seriously about the consequences for people who might end up unable to make a mortgage repayment or with a pension much lower than they had been led to believe, and far lower than if they had stuck with their employer schemes. And in the case of personal pension plans, the commissions to IFAs were set, intentionally or otherwise, at a level that was bound to compromise their independence and thus reduce the customer's ability to make rational informed choices.

Whatever the small print, the marketing message with these promotions was as follows: these products are good for you; trust us; you can trust us because we are the people who protect you by insuring your lives and homes; and you can also trust your friendly IFA. The ethical problem was partly that the firms, while exploiting people's trust, do not seem to have acted in a trustworthy way. As we have noted before, breaches of trust fail the test of Kant's Formula of Universal Law. In the case of split-caps there was also a play on trust, but of a different kind. In this case the products were quite complex and the investment firms promoting them asked customers to trust them on the technical side: you may not understand the details of these products, but they will do what they say on the packet. They didn't do what they said on the packet, of course, because market conditions turned out unlike anything their designers had envisaged, so again we have to ask whether their expectations were reasonable and whether they gave sufficient attention to the impact on customers of different market scenarios. For investment firms making their money primarily as intermediaries, taking fees rather than relying on market gains, market outcomes matter much less than they do to individual customers. Putting themselves in the place of those customers is difficult, but when customers rely on their technical judgments, it is something they should surely be doing.

In the cases of payment protection insurance and the sale of interest rate swaps to small companies, an additional factor to those already considered seems to have been confusion between the interests of bank and customer. Both were presented as products that served the customers' interests, insuring them against being unable to make repayments in one case and against rising interest rates in the other. But both also protected the bank against the risk of default, in one case directly and in the other case by frontloading the costs to the customer. Usually, when we seek to insure ourselves against default, we have to pay, but here the bank was actually paid by the customer – and paid handsomely – to be insured!

These products were designed to meet the interests of the banks, ensuring that they were protected whatever happened to interest rates. Therefore, the banks had no reason to think about the consequences of different interest rate scenarios for themselves, and it is not clear that anyone thought about those consequences for their customers. As before, the failings can probably be attributed to negligence rather than intent, perhaps the unintended effects of the banks' internal incentive systems. But the end result was that the ways in which the products were sold took little account of the customers' needs or of their being in a position to make rational informed choices. In some cases, customers certainly sought to blame the banks for their own bad judgments, but complex swaps should never have been sold to small businesses and the mis-selling of payment protection insurance was far too widespread to be anything other than the banks' responsibility.

The most interesting case in respect of customer or client relationships is the Goldman Sachs one. Set aside John Paulson's involvement, which was ethically dubious, and the omission to mention his role, which was clearly wrong but probably unintended, what we have here is a bank selling its clients a complex product that it is convinced will lose them money. The senators investigating the case seemed to take the view that by taking a position against that of its clients, even though that position was declared in the prospectus, the bank was de facto in breach of its ethical responsibilities to those clients. The press and public seem to have agreed, and given what has emerged since about Goldman's attitude to its clients more generally, it is tempting to follow suit.[6] The bank sold a product in the confident expectation that it would harm its customers, and in the normal run of things, that would clearly be wrong. Two things distinguish this case from the normal run of things, however. Goldman's clients on this occasion were hedge funds and other sophisticated investors with no excuse for not understanding what they were buying. And part of the service provided by investment

[6] See, for example, Greg Smith 2012.

banks like Goldman Sachs is to act as a counterparty for gambles their clients wish to make.

Usually the investment banks act as bookmakers and try to lay off the bets they take, but not always. When Bankers Trust acted as a counterparty to the products it sold P&G, the problems lay in the lack of price transparency and the ways in which it exploited this (and kept its clients in ignorance), not in its interest as counterparty. In the Goldman Sachs case, the pricing was transparent and out of its control, and the situation was little different from that which would have arisen had it been trading in third-party products. In a sense, it was taking the role of the bank in a casino and, as in a casino, it expected to win. Like a casino, it was giving its clients something they really wanted and something that was essentially no different, and no riskier, than other banks were supplying. The investors, hungry for this type of gamble, would have found ways to lose their money anyway. All Goldman Sachs did was to set things up so that it took, or shared in, the profit. From its perspective, it was playing the same game as everyone else in the industry and by the same rules, just playing it better.[7]

Having said all that, Goldman did misrepresent Paulson's involvement in the deal, both when setting it up and when promoting it, and rather like the sellers of private pension plans, they did play on a reputation for integrity that was based on quite different historical activities and attitudes.

In both Kantian ethics and virtue ethics, we will distinguish between intentional misrepresentation and unintended or accidental misrepresentation. What we typically have in the cases in this chapter, however, is something in between, which we might call negligent misrepresentation. We also have negligence in respect of the product itself and its possible effects and outcomes, in respect of the needs, interests and informedness of the clients, and in respect of the match between product and client. So when is negligence – neglecting to think through the consequences of what you do or say – unethical?

The concept of negligence is most familiar from the law of tort, where it is invoked to allocate responsibility for restitution or compensation. However, when used in this context, it carries neither ethical nor criminal connotations. When the neglect is of human life and safety and the damage done goes beyond what can be compensated for financially, negligence also

---

[7] For a more hostile take on Goldman Sachs, see Santoro and Strauss 2013.

becomes a criminal offense (in US and UK law), but only in extreme cases: manslaughter, death by dangerous driving, child neglect. In general the criminal law requires at least recklessness, taking risks that impact on other people when fully aware of the possible consequences, and even then it is mainly brought to bear only when the consequence is physical harm or injury, not when it is financial.

The difficulty in treating negligence from an ethical perspective, reflected in this criminal law approach, is that two people can be equally negligent with dramatically different consequences. Indeed, for every person whose negligence causes harm, there may be thousands who are equally negligent but with no adverse consequences. The civil law offers a pragmatic solution: compensation is required, but no moral blame is imputed. But it still leaves us with an ethical question. If a negligent provider of financial products that turn out badly for customers is ethically wrong, are not the equally negligent providers of products that turn out OK (as most of these products might well have done) equally wrong? And are we not in danger, then, of condemning most product providers and, more broadly, most people? Who can claim, after all, never to have been negligent when driving a car?

The ethical problem to which this relates is the problem of moral luck.[8] On the one hand, it seems evident that people shouldn't be judged differently from an ethical perspective on the basis of factors that are outside of their control. How markets turn out would be one such factor. On the other hand, it seems evident that we often do judge them differently. We seem to judge those who rob us as worse than those who try but fail, and those whose negligence causes an accident as worse than those whose equal negligence does not.

Philosophical responses to this problem vary. Some suggest that consequences are rarely due just to chance and that in many cases people *should* be judged differently according to how things turn out. We might argue, for example, that financial institutions cannot just blame outcomes on market movements, since accommodating these movements lies within their claimed area of expertise and control. Just as we hold airlines and pilots responsible for the safe flying of their aircraft, regardless of weather

---

[8] For the classic treatments, see Nagel 1979, Chapter 3; and Williams 1981b. For a review, see Nelkin 2008.

conditions (if the conditions are too uncertain, they shouldn't fly), so we should hold financial institutions responsible for the safety of their clients, regardless of market conditions. We are still in the realm of civil negligence here, and it remains debatable whether the institutions we have reviewed were ethically wrong or simply owed compensation, but this argument would at least hold them responsible for outcomes.

Others suggest that we do not in fact judge cases differently according to chance outcomes; we only appear to do so. We might argue, for example, that we have *evidence* of negligence on the part of the providers of failed products that we do not have in other cases. We might reasonably judge people ethically negligent given this evidence, but could not reasonably do so without it.

However we might resolve the question of moral luck, it would seem reasonable in looking at the cases in this chapter, many of which came to light only because things turned out unexpectedly, to look both at the cases as presented and at those with which we would have been presented had things worked out differently. Where we draw the line between negligence as conceived in civil law and negligence as ethically wrong is always going to be hard to judge. We can look for indications of greed, recklessness and disdain or contempt for clients on one hand, and of honest misjudgments on the other, but we rarely know exactly what people were thinking, what they were intending or what maxims they were following.

9 Financial reporting and corporate governance

In this chapter we shall conclude our survey of specific topics in finance by looking at some issues that cut across finance and accounting. We begin with financial management and financial reporting. A major ethical concern within financial reporting is earnings management, which can be a simple matter of accruals, but also uses financial products to alter the way in which a company's performance is reflected in its financial accounts. Financial products also play a part in the way in which the accounts of both companies and individuals are presented to the revenue authorities for tax assessment. Questions of corporate governance have come to be dominated in recent years by arguments drawn from finance theory and by the interests of financial institutions. General ethical concerns have focused on the relationship between shareholders and other stakeholders, and we shall look at this with particular reference to institutional shareholders. A more specific ethical concern has been with CEO pay and performance, and we shall look at this with particular reference to the performance and pay of bank CEOs.

Earnings management

A company's financial reports are supposed to give a true and fair view of its financial position to shareholders, creditors and other interested parties. Shareholders rely on these reports to monitor the company's management. Investors and potential investors rely on them to determine the company's value, and lenders, suppliers and customers to assess its viability. A company's directors and senior officers are both legally and ethically bound, whatever ethical criteria may be chosen, to produce reports that are as accurate as possible and in no way misleading. (Under the Sarbanes-Oxley Act, an American company's CEO and CFO now have to personally certify the accuracy of financial reports.) External auditors are also bound to give an honest and competent assessment of the accuracy of the reports. Accounting procedures are not so rigid, however, as to uniquely determine what the figures contained in the financial reports should be. In particular, both assets and liabilities may be of uncertain value, and the attribution of gains and losses across accounting periods may be open to interpretation.

In these circumstances, many firms seek to smooth their reported earnings across periods, knowing that each reported performance acts as a benchmark for the next one; that shareholders react much better to stable or steadily improving performance than they do to alternating good and bad periods; and that they react badly when analysts' consensus earnings estimates are not met. This is common industry practice and to the extent that short-term performance figures may actually be misleading or reflect arbitrary circumstances, it seems unobjectionable. However, in any case of smoothing, there is always a possibility that future performance may not move in the direction anticipated and that the adjustment may deviate from the mean instead of approaching it. When the earnings adjustments are intended to mislead, whether to increase executive compensation or to mislead regulators or contractual parties (e.g., by manipulating capital ratios in a bank or evading breach of a debt covenant), there is clearly an ethical problem.

Most of the techniques of earnings management lie within the realm of accounting rather than finance. Accruals are used to shift costs or revenues from one period or another. Year-end asset values are over-stated or under-stated. Profits and losses are taken on a mark-to-market or mark-to-model basis when it is convenient to do so, but are not when it isn't. Expenses are booked as capital when they should be revenue. One-off acquisition or restructuring costs are inflated (the "big bath") to hide operating losses, create hidden reserves for future adjustments (the "cookie jar") or just manipulate shareholder expectations. Assets are sold at inflated prices with an unstated promise to buy them back again the following week. The auditing rules on materiality, which allow auditors to ignore errors that are not "material" with respect to the overall accounts, are cynically exploited.[1]

[1] Jennings 1999. See also Jennings 2011, pp. 218–28 (Tyco), 233–46 (Enron) and 293–310 (WorldCom) for well-documented case studies of earnings management practices. The WorldCom case makes particularly interesting reading, especially when set alongside Jack Grubman's puffing of the stock, discussed in the previous chapter.

Nevertheless, in some cases, firms resort to financial management or to the valuation of financial products to manipulate their reports. General Electric reported increased earnings for 50 straight quarters, and so long as earnings were generally heading upwards, nobody particularly minded if there was some period-to-period massaging. From 2000 to 2005, however, by which time the business was no longer growing as it had in the past, the financial statements suggested that it was. This required some creativity, in this case around its quarter-end valuing of interest rate swaps.[2] At the height of the CDO boom, Citigroup, which as a bank regulated by the Federal Reserve was subject to much tighter leverage ratios than its investment bank competitors, concealed its CDO holdings in off-balance-sheet SIVs. The CDOs were bought by the SIVs, using repo finance, with Citigroup committing to re-buy them should they fall in value.[3]

SIVs also played a big part in Enron's accounting in the late 1990s, and another earnings management technique used here, and provided by Enron's bankers, Citigroup and JP Morgan Chase, was the prepaid swap, which effectively disguised a loan as an asset by taking the cash borrowed into the accounts and concealing the repayment obligation (see Box 5.3). In the 2000s, something similar was achieved by Lehman Brothers, which used year-end repo transactions initially to manipulate its balance sheet to meet regulatory criteria, but then to increasingly misrepresent earnings. Box 9.1 summarizes the Lehman case.

An initial take on the ethics of earnings management might be that it is simply telling lies and is doing so, moreover, to people who have a strong and legitimate interest in knowing the truth: shareholders, creditors and regulators. In the more extreme cases highlighted here, we probably need to go no further. Arguments for utility or virtue will likely lead to the same conclusion. However, less extreme cases are much harder to judge.

From a utilitarian perspective, for example, it seems likely that a modest amount of earnings management might be beneficial. Some smoothing of results from one period to the next reduces the emotional responses that can easily arise from small but insignificant movements in measured results, allows the managers to get on with managing the firm free of too many distractions and reduces unproductive share trading. At what point these benefits turn into costs, as the misrepresentation of earnings leads to

---

[2] www.sec.gov/news/press/2009/2009-178.htm.   [3] Madrick 2011, p. 390.

Box 9.1. Lehman Brothers and Repo 105s

The iconic event of the 2008 financial crisis was the collapse of the investment bank Lehman Brothers on the night of September 14. Everybody knew that Lehman Brothers was in trouble. It was the most heavily indebted of the major investment banks and the most exposed to the property markets. Already a high-risk operation, it had decided in spring 2006 to increase its risk profile further by moving away from the traditional investment banking activities of broker-dealing, securitizing and underwriting, and increasingly trading and holding assets on its own account. In 2007 it had paid over $5 billion for a highly leveraged real estate investment trust. And when the housing market had faltered in the summer of 2006, it had not only continued to acquire subprime mortgages but had stepped up its activities in pursuit of what it called a "countercyclical growth strategy," routinely disregarding its own risk policies and risk limits. Between 2006 and 2007, it almost doubled the mortgage-related assets on its books to $111 billion. In 2008 it ceased purchasing property assets and tried to restore both its capital base and its liquidity. Nevertheless, it failed a liquidity stress test conducted by its regulators, and the trade in CDSs on its debt suggested that the markets expected it to fail – which it ultimately did when its lenders refused to renew their credit lines.

Remarkably, however, Lehman Brothers kept giving out positive statements about its financial position right up to the end of August 2008, just days before its collapse. It insisted that it had passed its own severe liquidity stress tests and that its balance sheet was in good order.

The major factor in the discrepancy between the financial position of Lehman Brothers as presented by the company and its financial position as increasingly perceived from outside was an over-stating of its assets by a figure of, as far as we can now tell, around $50 billion – a figure almost double its capital base of $28 billion (meaning that it was for some time technically insolvent). And the main way in which it maintained that over-statement was through a quarterly manipulation of its accounts using what were known as "Repo 105" transactions. Essentially, this practice, which had been ongoing for about seven years, involved a sale and repurchase agreement. Assets would be sold before the end of an accounting agreement and treated in the accounts as sold, but the firm also had an obligation to repurchase them the following month. The initial aim was to temporarily replace one class of asset with another so as to meet the capital ratios required by regulators. Where the assets had no clear market price, however, the practice could also be used to artificially inflate asset values by using a high value for the repo transaction, and by 2008, it was effectively inflating assets by about $50 billion. And, of course, none of this was disclosed; indeed, the footnotes to Lehman's audited financial statements falsely stated that it accounted for all its repo transactions as financings (i.e., as loans to be repaid), not as sales.

Where, one might ask, were the auditors in all this? As Jonathan Weil stated in a later Bloomberg report, "any freshman accounting major can tell you that ... it's a violation of accounting principles for a company to tell investors it's using one type of accounting treatment when it's actually using another, especially when the method it's secretly employing makes its balance sheet look stronger." Given the publicity afforded the Enron malpractices, which came to light around the time the Repo 105s were first used, one would have expected a top accounting firm to have been watchful. But while Ernst & Young, which was Lehman's auditor from the time this practice was initiated to the firm's collapse, knew of the Repo 105 practice, it did not question Lehman's failure to disclose it. According to the bankruptcy examiner's report, it "took no steps to question or challenge the non-disclosure." Even when it was told explicitly by a Lehman executive in May 2008 that the practice was improper, it seems to have done nothing to investigate the allegations.

In December 2010, just two weeks after issuing a press release promoting its services in fraud prevention, Ernst & Young was sued for fraud by the New York Attorney General. The company vigorously denied any wrongdoing.

Sources: Financial Crisis Inquiry Commission 2011, supplemented by news coverage of the legal action. The Weil quote is from "Ernst & Young is nuts to say Lehman was clean," December 23, 2010, available at: www.businessweek.com/news/2010-12-23/ernst-young-is-nuts-to-say-lehman-was-clean-jonathan-weil.html.

inappropriate risk-taking or unsound investment decisions both in the firm and amongst those relying on its reported results, is hard to say. The auditing standards provide one pragmatic way of drawing the line with their reference to materiality. There are no rigid rules here, but auditors will generally overlook errors in net income statements or asset valuations of 5 percent or even 10 percent, the underlying idea being that accounts drawn up on any particular date are only approximately representative and that worrying about detailed changes within these error margins is productive for neither the company nor the auditors, nor those using the accounts.

This last observation is also important from a Kantian perspective, the point here being that there is no such thing as a perfectly "true" or accurate set of financial accounts. When auditors opine that a company's accounts give a "true and fair" view, they are referencing a rather approximate notion of truth. Accounting statements are better understood as constructions of knowledge according to a myriad of conventions, assumptions and social practices than as revelations of some independently existing knowledge. Almost nothing in accounting is black and white, and many of the things that are included in a set of company accounts could plausibly have been accounted for differently.[4] The accounts are rather like a photograph, taken at a particular time in a particular light and from a particular angle. They are standardized according to certain conventions so as not to misrepresent, but can never be a perfect or unique representation.

In this context, we probably need to judge earnings management on two dimensions. First, what is the intention? Is the intention to provide a fair account of the state of the company around the year-end, perhaps ironing out some of the quirks that arise from the year-end being one day rather than another and making adjustments where the standard valuation procedures would, in the circumstances, have been misleading? Or is the intention to deceive, to encourage readers to think that the state of the company is other than the managers honestly consider it to be? Second, what is the extent of the adjustment? Is it within the effective error margins of the accounting process and the standards adopted, or is it materially beyond those margins?

If the adjustments are immaterial and are intended to give a fair view, then no ethical problem would seem to arise. The practice can be universalized and perhaps beneficially so. If they are material and intended to deceive, then they are clearly unethical on Kantian grounds. There is an intention to deceive and that intention would be thwarted if the practice were universalized, giving a contradiction of conception. Adjustments that are intended to deceive but immaterial are more problematic. A maxim of using earnings management to deceive so long as the effect is not material is

---

[4] Gill 2009.

rather like a maxim of telling lies so long as they are only small ones. If it were universalized, we could still count on a kind of truth-telling, but what is a small matter to the liar may not be such a small matter to the person being told the lie. Similarly, what is immaterial to the people preparing the accounts may be material to those relying on them. Earnings management, in this context, would seem to carry a responsibility of care and an associated risk of negligence.

Adjustments that are intended to give a fair view but are material are also problematic. The presumption here is that the normal accounting procedures would not give a fair view, but if that is the case, it should probably be stated explicitly and the accounts presented, using notes, on both views. The accounting system relies heavily on the normal rules being followed and people reading accounts assume that this is the case, making their own adjustments for any special circumstances of which they are aware. Suppose, going back to the photograph analogy, that a photograph was being used to judge someone's health, that the photograph was taken, according to standard practice, on a particular day and that, owing to an earthquake, the person had been awake for 72 hours. In this situation, doctoring the photograph to make the person look as they usually did would mislead someone who knew about the earthquake and assumed that what they were looking at was someone who had been awake for 72 hours. Materially doctoring the accounts to make them fair can mislead just as much as materially doctoring them to make them unfair.

Tax avoidance

As well as providing financial accounts for shareholders and others, companies also provide such accounts for the purposes of taxation. So do individuals. In some countries, tax accounts take the form of an opening bid in a negotiation with the revenue services, but the systems used in the USA, the UK and elsewhere are based on self-assessment, the onus being on the firm or individual to make an accurate declaration of taxable income.

When it comes to avoiding taxes, the simplest, if blatantly illegal, way has traditionally been to not declare the income and to hide the money away in numbered Swiss bank accounts, one of the services traditionally provided by the Swiss banks being absolute confidentiality. This option has recently been closed off after persistent pressure from the US government and heavy fines from the US Inland Revenue Service (IRS). In 2009 the Swiss bank UBS was fined \$780 million by the IRS for assisting US citizens in evading taxes on an estimated \$20 billion of account holdings. Swiss law was subsequently changed to allow it to pass over details of US client accounts.[5]

The other common way of avoiding tax is to own up to the income but find legal and regulatory loopholes to avoid paying tax on it, typically by taking out matching financial products that cancel each other out but are taxed differently. Box 9.2 explains a scheme used by the accountants KPMG in conjunction with investment banks, which is typical of the genre.

There are two ethical issues here. One concerns the professional ethics of accounting. According to their professional codes of conduct, tax account-ants have two potentially conflicting duties: to ensure so far as possible that tax returns are "true, correct and complete"; and to assist the taxpayer in paying no more tax than is legally required. Truth here is easier to deter-mine than in financial reporting, as tax law allows much less discretion than financial reporting standards. What is due is what the rules stipulate, not what might be "fair." But the rules are never perfect. They are always trying to catch up with financial practices and there are always loopholes that have yet to be closed. In respect of loopholes, the Statement on Standards for Tax Services issued by the American Institute of Certified Public Accountants (AICPA) in 2009, the relevant professional code here, states that "a member should not recommend a tax return position … unless the member has a good faith belief that the position has at least a realistic possibility of being sustained administratively or judicially on its merits if challenged," which clearly allows for tax return positions that are contested by the IRS but are legally untested, and even for those that might probably fail, should they be challenged, provided there is a "realistic possibility" of their succeeding.[6] In this case, however, it is evident that there was no such possibility. The IRS had declared against the loophole and it was only a matter of time before this was upheld in the courts.

---

[5] www.justice.gov/opa/pr/2009/February/09-tax-136.html. Investigations have since opened up at the second of the large Swiss banks, Credit Suisse.

[6] AICPA, 2009, Statement on Standards for Tax Services, at www.aicpa.org/InterestAreas/Tax/Resources/StandardsEthics/StatementsonStandardsforTaxServices/DownloadableDocuments/SSTS,%20Effective%20January%201,%202010.pdf.

Box 9.2. KPMG's "Son of BOSS" tax avoidance schemes

In 2005, after a hotly contested legal argument, global accounting firm KPMG reached a deferred prosecution agreement with the US IRS, paying a fine of $456 million in respect of tax avoidance schemes. A few months later, a total of nineteen KPMG partners and managers (who were not protected by the deferred prosecution agreement) and others involved in the scheme were indicted by the Department of Justice, four being eventually convicted. KPMG's tax specialists had come up with a range of tax shelters for high-net-worth individuals seeking to offset tax on a minimum of $10–20 million of taxable gains. From 1996 to 2003, the IRS estimated that a total of at least $11 billion of phony tax losses were generated, depriving the IRS (and thus the American public) of at least $2.5 billion of evaded taxes, but earning KPMG over $500 million in fees.

To understand this case, we need first to understand the nature of the tax shelter offered. In general terms, the KPMG shelters were deemed by the IRS to fall into the "Son of BOSS" class. Here the taxpayer typically buys matched long and short stock options. These are then put into a partnership. The options are sold and the partner's funds returned. In economic terms, the taxpayer makes a loss on the deal, but under traditional partnership accounting rules, "contingent liabilities" – liabilities that might never arise – are treated differently in the valuation of partnership stakes from ordinary liabilities or assets. So when the partnership is wound up, the taxpayer declares a tax loss in respect of the asset side of the options, but no matching profit in respect of the liability side.

The basic structure of this kind of tax shelter is simple and ages old. For a fee, and with the help of bankers (in this case reportedly Deutsche Bank), your tax advisor divides $zero into a pair of large matching profits and losses in such a way that the loss is chargeable against tax but the profit is not, either because it is artificially deferred to the distant future or because of some quirk in the tax rules. In 2000, the IRS announced that Son of BOSS arrangements lacked economic substance and were an abuse of partnership laws, that it was changing the rules on contingent liabilities and that losses of this kind would not be tax deductible. Moreover, if transactions of this kind were not explicitly identified on tax returns, taxpayers would be liable to harsh negligence penalties and possible legal action, as well as the tax due. In 2004, in a kind of amnesty, it offered taxpayers who had used the device the chance to settle up without prosecution and with reduced penalties, and by 2005 had reclaimed $3.7 billion of tax due. However, it was not until the end of 2007 that a Son of BOSS scheme was found to be illegal in the courts.

The KPMG schemes seem to have been more sophisticated than that described, and at the time of the IRS and Department of Justice actions had not been found to be illegal. Moreover, the prosecutions of most of the individuals were subsequently dropped, albeit for largely technical reasons. The main components of the KPMG fine were for failure to disclose and register the tax shelters, and for delays in passing information to the IRS when it investigated the scheme in 2002–3, as a result of which some tax was too long overdue to be recovered.

From 2000 on, the scheme was almost certainly in violation of IRS rules, but those rules, and their detailed interpretations, can be and are challenged in the courts. The charges raised included the issuing of false legal opinions in respect of the schemes, but it could well be argued that these were perfectly legitimate legal opinions. In the course of the trial of the four individuals that went ahead in 2008, defense lawyers insisted that their clients acted in good faith, that what they were doing was legal and that they made no effort to hide it: the schemes were not registered as tax shelters precisely because, in the opinion of accountants and tax lawyers, they were not tax shelters but allowable investments. The investments were not kept secret from the IRS, but on the contrary were quite openly declared to them, so that the clients could claim the tax losses. The prosecution argued that investments that were sold in significant numbers over many years and from which no client ever made a profit – all declared large losses – could not be construed as genuine investments, but the prosecution eventually succeeded on the basis of a *judgment* that the accused could not reasonably have believed the schemes to be legitimate, not on a demonstration that they had knowingly acted illegally.

Source: this case is described in Duska et al. 2011, pp. 151 ff. The core information comes from an IRS press release 2005–83 (www.irs.gov/uac/KPMG-to-Pay-$456-Million-for-Criminal-Violations) and a Department of Justice press release no. 05-547 (www.justice.gov/opa/pr/2005/October/05_tax_547.html).

The other issue concerns the use of tax loopholes more generally. Duska *et al.*, analyzing this case, argue that taking advantage of loopholes goes against the spirit of the law and is unethical on Kantian grounds:

> The tax laws were developed with certain purposes in mind, certain objectives that were deemed desirable by duly elected officials. Now in any law there are loopholes that can be exploited … But applying the Kantian universalizability principle we see that if everyone exploited the loopholes the system would not accomplish what duly elected officials thought we needed to accomplish, and indeed might collapse. It is only because most people abide by the spirit of the law and don't exploit the loopholes that the laws continue to function. Those who exploit the loopholes are *free riders* who take advantage of others. That is patently unfair.[7]

This argument is debatable, to say the least. If the practice of exploiting loopholes were universalized, there would be no contradiction in the Kantian sense. Tax rates might have to be increased slightly to compensate, but the system would most likely still function and tax avoiders would still be able to meet their objectives.

The reference to free riders is implicitly to Rawls's principle of fairness or fair play, which seeks to obligate the citizens of a just society to contribute fully to that society, even if doing so doesn't accord to their own narrow interests:

> The principle of fair play may be defined as follows. Suppose there is a mutually beneficial and just scheme of cooperation, and that the advantages it yields can only be obtained if everyone, or nearly everyone, cooperates. Suppose further that cooperation requires a certain sacrifice from each person, or at least involves a certain restriction of his liberty. Suppose finally that the benefits produced by cooperation are, up to a certain point, free: that is, the scheme of cooperation is unstable in the sense that if any one person knows that all (or nearly all) of the others will continue to do their part, he will still be able to share a gain from the scheme even if he does not do his part. Under these conditions a person who has accepted the benefits of the scheme is bound by a duty of fair play to do his part and not to take advantage of the free benefit by not cooperating.[8]

---

[7] Duska *et al.* 2011, p. 155, emphasis in original.   [8] Rawls 1964.

"Doing his part" here might mean paying the taxes intended and not using loopholes. It might, however, mean simply paying the taxes legally due. For libertarians like Robert Nozick, even this requirement can be construed as an infringement of liberty. On Nozick's view, all imposed (as opposed to voluntary) taxes are unethical, beyond those needed for defense and possibly policing. Taxation, according to Nozick, is "morally on a par with forced labor."[9]

Although this view is widely shared among the super-rich, it is hard to sustain in practice. It would be quite possible to have a society in which all public services (from roads to emergency medical services, schools to weather forecasts) were replaced, in effect, by private subscription services. But it would certainly fail ethically on Rawlsian grounds as leaving the most disadvantaged worse off, and also on utilitarian grounds. Indeed, the strongest case that can be made against tax avoidance may well be a utilitarian one. A tax system represents, roughly speaking, a nation's current consensus (backed in this case by an open democratic process) as to what redistribution of wealth is most likely to maximize overall utility. Not taking advantage of loopholes would therefore be a reasonable ethical rule to impose from a rule utilitarian perspective. It is sometimes argued that people and firms taking advantage of loopholes is an essential part of the process by which tax law is refined, but that end could be achieved much more easily and much more cheaply by people simply pointing out the flaws.

Tax avoiders may not share their society's consensus, and some will argue that they add more to utility by using the loophole and investing the money productively, or giving it to their chosen good causes, than by paying the tax. However, very few do this in practice. Indeed, there is not normally any suggestion when people avoid paying tax through loopholes that the resulting distribution is more beneficial for total utility than that intended by the tax laws; it is just more beneficial for them. Taking advantage of loopholes is legal, but from a utilitarian point of view, it appears to be unethical.

A virtue approach would lead to a similar conclusion. From this perspective, each case would have to be treated on its merits, but tax avoidance is typically selfish, insisting on different rules for the avoider than those agreed by society at large. It is generally motivated by greed or avarice and it shows a lack of benevolence or charity.

---

[9] Nozick 1974, p. 169.

Wealthy individuals are not the only ones to avoid tax. Many companies also seek to minimize their tax bills by taking advantage of any loopholes they can. However, the most prominent form of tax minimization by companies is through the use of low-tax jurisdictions and international transfer pricing. Individuals can also make use of low-tax regimes, but only at considerable inconvenience as they have to adjust their lives to meet complex residence restrictions. Companies can move residence much more easily, and to a large degree they can use internal pricing agreements to take their taxable profits where they wish, especially if their operations require little physical presence. The large banks all attribute significant proportions of their profits to offshore tax havens. Amazon takes its European profits in Luxembourg and Google, which used to take them in Ireland, now takes them in Bermuda. Even Starbucks reduces its UK taxable profits virtually to zero by charging royalties from a subsidiary in the Netherlands.[10]

These arrangements attract moral opprobrium, but the principles of international tax minimization are long established and, unlike the tax avoidance discussed above, they are largely accepted by the tax authorities. This is partly because doing anything about them would be incredibly difficult and partly because they serve more to defer tax than to avoid it. Corporate profits are in a sense unrealized gains. Although they accrue to the shareholders, the shareholders cannot take and use them without paying tax again in the form of personal income tax if they take them as dividends or capital gains tax if they sell their shares. Acceptance by the revenue services doesn't necessarily make these tax practices ethical. We might well argue, for instance, that virtuous business owners would endeavor to pay their full share of taxes in countries in which they did business, rather than to minimize their total tax bills. But the practices don't typically involve any deception and the rule utilitarian argument that we used above becomes less straightforward in this context. We leave further analysis as an exercise for the reader.

Corporate governance: shareholders and other stakeholders

Fifty years ago, questions of corporate governance would probably not have been seen as part of finance. Over the last two generations, however, the

---

[10] www.bbc.co.uk/news/business-20288077.

problems of corporate governance have increasingly been portrayed as arising from an economic agency relationship between shareholders (as principals) and managers (as agents). The duties of corporate managers have increasingly been cast in terms of a duty to shareholders. Shareholding has become increasingly dominated by financial institutions, and the duties of management have accordingly been cast in financial terms.

One result of these developments is that the ethics of corporate governance have become very confused. On the one hand, the agency theory of corporate governance, like the rest of finance theory, is morally neutral. The problem it addresses is how shareholders can get managers to act in their (the shareholders') interests, on the assumption that the managers are opportunistic self-seekers. Technically, at least, there is no place in the theory for "duty." On the other hand, there is an underlying assumption that the shareholders are the people or institutions whose interests really count, and while this is sometimes expressed in terms of company law or in terms of the overriding logic of shareholder capitalism, it is also often expressed in terms of an explicitly ethical duty on managers.

Expressed in terms of an agency relationship between shareholders and managers, the problem of corporate governance is largely one of the quoted company with diversified shareholdings. This form, which is distinctively Anglo-American, emerged in the late nineteenth and early twentieth centuries as new technologies created the potential for massive economies of scale. First in the USA, then in the UK, companies grew and merged to exploit these, and as they did so, the link between the ownership of companies and their management was broken. Whereas once all companies had been managed by their founders and then by their families, and had been localized in a town or city, the large corporations of the twentieth century were diversified in both ownership – first through multiple mergers and then through the issue of stock on the exchanges – and geography.

The result was a separation of ownership and control. In the early 1930s, the American lawyer Adolph Berle and the economist Gardiner Means identified what we now think of as the agency problem of corporate governance, pointing to a potential divergence between the interests of a company's owners or shareholders, now a diversified group with no direct contact with the company's operations, and its professional managers. Responding to their work, another lawyer, Merrick Dodd, pointed out another consequence. Whereas family-owned companies tended to make significant social contributions to their local communities, the managers of the new corporations, if they ran the business in the interests of shareholders whose interests were merely financial, had no license to do this. Quite right, said Berle: the managers' duties should be to their shareholders. The company was their property. Besides, if managers did not have a clear responsibility to one party, they would end up being responsible to no-one. Not right at all, said Dodd: companies have a broad range of social responsibilities and these should be reflected in the responsibilities of their managers.[11] Thus began the debate that dominates contemporary discussions of corporate governance: should the managers run a company for the financial benefit of the shareholders alone or for a multiplicity of stakeholders, also including customers, suppliers, employees and communities?

Free market economists argue, and the financial community generally assumes, that a company should be run solely for the financial benefit of its shareholders. The classic formulation is due to the economist Milton Friedman:

> The primary and only responsibility of business is to use its resources and engage in activities designed to increase its profits so long as it stays within the rule of the game, which is to say, engages in open and free competition without deception and fraud.[12]

The business ethicist Elaine Sternberg puts it even more strongly:

> Managers who employ business funds for anything other than the legitimate business objective [meaning the maximization of shareholder wealth] are simply embezzling: in using other people's money for their own purposes, they are depriving owners of their property as surely as if they had dipped their hands into the till.[13]

The financial economists Andrei Shleifer and Robert Vishny, in an authoritative review of corporate governance from the perspective of finance theory, sum up the aim of corporate governance research as being "to know how investors get the managers to give them back their money."[14]

This perspective is evidently closely related to the prevailing ideology of financial capitalism, with its broadly utilitarian justification. Wealth (and

---

[11] Berle and Means 1932; Berle 1933; Dodd 1932.   [12] Friedman 1970, pp. 32–3.
[13] Sternberg 2000, p. 41.   [14] Shleifer and Vishny 1997, p. 738.

hence utility) is maximized by free market competition driven by financial self-interest. Where there is no single owner whose financial self-interest can be invoked, the shareholders stand in. Overall wealth is maximized by free market competition driven by shareholder wealth maximization. However, this argument is overlaid with other normative considerations. In particular, following Berle, both Sternberg and Shleifer and Vishny invoke the property rights of the shareholders, interpreting the ownership of the company as being just like the ownership of any other goods.

Against this, critics of the shareholder view have argued on Kantian grounds that, regardless of any considerations of ownership, treating people as ends rather than merely as means imposes a duty on managers to take seriously and give weight to the interests of all of a firm's stakeholders to the point of engaging them in the decision-making process.[15]

Other views of the problem take a more nuanced view of property rights and ownership. In line with contemporary economic theories of the firm, the firm is envisaged as a nexus of contracts involving shareholders, managers and other stakeholders, each of whom may have a bundle of contractually based property rights.[16]

Many financial and economic treatments accept this nexus of contracts model, but still treat shareholder interests as paramount. Oliver Williamson, whose transaction cost economics has been particularly influential on legal debates, recognizes that shareholders are not the only people with a claim on a company, but argues that since they have only a residual claim on a company's assets and no contractual protection, their interests can only be protected if they are given priority.[17] Finance scholars typically follow an agency theory approach and adopt the perspective of financial capital, with shareholders as the focal principals. When Shleifer and Vishny write of investors getting their money back, as in the quote given above, this is strictly speaking an account of the world as seen by shareholders, but it segues into an account of how the world should be seen. One of Berle's arguments for shareholder dominance, against Dodd's stakeholder view, was that it was the only practical way of disciplining managers, and this argument is often invoked today. Reference is also made in the US context

---

[15] See, for example, Bowie 1998; Freeman and Evan 1990.
[16] Alchian and Demsetz 1972; Cheung 1983; Jensen and Meckling 1976.
[17] Williamson 1985.

to a legal or fiduciary duty on the directors of the company to run it primarily for the benefit of its shareholders.[18]

On the stakeholder side, the nexus of contracts approach is used to model the firm as a cooperative venture in which willing participants, including shareholders, take on obligations of fair play. Reference here is typically to Rawls. Robert Phillips, for example, has drawn on Rawls's discussion of fair play cited in the last section. In the case of a cooperative business venture, Phillips argues, the obligation to fair play is even stronger because the venture is voluntarily entered into.[19] In Tom Donaldson and Thomas Dunfee's Integrative Social Contracts Theory, business is set in the context of a just society modeled on Rawlsian lines and governed by the broad moral norms that would be agreed to by hypothetical contractors in a Rawlsian initial position. This is not enough, in their view, to resolve specific questions of corporate governance and business ethics, beyond basic questions of human rights. But they argue that a social contract argument can also be applied at the micro level of the business acting within its community of stakeholders, and that by taking part in a business venture, shareholders tacitly consent to the norms that would be agreed for the community by actors ignorant of their roles in it.[20]

Let's look at the arguments in favor of shareholder dominance. These can be split into two parts: an argument that makes managers ethically obliged to follow shareholder interests, either on account of their legal or ownership status or as a matter of pragmatics; and an argument that expresses shareholder interests in terms of wealth maximization. With respect to the first part, arguments from law and ownership are both problematic.

Under English law, shareholders are not actually owners of the company, but "members": all they own is a right to the residual assets. Under American law, shareholders are cast as owners, but mainly because the legal form of the private company has been carried over to the very different entity of the public company. Historically, this is perfectly understandable. As the modern corporation evolved, there was no single point at which it became different from the private company. In practice, however, it is very different.

---

[18] For a comprehensive treatment from this perspective, see Monks and Minow 2011.
[19] Phillips 1997. For a fuller review of these debates, see Hendry 2001a, 2001b.
[20] Donaldson and Dunfee 1999.

We tend to take our model of ownership from the simplest cases. I recently bought some potatoes. I now own them and can do more or less anything I like with them, bar assaulting someone or smashing their windows. In more complex cases, however, where ownership is shared or where it is applied to entities that are not just "things," it is much less straightforward. In the corporate context, it is, in effect, a short-hand term for a rather complex bundle of property rights, and while describing these as "ownership" is convenient, it masks the fact that other stakeholders in the firm also have complex bundles of property rights and that the rights of one party are often constrained by the rights of another. The law gives owners a relatively privileged position and there is a duty on managers to respect that, but the privilege is relative. It does not negate the managers' responsibilities to other stakeholders.

In the case of institutional shareholders, who are the principal claimants of ownership rights, the reference to ownership is even more misleading. Trading speculatively on the markets, they happen at any moment to hold shares in listed companies, but this is almost entirely accidental to their main purpose, which is to profit by trading. This is most obviously the case with hedge funds, but is true to a large extent of all actively managed funds.[21] It seems perverse to claim ownership rights for institutions that might own stock only for days or months as part of an automated trading program.

Even allowing for these critiques, there is still the pragmatic argument for shareholder dominance, without which self-interested managers would be left free to juggle the various stakeholder interests to their own advantage. If we accept the dominance of shareholder interests, there is also a pragmatic argument for treating these as tantamount to wealth maximization. The actual interests of the ultimate beneficiaries of pension funds and other institutions may vary widely, and it might well be that some would prefer the companies in which they invest to be run cooperatively with stakeholder interests in mind. But all will be interested to a large extent in wealth maximization, and for most this will be the overriding objective. However, even if we accept the shareholder model on these terms, it does not absolve either shareholders or managers from moral obligations to other parties.

---

[21] Hendry *et al.* 2006.

In another context, the philosopher Thomas Pogge has argued that institutional arrangements such as the agency relationship between shareholders and managers cannot be used to evade moral responsibility.[22] If, as we generally believe, private business owners have moral responsibilities beyond profit-maximization, these responsibilities should apply to the multiple owners of the large corporation as well, *and* to their agents, the managers. To say that the managers should run the company purely in the financial interests of shareholders is, on this view, a straightforward evasion of moral responsibility. To see how this may work, consider a simpler example (not Pogge's) of joint ownership – the joint ownership by several people of a racehorse. The racehorse is purchased for profit and its management is contracted to a trainer, but the profit motive doesn't in any way diminish the normal moral responsibilities associated with keeping an animal, and nor does the division of ownership. All the owners are responsible; indeed, they are in some ways more responsible than they would be as sole owners, because they cannot simply do as they wish (exercising their property rights) with their bit of the horse, but have to have a regard for the whole. The trainer, as agent, is also responsible; again, indeed, even more responsible, because with the division of ownership, the trainer is the only person who can practically take on their collective responsibility.

From this perspective, the pension fund and insurance fund beneficiaries who are the ultimate owners of company shares have the same moral responsibilities as any other owners, the exercise of which is delegated to the institutions and again to the company managers. There is just one more link in the agency chain. Moreover, the fact that the institutions are traders doesn't absolve them from those responsibilities any more than someone who trades in animals is absolved from responsibility for the brief period they are in her care.

This example also suggests a response to the weaker forms of shareholder theory. While at first sight it might seem that the managers of a quoted company, who cannot possibly know what all their shareholders might want, should as fiduciaries restrict themselves to the common goal of maximizing shareholder value, this embodies an implausibly thin notion of fiduciary responsibility. The essence of the fiduciary responsibility of an agent, as more generally conceived, is to act *for and on behalf of* the principals,

---

[22] Pogge 2002, Chapter 3.

using judgment to interpret their interests and responsibilities in any particular circumstances.

There are limits on agent discretion. David Rodin, building critically on Pogge's observations, points out that managers cannot just take it on themselves to make moral judgments.[23] They must be very careful not to substitute their own aims and values for those of their shareholders, and to the extent that they may be tempted to do this, the Friedmanite admonition is correct. There should always, perhaps, be a presumption in favor of shareholder value as a priority. But while the managers should not impose their own moral values, they cannot evade moral responsibility. To the extent that responsibilities to stakeholders (or corporate social responsibilities) are in line with the ethical standards we would normally expect from privately owned businesses, it would seem to be not only legitimate but, in the absence of any counter-indication, mandatory for managers to act in accordance with them.

Concluding this section, we should note again that the reference is primarily to quoted US and UK firms. Elsewhere in the world, the typical quoted firm remains closely controlled by majority shareholders who can dictate directly to management. Here the ethical issues are more concerned with the obligations of the majority owners to minority shareholders, who are effectively riding on their coat tails. From an ethical point of view, this places the majority owners in an additional relationship as fiduciaries for the minority shareholders. To go back to the racehorse example, if I were to buy a racehorse and then sell one-fifth of it to someone else, that person would have to concede to me the right to determine how the racehorse was trained and managed, but would also expect me to take full responsibility for how it was treated, from an ethical perspective. They would also expect me to respect their ownership share – by not privileging, for example, another racehorse that they owned outright.

In practice, majority shareholders often treat the company as wholly theirs, and this can easily lead to abuses. In this situation, however, the minority shareholders rarely claim ownership rights. They recognize that they are in effect gambling on the company and its owners to deliver them a return.

---

[23] Rodin 2005.

The responsibilities of the CEO

The main focus of the finance literature on corporate governance has been on tying the pay of CEOs and other top executives to shareholder gains, so that the shareholders' interests become their interests. In the early 1990s, this logic was transferred from the world of the finance journals to the world of practice,[24] and in the ensuing twenty years, executive pay has risen inexorably as more and more is paid in the form of incentives. By 2008, the average pay of an S&P 500 CEO exceeded $10 million, nearly 300 times as much as the average pay of American full-time employees in general.[25] CEOs of similar-sized companies elsewhere in the world earn less, but their pay too has risen massively, both in absolute terms and relative to the average employee. In 2011 the average pay of a UK FTSE 100 CEO was over £4 million, about 150 times that of the average worker.[26] Moreover, from 2010 to 2011, a time of economic recession, it soared by a reported 50 percent, while ordinary workers' pay was effectively frozen.[27]

In the public mind, CEO pay is often linked with the bankers' bonuses discussed in Chapter 7, with an extra element of moral indignation arising when CEOs get large pay-offs on being fired from the job: so-called payments for failure. Compared with the bonuses used to incentivize bankers, CEO incentives are in fact much better constructed. They are mainly tied to medium-term share price performance and increasingly include required stockholdings to ensure that, even though they might still be very well paid, CEOs will suffer a loss of wealth when shareholder wealth declines. On the other hand, CEO performance is much less easily measurable than the performance of traders, depending heavily on the work of colleagues and the actions of competitors. With these two effects pulling in opposite directions, we are again left asking whether the incentives are genuine attempts to maximize wealth (and, on the model of financial capitalism,

---

[24] A critical event was the popularization of the agency theory arguments in Jensen and Murphy 1990.

[25] www.aflcio.org/corporatewatch/paywatch/pay/index.cfm. It then dropped back slightly, but had recovered by 2011.

[26] Report of High Pay Commission, 2011: http://highpaycommission.co.uk/wp-content/uploads/2011/11/HPC_final_report_WEB.pdf.

[27] *Ibid.*

utility) or whether they are the products of collusion and an unethical appropriation of wealth from other stakeholders.

CEO and top executive pay is set by firms' compensation committees. These are made up mainly of past and present CEOs and are advised by compensation consultants, whose role is to inform the committees of current "market" rates. There is no evidence of collusion as such, but since every firm and every CEO has to be seen as above average (no board would admit to its shareholders that its chosen CEO was below average), there is an inbuilt inflator or ratchet mechanism.[28] Pay simply rises to the point at which something stops it. In Germany and some other countries, it is limited by what is considered socially acceptable. In the USA, the only limitation would be if the senior management pay eats up so much of the profits that increasing it would be directly counterproductive to shareholders.

This process is of course collusive in a weak sense. The CEOs take the pay they are offered, even though they often say, recognizing the way pay packets have spiraled, that they would do the job for half the pay. Jeffrey Moriarty has argued that they should act on these words: that to permit any organizational costs for which there is no corresponding benefit, including their own, is a breach of their fiduciary duties. On this account, CEOs have a moral duty to take *only* that pay which would be necessary to reward and incentivize them, as self-interested actors, to do the job to the best of their ability.[29]

This is an interesting argument, the validity of which seems to rest mainly on whether or not a separation should be made between the CEO who is accepting a pay package and the (same) CEO who is running a company: is the pay package within or outside the fiduciary responsibilities? Most people would probably see it as lying outside, and beyond the charitable or public sectors, few people would consider it immoral to take any pay they were offered. Interviews with large-company CEOs also suggest that when they say they would do the job for half the pay, what they really mean is something like "I would do the job for half the pay, but only if all my peers did likewise. The extra money doesn't matter to me, but my relative status does."[30]

[28] Ezzamel and Watson 1998.   [29] Moriarty 2009.   [30] Hendry 2012.

However, those same interviews also suggest that many CEOs are highly ambivalent when it comes to both shareholder dominance and incentive pay. Taking a stakeholder view of the corporation in which shareholder interests are important but not overriding, they question whether the kinds of people who would be motivated by incentive pay are the kinds of people we should want, as a utility-maximizing society, in charge of our business organizations. The concern being expressed here is partly that the interests of actual shareholders (as opposed to hypothetical long-term owners) tend to be relatively short-term, and partly that the link between business performance and share price performance (which is subject to all sorts of extraneous influences) is too tenuous. Ethical CEOs should ignore any personal incentives and focus their attention as dutiful stewards on using their impartial judgment to look after and develop the business.

A similar line of argument lies behind some CEOs' defense of payments for failure. Properly conducted, they say, the CEO's job is an extraordinarily difficult and very exposed one. The chances of being fired are quite high, especially if the CEO is acting for the business as a whole rather than responding to immediate shareholder pressures, and the consequence is often the end of a career. They might do the job for half the salary (especially if their rivals did the same), but they wouldn't do it without the insurance of a generous severance package built into their contracts, freeing them to focus clearly on the job in hand rather than just their own survival. Although there are surely exceptions, these payments generally do seem to be the result of efficient market contracting.[31]

This apparent rejection of self-interest may of course be self-serving, in that it leaves the managers in control, but the recent history of the banking sector suggests that the view may have some substance. The management of banks has traditionally been entrusted to people whose primary concern was to ensure the bank's solvency and security. On the commercial and retail side, this reflected a belief that the overriding duty of a bank was to its depositors. On the investment banking side, it reflected a professional ethic according to which banks owed a duty of care to their clients, allied to the commercial judgment of an unlimited partnership that the partners' own interests were served by such a professional positioning. In the last thirty years, the shift in emphasis in investment banking from advice to trading,

---

[31] *Ibid.*

the acquisition and absorption by commercial banks of investment banking subsidiaries and the growth of the remaining investment banks, together with their adoption of limited liability status, have all impacted on this traditional approach. It has become relatively common for banks to be led by CEOs from a trading background, focused on risk-based return rather than sound finances and committed to the incentive system.

One of the problems addressed by the agency theory of CEO incentive pay is that CEOs, whose wealth is tied up largely in the company, are perceived as much more risk averse than shareholders, who hold diversified portfolios. One of the aims of incentive pay is, accordingly, to encourage them to take more risks. Conversely, one of the intuitions underlying many CEOs' adoption of a stakeholder perspective and their criticism of incentive structures is that they are not the only ones whose wealth is tied to their companies. The shareholders' risk preferences are influenced by their ability to switch their investments elsewhere in a way that employees and customers cannot easily do. This applies especially in the case of banks, where a company failure can have devastating effects across society, while impacting relatively little on shareholders with diversified portfolios.

In recent years, the agency theory view has dominated, banking regulations have also been relaxed and banks have generally been run in a much less risk-averse way. One of the consequences of this is that banks have got into much greater trouble. Some have gone under and many have had to be rescued by government intervention. What is striking is that the banks which have got into the deepest trouble and those most costly to society as a whole appear to be those that have been run by highly incentivized CEOs, typically from a trading background.

Richard Fuld's "countercyclical growth strategy" for Lehman Brothers was at root no more than a long-odds gamble, but with the whole company as the stake. Jimmy Cayne at Bear Stearns was another aggressive and risk-taking trader. Merrill Lynch's Stan O'Neal was not a trader by background, but became one on assuming the CEO role, taking extreme high-risk, high-return positions. The same can be said of James Crosby at HBOS, who equated strategy with risk-taking and fired his head of risk for questioning the amount of risk the bank could take on. All four banks effectively went bust. Mark Ospel built up UBS through an aggressive acquisition strategy, but never developed an organization that could handle the resulting risks, resulting in a series of costly disasters arising from a lack of organizational control. Sandy Weill's creation of Citigroup was based on the principle that the larger the company grew, the larger the risks it could take on. His successor Chuck Prince was an administrator rather than a trader or entrepreneur, but he inherited a high-risk bank without seeming to understand the implications. In 2007, he famously said, referring to the dangers of highly leveraged lending for corporate buy-outs, that "as long as the music is playing, you've got to get up and dance. We're still dancing."[32] Citigroup has repeatedly had to be rescued by the US government. Meanwhile, the most successful banks, such as Morgan Stanley in the USA or Lloyds in the UK (before it took over HBOS), were run on much more traditional lines. Goldman Sachs, though it may no longer care for its clients, remained in careful control of its risks – and profited greatly as others didn't.

The 2000s were, of course, exceptional years for the financial sector, and many of the participants saw themselves as the victims of unforeseen and unforeseeable circumstances. The press and public saw things rather differently, blaming the crisis largely on the banks. There were, however, other actors involved whom we have yet to consider: the regulators and the politicians who appointed them.

---

[32] www.creditwritedowns.com/2010/04/citigroups-chuck-prince-confirms-that-risky-behavior-drives-out-prudent-when-risk-is-rewarded.html.

10 Epilogue: the ethics of financial regulation

Throughout this book, the financial regulators have emerged as key players. Sometimes we only find out that something is wrong when the regulators act. Often they act in response to public concerns, but it is only when they act that we get enough information to work out what went wrong. Sometimes things seem to go wrong because – or partly because – the regulators fail to act, act too slowly or too softly. One of the conclusions suggested by our discussion of the financial system was that utility might be significantly enhanced by a more effective system of global regulation. Many of the specific ethical problems we have discussed appear to have arisen either from deregulation (e.g., of the banking system and the capital requirements and other constraints under which it operates) or in areas that are effectively unregulated (derivatives trading, ratings agencies, hedge funds, parts of the mortgage industry, etc.), but look like they probably should be regulated.

From the amoral perspective of the financial sector, regulation is no more a moral issue than anything else to do with finance. In line with public choice economics, financial theorists and financial practitioners alike tend to see the regulators as self-interested actors seeking to maximize their own utility. They are part of the economic competition, on this view, not arbiters of it, and while the rules of the game give them certain rights, in particular the right to impose fines or even, *in extremis*, to ban players from the game, they don't give them any moral authority or any particular moral responsibility.

An alternative theoretical perspective, rooted in pluralist conceptions of political action, sees regulators as mediating between political interests. Depending on the particular theoretical viewpoint adopted, they might be seen as mediating between industry and the state, or as representing the state and mediating between competing private sector interests. This gets us closer to moral concerns, but in the political science literature, it rarely gets very close. It simply replaces an economic equilibrium with a political one, the role of the regulator being to find a pragmatic political accommodation between the various interests represented.[1]

These theoretical views provide us with useful descriptions of the regulators' role and useful insights into the process of regulation. The economic view helps us to understand how financial firms respond to their regulatory environments by pursuing their own interests and treating regulatory intervention as an attempt to extract economic rents from them. The political view helps us to understand the challenges posed for regulators by the banks' power and political influence, which severely constrain their scope for action. Neither theory, however, gives a normative account of what regulators should do. To obtain such an account, we need to pick up on the description of regulators as somehow representing the interests of the state, which is how they are seen by society at large, and ask what this entails. To whom are such regulators accountable, and for what are they responsible?

To sharpen this question, consider the deregulation of derivatives trading as summarized in Box 10.1. As far as we know, Phil and Wendy Gramm did nothing illegal, nor was there anything illegal or even unusual about Enron's payments to them. This is how US regulatory politics works. But when the roles of politicians, regulators and the regulated get mixed up in this way, the particular accountabilities and ethical responsibilities of the regulator inevitably get confused.

The responsibilities of regulation

The primary accountability of regulators is surely to the government of the day, but saying this leaves important questions unanswered. In particular, we need to ask to what extent they should be accountable to the committees or ministers to whom they report, and to what extent to the wider public. And insofar as they may be accountable to the public, should their responsibility be expressed in terms of a utilitarian conception of the public interest as an aggregate of individual utilities or a republican conception of the public interest as the common good?

The first of these questions overlaps with a similar question in respect of politicians in government office. Politicians in government may feel duties

---

[1] For an introduction to theories of regulation, see Baldwin *et al.* 2011.

Box 10.1. Derivatives regulation, Enron and the Gramms

By the early 1990s, trading in OTC derivatives had been building for a decade and had spread from purely financial derivatives such as Forex and interest rate swaps to a range of commodity derivatives, including those based on energy prices. Exchange trading of commodities futures were regulated by the CFTC under the Commodities Exchange Act (CEA). Certain financial swaps had been explicitly excluded from the CEA in the 1970s, but there remained some legal uncertainty in the middle. In 1989 the CFTC issued a statement to the effect that it thought it had the authority to regulate swaps but wouldn't do so, and it took no action in particular to regulate energy derivatives, which clearly fell within the CEA and were arguably prohibited unless authorized by the CFTC.

This was the period of the elder Bush administration. The Chair of the CFTC, appointed by President Reagan in 1988, was Wendy Lee Gramm, an academic economist and passionate believer in free markets whom Reagan described as his "favorite economist." Phil Gramm, her husband and also an academic economist, had earlier represented the Democrats in the House, but had jumped ship to join Reagan and had sponsored the first Reagan budget. By 1989, he was a Senator and a member of the Senate Budget Committee. Wendy Gramm's attitude to conduct regulation appears to have been slightly unusual. On resigning as one of the CFTC lawyers many years later, Judge George Painter described how his colleague Judge Bruce Levine had promised Gramm on his appointment that he would never rule in favor of a complainant – and indeed he never did.

In 1992, to clarify the situation, Congress gave the CFTC authority to exempt OTC derivatives from its regulation. At the beginning of 1993, on the back of this authority, with days to go before the Clinton administration took office, and on the basis of a 2:1 majority (including her own vote) of the nominally five-person lame duck Commission, Wendy Gramm issued a clarification of the CFTC's earlier swaps exemption and also a specific exemption for energy-based OTC derivatives. Six days later, she resigned from the CFTC, and a month after that, she was appointed to the board of Enron, an energy company that was moving heavily into derivatives trading.

Move forward seven years to 2000. Enron by this stage was trading heavily in energy derivatives and was making full use of its regulatory freedom, creating false markets in derivatives and falsifying its accounts to show fictitious profits. As a President's Working Group again considered derivatives regulation (by this point, the Clinton presidency was nearing its end), it had also spent $3.4 million in the past two years on lobbying expenses. Wendy Gramm was still on the Enron board and had been serving on its Audit Committee, signing off the accounts. By this time, Phil Gramm was now Chair of the Senate Budget Committee and the second largest recipient of Enron campaign contributions.

Meanwhile, in 1998, the SEC had flagged up the possibility of bringing OTC derivatives traders under its own regulatory wing. The then Chair of the CFTC, Brooksley Born, had responded by inviting comments on whether OTC derivatives regulation should be tightened within the CFTC regime. This elicited extremely strong opposition from derivatives traders, from other regulators, in particular Alan Greenspan at the Federal Reserve, and from Treasury Secretary Robert Rubin and former SEC Chair Arthur Levitt. In response to the outcry, Congress put a hold on any CFTC action and a President's Working Group drawn from the Treasury and the main regulators was set up to report. The report recommended that in the interests of encouraging innovation and providing legal clarity, both of which were essential to the competitiveness of the US financial sector, all non-commodity OTC derivatives should be explicitly excluded from the CEA and from CFTC jurisdiction, but that commodity-based derivatives should remain under the CFTC. This latter point was explicit and unanimous. However, the legislation proposed by the Senate Banking and Agriculture Committees, propelled by the then Chair of the Banking Committee, Phil Gramm, removed the distinction, excluding energy derivatives from CFTC control. And despite the opposition of the CFTC, now chaired by William J. Rainer, who argued, in effect, that unregulated trading in energy derivatives was open to manipulation, that was what was enacted.

Sources: Jickling 2006; Public Citizen 2001; Rainer 2000.

of at least three kinds: duties of reciprocity to the people who put them there (the interest groups they represent or the providers of funding); duties to follow the manifesto policies on which their government was elected; and duties to the public at large, including those who voted for rival parties.

Most people would probably argue that the second and third of these should override the first. The banks, for example, may legitimately lobby for policies that favor them, and in the USA may legitimately give cash support for candidates whose policies they support; moreover, it is accepted as a fact of life that individual politicians will represent or repay them by arguing their case in government. Whether even this is ethical, however, is open to question: many would argue that elected politicians should represent their constituents and the wider public, and not succumb to influences outside the ballot box. And it is generally held that government as a whole should not give such interests special treatment (although in the US case they evidently do), especially if this runs against the public interest, or declared public policy. There is a difference in principle, even if there doesn't always seem to be one in practice, between supporting free financial markets and advancing the interests of the banks. However, the appropriate balance between the first and second duties to declared government policy and the wider public interest is much harder to determine.[2]

Regulators face a similar balance of duties, with the tension between them taking different forms in different political systems. In the UK, regulators are not generally political appointees, and while they clearly have a duty to implement government policy, they also have a strong sense of responsibility to the public interest. The governors of the Bank of England are accountable to the Treasury Committee of the House of Commons, which as a "select committee" has cross-party membership and no decision-making powers. The board members of the FSA are formally appointed by the Treasury itself, part of the civil service. In both cases, appointments are based on expertise rather than politics and members serve fixed terms, cutting across periods of government office. In the USA, in contrast, regulators are mainly political appointees. The board of the Federal Reserve and the commissioners of the SEC, for example, are appointed by the president and their appointments expire on a change of government.

One consequence of the US system has been the appointment by Republican Party presidents of regulators who don't really believe in regulation, or at least believe that it should be kept to an absolute minimum. The prime example here is Alan Greenspan, Chairman of the Federal Reserve throughout the period of bank deregulation and in the years leading up to the financial crisis (see Box 10.2).

---

[2] For an extended commentary on these issues that is still hard to beat, see the founding documents of American political philosophy: Madison *et al.* 1788.

Box 10.2. Alan Greenspan: profile of a regulator

Initially appointed by President Ronald Reagan, Alan Greenspan served as Chairman of the Federal Reserve Board of Governors for almost twenty years from 1987 to 2006. A free market ideologue and member of the Ayn Rand circle, the young Greenspan was an outspoken critic of both consumer protection and antitrust legislation: an unlikely candidate, one might think, for a regulator. He ran a successful economic forecasting consultancy and campaigned for and advised the Nixon administration before serving in the Ford administration. Returning to private practice, he remained politically active and in 1985 wrote a notorious letter to the Federal Home Loan Bank Board (for a reported fee of $40,000) asking for a waiver of Charles Keating's Lincoln Savings & Loan Association from new prudential state regulations that would have limited its investments in non-mortgage investments, and stressing in particular Keating's management qualities. Whether the letter had any effect is unclear – the Reagan administration had been active in deregulating the savings and loans and was already inclined to resist any attempts at new controls. But Keating got his waiver. Within a few years, Lincoln Savings & Loan Association was bust, costing the government $3.4 billion, as indeed were many other savings and loans (the total cost to the government was around $150 billion). Thousands of customers were left with worthless bonds and Keating was eventually jailed. Meanwhile, Greenspan had been appointed by Reagan to chair the Federal Reserve.

Greenspan's priorities at the Fed were concerned more with monetary policy than bank regulation, but he remained a strong opponent of conduct regulation, contributing to the rejection of derivatives regulation in the late 1990s, and also a strong friend of Wall Street, helping to keep the banks protected from the consequences of their own misjudgments through repeated federal bail-outs (though he vociferously opposed bail-outs in other sectors as market interference). In supporting the sector, he was helped by a series of key government appointments of Wall Street insiders to senior policy positions. Reagan had already appointed as his Secretary to the Treasury Don Regan, CEO of investment bank Merrill Lynch. Clinton's appointment to the same position was Robert Rubin, formerly Co-Chairman of Goldman Sachs and subsequently Vice-Chairman of Citigroup.

Sources: Greenspan 2007; Martin 2000.

Greenspan has been strongly criticized for repeatedly bailing out American banks using state funds and for his role in the financial crisis, in particular for engineering the housing bubble through his low interest rate policy and for his relaxed attitude to banking regulation. However, he clearly acted in line with the policies of the Republican administrations he served and could reasonably take his reappointment by the Clinton administration as an endorsement of the policies he had pursued under Reagan and George Bush Sr. He also acted in line with his own strong belief in what served the public interest. An ardent defender of free markets with minimal regulation, he believed that these served the public interest both in a utilitarian sense – in line with the arguments for the financial system outlined in Chapter 4 – and in a republican sense. Unregulated free markets, in his view, encouraged virtues of self-reliance and norms of individual freedom, the adoption of which was critical to the common good. Free markets were good for everybody, even if they suffered financially from them, because of the virtues and values they instilled.

Greenspan was surely acting ethically as he saw things, and we might say that that is all we can ask of someone, but the consequences of his policies do not in fact seem to have been good from a utilitarian perspective – indeed, they probably caused considerable harm – and it is arguable that the common good was not served even on his own interpretation, let alone on more liberal interpretations. There is a striking contradiction between the imposition of free market discipline on ordinary people, through the minimization of con- duct regulation, for example, and repeated government rescues of the banks. This seems to say something along the lines of "you are responsible for looking after yourselves, *unless* you're rich and powerful, in which case the state will look after you," a message that seems rather unlikely to advance the common good. The ethical problem here is blindness to the problems arising from one's policies. Whether one follows rules or guidelines based on utility, virtue or Kantian laws, there is surely some ethical responsibility to monitor the out- comes and reconsider the rules or guidelines, and the arguments by which they were derived, if things appear to go badly.

Turning to the other regulatory bodies, the key figures in recent Republican administrations have all held strong political views. William H. Donaldson and Christopher Cox, who between them chaired the SEC from 2003 to 2009, had both held government office in Republican administrations and Cox had been a Republican Member of Congress. Under their chairmanship, the SEC, despite a budget of over $900 million by 2005, failed to monitor the broker-dealers' maintenance of capital ratios, both failing to ask for the relevant information and failing to review the information supplied.[3] John M. Reich, who chaired the OTS from 2005 to 2009, was a staff officer for a Republican senator before becoming a regulator and an outspoken champion of lighter regulation. Under his direction, the OTS failed to do anything much to oversee the doomed insurance giant AIG, even though the creation of a savings subsidiary in 1999 had brought the company under its supervision. A 2009 report by the US Treasury also found it culpable of adding significantly to government losses from the failure of IndyMac Bank through lax oversight and knowing acceptance of regulatory misdemeanors.[4] John Dugan, appointed OCC Comptroller in 2005, had served in the administration of Bush Sr. and had been one of the architects of banking deregulation. Though an able and well-respected figure, Dugan seems to have had little financial expertise himself and, defending his agency in 2008, he gave accounts of the trading in CDOs by the banks under his supervision that have been described as "alarming" in their naivety.[5]

There is no reason to doubt that these were all honorable men doing what they thought best. But they were also people with a strong political commitment to the minimization of regulation, put in charge of regulatory agencies each of which was treated by the firms it regulated more as a nuisance and as a competitor than as an authority. This inevitably compromises the regulatory role. Even if the politicians and regulators are acting with good intentions, it opens the way for unchecked unethical behavior on the part of the firms being regulated.

The appointments of Democrat presidents have generally been much less political. Bill Clinton left Greenspan in charge of the Fed despite his strong Republican convictions. His SEC Chairman, Arthur Levitt, was a Democratic Party member, but had not been politically active. Barack Obama left Dugan in post at the OCC, left Ben Bernanke, a Republican Party member, in post as Chairman of the Federal Reserve, and appointed the politically independent career regulator Mary L. Shapiro to the SEC. The issue for the Democrats is that their political supporters are too busy making money on Wall Street to want to regulate it. Whereas the Republicans are supported financially by the oil sector

---

[3] Soule 2010.
[4] *Ibid*; www.ustreas.gov/inspector-general/audit-reports/2009/oig09032.pdf.
[5] Soule 2010. For general discussion, see also Davies 2010.

and the military-industrial complex, Democrat support comes largely from the financial sector, and while the party may preach stronger regulation, it serves its interests not to practice it. This poses its own problems, of course. In the US context, both the amount of regulation and the interpretation of the public interest are highly politicized. If a Republican regulator, with well-known views on the need for deregulation and on what is good generally for the country and the public interest, is appointed by a Democrat president, with rather different views on these issues, how should he act?

The situation in the UK is very different. With politics dominated by centrist and broadly social democrat parties, there is a broad political consensus on the appropriate extent of regulation. There also seems to be a general if rather fuzzy consensus on the nature of the public interest, corresponding to what in the USA would be termed "liberal values": a balance between individual freedom and social justice in a caring society. Howard Davies and Callum McCarthy, who between them chaired the FSA from 1997 to 2008, both combined extensive private and public sector experience and commanded cross-party support. So too did their successor Adair Turner, who was more politically active (he was a member of the centrist Social Democratic Party) and had built his career in the private sector, but was widely respected for both his ability and his independence. When a new Governor of the Bank of England was appointed in 2012 to succeed Mervyn King (an academic and long-serving bank staffer), the UK Treasury turned to a Canadian, again seeking the most able regulator rather than one who would toe a particular line.

The ethical challenge for the UK regulators is that with no strong political guidance, and in a regime in which regulation is conducted through broad principles rather than detailed rules, they have to make their own judgments as to how current government policy and the public interest are to be interpreted and combined.

The challenges of financial regulation

Whatever the political context, financial regulators are faced with a number of practical challenges that between them make the regulation of the financial sector especially difficult.

The first practical challenge, easily forgotten, is that posed by the amoral character and values of the sector. In a talk given in 2000, Howard Davies, then Chairman of the FSA, made the point that regulatory compliance, even if it could be achieved, would never be enough for the system to work effectively. Only if there were an ethical culture and a commitment to integrity in the banks and other financial institutions would the regulatory aims of the FSA, primarily the protection of customers, be achievable.[6] More recently, in the wake of the recent financial crisis, many political leaders have made the same point. But as we have seen, banks no longer do ethics. They do technical compliance, and even that they sometimes do only half-heartedly. This has two consequences. First, even if regulators are able to make ethical judgments as to what should be done, they can only communicate these effectively by translating them into technical requirements. Second, they can rarely rely on industry insiders to blow the whistle when something is going wrong. The cultures of financial institutions, privileging technical means to a given end (profit) over any consideration of appropriate ends, effectively suppress any discussion of moral issues.[7]

A second practical challenge, discussed in Chapter 4, is posed by the global nature of the financial sector, as compared with the national basis of regulation. The major banks and investment banks, hedge funds and asset managers have globalized their activities much more rapidly than governments have been able to coordinate their regulatory requirements. It is relatively easy for them to escape the reach of a particular regulatory regime and to respond to the threat of more onerous operation by moving their operations elsewhere.

This poses particular problems for developing or emerging economies. Following the collapse of communism in Eastern Europe, many of the local banks were taken over and became subsidiaries of banks from Western Europe, in particular Italy and Austria. When the crisis hit in 2008, these quickly took their liquidity back to the home country, deepening the effects of the crisis on the vulnerable emerging economies.[8]

There are moves towards more connected international regulation. The EU has been pushing for regulatory standardization, but as yet to no effect. And the USA has been using its economic power to impose its regulatory requirement on any bank with a US office – and a global bank cannot be without a US office. This has resulted in some tightening of practices, most

---

[6] Davies 2001.

[7] For a rich discussion of this phenomenon in business more generally, see Deetz 1992.

[8] Davies and Green 2010, pp. xxiv–xxv.

noticeably in respect of money laundering and enhanced disclosure requirements on the Swiss banks. In general terms, however, American regulation
is probably not the most effective. Other countries, even those with large
economies and banking sectors like Germany (which has a very strong
regulatory record) and the UK, have not been able to impose themselves in
the same way. Attempts at the international harmonization of regulation
have made little progress apart from Basel II, which relied on the commercial banks acting responsibly and was exploited with gross irresponsibility
by both US and UK banks.

The complexity of the financial system also poses regulatory challenges
unlike those found in other sectors. However regulatory regimes are structured, there are always likely to be trade-offs between the requirements of
monetary policy and those of prudential regulation, and between the
requirements of prudential and conduct regulation. When a government
needs to get money flowing through the economy, it needs the banks to lend
more freely (and thus more riskily) than they would otherwise do and that it
might, from a prudential point of view, want them to do. Strong actions to
curb illegitimate conduct threaten a bank's profits and are seen by the
banks in that light, damaging economic confidence and potentially putting
the system at risk.

At the prudential level, both risk and risk management are inherently
pro-cyclical. As we saw in Chapter 4, movements in financial markets are
self-reinforcing leading to vicious circles that risk management measures
tend only to exacerbate. In falling markets, for example, the enforcement of
margin requirements reduces the immediate risk to lenders, but forces
traders to sell, thus pulling the markets down further, leading to still tighter
margin requirements and so on. The regulatory enforcement of capital
requirements on banks has precisely the same effect, reducing individual
risk but adding to systemic risk.

In many cases, systemic risk arises from limited liquidity rather than
limited capital, and this is difficult if not impossible to regulate effectively.
The issues are essentially the same as with capital ratios: if a regulated
liquidity ratio requirement is breached, the actions necessary to restore the
ratio (sell assets to release cash) tend to make the situation worse, both for the
bank in breach, which is forced into a fire sale which reduces its asset values,
and for the other banks with which it does business. The difference between
liquidity and capital crises is that liquidity crises are by definition very short

term, and with the financial system fueled by high levels of short-term (typically overnight) inter-bank lending, things can unravel very quickly indeed. In the wake of the 2007 crisis, which became in part a liquidity crisis in 2008, some countries have tried to impose significant liquidity ratios, but in general banks depend on their central banks as lenders of last resort to get them out of liquidity problems. Whereas in the post-war period, a commercial bank might hold 30 percent of its assets in liquid form, a typical level today would be more like 1 percent.

Another aspect of liquidity that is almost impossible to regulate is market liquidity, or the ability to find a counterparty to trade with. This is a form of liquidity on which the markets depend and which everyone in the industry wants, and the operating systems of the large exchanges are designed to maintain it. But in the case of OTC-traded derivatives, there is nothing whatsoever that regulators can do to force people to trade, and when these markets grind to a halt, as that for CDOs did in 2008, the traded assets effectively lose all value (since whatever their notional value might be, no-one will actually buy them). Since these assets may be security for other assets, the systemic effects can be fast and severe.

Besides these specifically financial issues, the financial regulatory system also faces a number of challenges common to the regulation of other technical industries, such as food and drug regulation, but in each case to a much greater degree. First, the implementation of regulations tends to lag behind events. The sheer complexity of the financial system and its products and activities make it exceptionally hard to anticipate possible problems, so the regulation tends to be reactive, typically framed in response to crises, rather than proactive.

Second, and separate from the implementation problems, the regulators tend to be at least one step – and often many steps – behind the players. As in the pharmaceuticals industry, for example, the technical knowledge needed to evaluate and understand new developments and to regulate them appropriately lies overwhelmingly within the industry. The people who staff the regulatory agencies are often significantly less able (and are also, of course, much less well remunerated)[9] than the key players in the

---

[9] In 2012, the Governor of the Bank of England, the prudential regulator of the UK banking sector, which is the second largest in the world, earned about £350,000, plus pension contributions – in banking terms, a mere pittance.

banks. They are also at a significant informational disadvantage, as the competitive ethos of the industry ensures that innovators are unlikely to share potentially profitable ideas in advance of their execution. Indeed, one of the most valued and valuable skills in the sector is the ability to circumvent regulatory restrictions; to devise products, especially in an American context, that exploit gaps between regulators, gaps in the rules and the bits of drafting that were maybe clear enough in the context of the technologies around when they were written, but become less so as these evolve.

We might think that this last problem could be overcome in part by some kind of prior approval process such as that which operates in pharmaceuticals, but that is not something the banks and hedge funds would agree to. This brings us to the third, and perhaps most important, challenge: the firms being regulated are immensely powerful. Like large firms in other sectors, they make substantial political donations (in the US context), put a lot of effort into building relationships with key political figures and devote substantial resources to lobbying against regulatory controls. Unlike firms in other sectors, they are also very deeply interconnected both with each other and with every other sector of the economy.

One indicator of the power of the banks is their extraordinary record of serious regulatory breaches.[10] One view of this, and the view taken of it within the financial system itself, is that it shows that the regulators are able to act. When firms break the rules, they are punished. But while the fines imposed look substantial, they are not a serious drain on the banks. Nor, it seems, are they that great an embarrassment to the bankers. The world of finance is complex and criminal fraud can be hard to prove, so even in extremely serious cases, a compromise is often reached under which the firm pays a substantial fine but its executives escape any legal action, continue to take their salaries and bonuses, and move on to the next dubious engagement. No other industry has anything like this record of malfeasance.

Another example of the banks' power is a classic case of regulatory capture, the introduction of VaR models to determine capital ratios. Bank capital ratios were traditionally imposed by regulators in the form of a fixed percentage, but through the 1900s and early 2000s, the banks increasingly pressed the argument that their own mathematical models of risk

---

[10] These are dramatically cataloged in Ferguson *et al.* 2010.

assessment provided a much more scientific method of determining their appropriate capital requirements. Of course, what mathematical models put out is a function of the assumptions you put in, and it turned out here as elsewhere that the assumptions banks were making about the degree to which different risks were correlated – a key determinant of the overall risk measure – were quite unrealistic. They also had an inherent interest in keeping capital requirements to a minimum and were increasingly influenced by the pro-risk culture of their derivatives traders, responsible for an ever-increasing proportion of their profits. But they paid top academics to advance their case and gradually wore down any regulatory resistance. By 2005, the methodology was being applied in most of the leading economies. Moreover, as we saw in Chapter 1, the technical capacity to effectively supervise the application of VaR models was sorely lacking and when the new approach was introduced in the UK and the USA, the banks used it to ramp up their levels of leverage to quite unrealistic levels, massively understating the risks to which they were exposed.[11]

Perhaps the sharpest indication of the banks' power is the recognition on the part of the regulators that many of them are "too big to fail." The problem here is not just the size of the banks and the impact on their millions of retail depositors. Governments can and do provide forms of deposit insurance, though typically only for limited amounts. The real problems arise from the dependence of the whole economy on the smooth working of the banking sector and from the interconnectedness of the sector, which in that respect is like no other. The failure of one of the major banks would have massive consequences. In regulatory terms, the main effect is to compromise prudential controls. Knowing that they will be rescued by government if things go badly wrong, banks may take more risks than they would otherwise. This effect is compounded, some argue, by agency problems. When the risks pay off and the banks make high profits, the beneficiaries are the shareholders and the employees, traders and executives. When the risks don't pay off and the banks have to be rescued, the cost is borne by shareholders and the public through government bail-outs, but not by the banks' managers or other employees. In fact, things are not quite so simple. The public share to some extent in the good times, through taxation, and employees sometimes lose their jobs when

[11] See Madrick 2011; McDonald and Robinson 2009.

things go wrong, but it is striking that many employees do manage to ride through failures of their own creating with only a small check on their accumulation of wealth.

Two episodes in recent history that have resulted in large-scale bail-outs are the Mexican crisis of 1982 and the financial crisis of 2008. Beginning in 1979, American banks, led by Citibank, began to lend heavily to developing countries. The environment was one of high domestic inflation, global economic growth and rising oil prices, and under these conditions the business looked good, but the conditions were unsustainable. As the US government sought to bring inflation under control in the early 1980s, a global recession left developing countries, and in particular Mexico, unable to meet their debt payments. At this point, the government stepped in with emergency lending of $1.5 billion, not to save Mexico but to save the banks that were lending to it.[12]

Though this episode is often cited as an example of irresponsible lending by the banks, it says more about the symbiotic relationship between the banks and the government, which had been quietly encouraging their lend-ing in the first place. In the 2008 crisis, this relationship and the idea that banks were too big to fail were both dramatically tested. The first victim of the subprime mortgage derivative crisis was not one of the big conglomer-ate banks (though Citigroup and UBS had already taken massive losses), but Bear Stearns, an aggressive but relatively small investment bank. Bear Stearns was not too *big* to fail, but the view of the authorities was that it was too interconnected to fail. With federal help in the form of the govern-ment taking liability for $29 billion of toxic assets, the firm was sold to JP Morgan, making one of the largest banks larger still.

When a few months later Lehman Brothers, another investment bank, also went bankrupt, the government decided it was time to take a stand and let the markets take their course. This policy lasted about two days. Not only were most of the big-name banks too big to fail, the regulatory response was to make the biggest banks even bigger. Within 24 hours of Lehman Brothers announcing its bankruptcy, Bank of America had been pressed by the government to buy the investment bank Merrill Lynch, which was also in deep trouble, and a day later the government itself took an 80 percent share in insurance giant AIG at an initial cost of $85 billion. Over a short period,

[12] Madrick 2011 covers this episode well.

AIG received just short of another $100 billion, while Citigroup received $45 billion of capital together with federal guarantees over $300 billion of its liabilities. The other banks also benefited both from significant injections of capital, about $250 million being committed to this purpose, from a $700 billion program to relieve them of toxic assets and from a range of short-term guarantees on bank debt, money market liabilities and commercial paper – a commitment in all of around $12 trillion. The bank executives, by and large, kept their jobs.[13]

When the banks are so powerful, is there anything that regulators, however well-intentioned, can do? One of the more surprising outcomes of the financial crisis was the extent of exposure of German banks, traditionally cautious, conservative institutions operating in a cautious, conservative and self-consciously ethical culture. German banks lost at least $60 billion from their exposure to subprime CDOs, as well as making heavy losses from the collapse of Irish and Icelandic banks. In *Boomerang*, his account of how different nations responded to the easy money of the 2000s, journalist Michael Lewis tells the story of IKB, a small regional German bank that had bought some of the synthetic CDOs sold by Goldman Sachs. IKB's analysts were meticulous in researching which mortgage-backed assets they should invest in. As Lewis puts it, if some of these lost 97 percent of their value and others 98 percent, IKB was quite sure to have the safer, 97 percent ones. But it took it for granted that the American banking sector was well regulated and that the American ratings agencies were competent. It lost $15 billion on a capitalization of $4 billion. The regulatory response? The CEO, Stefan Ortseifen, was given a prison sentence and was required to refund his salary, all €850,000 of it.[14]

This story prompts two thoughts. The first is that the informal rules of a game are effectively set by the players. The Germans, accustomed to a form of the finance game in which the players chose to be guided by the regulators and in which certain standards of behavior could be taken for granted, were out of their depth, innocents abroad, in the game as played by the US banks. The second is that the rules that the players choose depend on the wider cultural context. Finance as a self-interested, amoral activity thrives partly because, whatever the protestations to the contrary, amoral self-interest has acquired a widespread social legitimacy. Where social

---

[13] *Ibid.*   [14] Lewis 2011, Chapter 4.

norms are tighter, as in Germany, and where the domestic financial sector is held morally to account by holding its managers to moral account rather than just fining their companies, it is still possible for the regulators to be effective. And it is still possible to treat finance as part of society and subject to the moral norms of society.

Possible, but very difficult. By 2013, US and UK finance industry insiders were claiming that the sector had learnt the lessons of the financial crisis and was reforming its ways. The flow of scandals showed no signs of ceasing. Investigations into LIBOR rate-fixing, in which bankers mis-reported the rates their banks were paying in inter-bank loans so as increase profits from securities that used the official LIBOR rate (which is based on the figures reported) as a reference, showed the practice to have been endemic. As one bank after another was found guilty of malpractice, it became apparent that the bankers had effectively been conspiring with each other to defraud their customers. This was presented, however, as a hangover from the bad old days. Although it was inevitably taking a while to clean out the stables, we were told, the banks *were* now being driven by the same moral norms as everyone else. But the fundamental characteristics of finance, as described in Chapter 2, have not changed, and nor have the societies in which it operates. Indeed, the legitimacy of self-interest is if anything increasing, while the business cultures of some emerging economies make the culture of American finance seem almost altruistic by comparison. The ethical challenges of finance are unlikely to go away.

Glossary

Arbitrage.	Exploiting a temporary price difference between the same security in different markets, or between near-identical securities, by buying one and selling the other.
ARM.	Adjustable-rate mortgage. An option ARM allows the borrower to choose how much to repay.
Asset-backed securities.	Financial instruments secured on some underlying assets. These can be physical assets, like mortgaged homes, or financial assets, such as unsecured credit card or student loan debts.
Basis point.	One-hundredth of 1 percent.
Bond.	A debt security paying a pre-determined rate of interest over a fixed term and repaying the capital cost on maturity, at the end of that term.
Broker-dealer.	US term for any institution that engages in the buying and selling of securities, on its own account or for clients.
Building society.	*See Thrift.*
Buy-side.	That part of the financial sector concerned with the purchase and management of investment, specifically the asset management firms.

CDO.	Collateralized debt obligation. A form of asset-backed security structured in tranches offering different risk-return profiles.
CDO^2.	A CDO in which the underlying assets are tranches of other CDOs.
CDS.	Credit default swap. A swap based on the risk of default of a given security.
CEO.	Chief executive officer of a firm.
CFO.	Chief financial officer or finance director of a firm.
CFTC.	Commodities Futures Trading Commission. US regulator.
Collateral.	Assets put up in order to secure a loan. In the event of the borrower failing to repay, the lender acquires a legal right to the collateral assets.
Commercial paper.	Short-term debt securities issued by large companies to cover current cash needs.
Counterparty.	In an agreement or trade between two parties, the one other than that being discussed.
Derivative.	A financial instrument that is based on the prices of underlying assets, but without conveying ownership of those assets. Derivatives include forwards, futures, options and swaps.
Fannie Mae.	Federal National Mortgage Association (US).
Fed.	Federal Reserve: the central bank of the US.
Forex.	Foreign exchange. Also known as FX.
Freddie Mac.	Federal Home Loan Mortgage Corporation (US).
FSA.	Financial Services Authority. UK regulator.
FTSE 100.	The 100 largest companies by market capitalization listed on the London Stock Exchange. The FTSE 100 index is an index of

	the share price of a weighted basket of the shares of these companies.
Future.	A financial instrument entailing a commitment to buy or sell assets at some future date.
FX.	Foreign exchange. Also known as Forex.
GDP.	Gross Domestic Product: the standard measure of a country's economic output.
Gearing.	*See Leverage.*
Ginnie Mae.	Government National Mortgage Association (US).
Glass-Steagall Act.	The Banking Act of 1933, or that part of the Act enforcing a separation in the USA between commercial and investment banking activities.
Hedge.	An investment designed to protect the investor against unwanted outcomes on another investment (as in hedging one's bets).
Hedge funds.	Lightly regulated investment funds, not open to the general public, that typically speculate on specific market movements by buying one kind of asset and selling a closely related one, magnifying the effects of small price differences by using high leverage.
IFA.	Independent financial advisor.
IMF.	International Monetary Fund.
IPO.	Initial public offering.
IRS.	Inland Revenue Service (US).
Junk bond.	A bond issued by a company offering a high interest rate with a significant risk that the issuer will be unable to repay the capital when it reaches maturity.

Leverage.	The use of borrowed money or derivatives to magnify the effects of an investment. Also known as gearing.
LIBOR.	London Interbank Offered Rate. A daily quoted measure of the interest rate at which banks lend to each other.
Margin.	Collateral deposited by a trader as security for a counterparty or intermediary when trading on credit.
Margin call.	Demand from a counterparty or intermediary for more collateral to cover a party's possible losses on a trade.
Mark-to-market.	In accounting, valuation of an asset according to its current market value rather than its historic cost.
Mark-to-model.	In accounting, valuation of an asset for which there is no current market price according to a mathematical model based on the prices of similar assets.
Money market mutual fund.	A mutual fund that invests in low-risk, short-term debt, such as government bonds and commercial paper.
Mortgage.	A loan secured on a property (real estate), such as the borrower's home, as collateral.
Mortgage-backed securities.	Asset-backed securities in which the asset is the right to receive interest and repayments on a mortgage, together with the mortgaged property as collateral.
Mutual fund.	An investment vehicle, put together and managed by an asset management company, in which the public can buy shares. Also known as a unit trust.
Mutual society.	Sometimes just called a mutual, an organization owned by and run for its

	members, typically its savers and borrowers in a financial context.
NASDAQ.	A US stock exchange originally run by the National Association of Securities Dealers and specializing in technology stocks.
NYSE.	New York Stock Exchange.
OCC.	Office of the Comptroller of the Currency. US regulator.
OECD.	Organisation for Economic Co-operation and Development.
Option.	Financial instrument conveying the right to buy or sell assets, but without obliging the holder to do so.
OTC.	Over the counter: used to describe financial trades where the price is agreed bilaterally between the parties rather than through trading in an open market.
OTS.	Office of Thrift Supervision. US regulator.
Plain vanilla.	The simplest version of a class of derivative.
Ponzi scheme.	A fraudulent investment scheme in which the money is never invested and any redemptions are paid from subsequent investments.
Repo.	Repurchase agreement. A sale of securities with a commitment to repurchase them, typically on a very short timescale.
S&P 500.	The 500 largest American companies listed on the major US stock exchanges as determined by Standard & Poor's. The S&P 500 index is an index of a weighted basket of the shares of these companies.
Savings and Loan.	*See Thrift.*
SEC.	Securities and Exchange Commission. US regulator.
Security.	Any tradable financial instrument, including stocks and shares, bonds and

derivatives of all kinds. The term was originally used to describe instruments secured on an underlying asset, but these are now described as asset-backed securities.

Securitization.   The repackaging of income streams from loans (mortgages, car finance, credit card debts, etc.) as financial instruments that can be sold to investors.

Sell-side.   That part of the financial sector concerned with the promotion and sale of securities, more specifically stockbrokers.

Short selling.   The sale of shares by someone who does not own them, with the intention of buying or borrowing the same number of shares before the settlement date.

SIV.   Structured investment vehicle. A pool of long-term assets funded by short-term loans and typically held in a separate company so as to be kept off the balance sheet of the company creating it.

Split-cap.   Split capital investment trust.

Stakeholder.   Someone with an interest in a company, either as affecting or (more generally) as being affected by its activities and performance.

Swap.   A derivative which has the effect of exchanging one security or cash flow for another, for example, between fixed and floating exchange rates or between differing maturities.

Synthetic CDO.   A security offering risks and returns modeled on a CDO. The issuer does not own the underlying assets, as in a CDO, but contracts with third parties to secure the benefits and costs that would arise if it did.

Thrift.	A mutual society holding savings for depositors and lending to borrowers for the purpose of buying a home.
Tranche, tranching.	Splitting asset-backed securities such as CDOs into segments with different risk-return characteristics in order to appeal to different investors. Super-senior, senior, mezzanine and junior tranches refer to the different classes of securities created from the lowest risk to the highest, respectively.
Unit trust.	An investment vehicle, put together and managed by an asset management company, in which the public can buy shares. Also known as a mutual fund.
VaR.	Value at risk. A measure of the risk exposure of a portfolio of assets expressed as the probability of a given loss over a given period.

References

Alchian, Armen and Demsetz, Harold 1972. "Production, information costs, and economic organization," *American Economic Review* 62: 777–95.

American Institute of Certified Public Accountants 2009. Statement on Standards for Tax Services, available at: www.aicpa.org/InterestAreas/Tax/Resources/StandardsEthics/StatementsonStandardsforTaxServices/DownloadableDocuments/SSTS,%20Effective%20January%201,%202010.pdf.

Appiah, Kwame Anthony 2006. *Cosmopolitanism: Ethics in a World of Strangers*. New York: Norton.

Argandoña, Antonio 2010. "Microfinance," in Boatright (ed.), pp. 419–34.

Aristophanes, *Wealth*, translated by George Theodoridis, available at: www.poetryintranslation.com/theodoridisgwealth.htm.

Aristotle, *Politics*.

Augur, Philip 2010. *Reckless: The Rise and Fall of the City*. New York: Random House.

Bainbridge, Stephen M. 2000. "Insider trading," in Bouckaert, Boudewijn and De Geest, Gerrit (eds.), *Encyclopedia of Law and Economics, Volume III*. Cheltenham: Edward Elgar, pp. 772–811, available at: http://encyclo.findlaw.com/5650book.pdf.

Baldwin, Robert, Cave, Martin and Lodge, Martin 2011. *Understanding Regulation: Theory, Strategy and Practice*, 2nd edn. Oxford University Press.

Bales, Kevin 2012. *Disposable People*, 3rd edn. Berkeley: University of California Press.

Barberis, Nicholas and Huang, Ming 2001. "Mental accounting, loss aversion and individual stock returns," *Journal of Finance* 56: 1247–92.

Barker, Richard, Hendry, John, Roberts, John D. and Sanderson, Paul 2012. "Can company – fund manager meetings convey informational benefits? Exploring the rationalisation of equity investment decision making by UK fund managers," *Accounting, Organization and Society* 37(4): 207–22.

Bech, Morten 2012. "FX volume during the financial crisis and now," *BIS Quarterly Review*, March, pp. 33–43, available at: www.bis.org/publ/qtrpdf/r_qt1203f.pdf.

Benhabib, Seyla 2003. "Discourse ethics and minority rights," in Pauer-Studer, Herlende (ed.), *Constructions of Practical Reason: Interviews of Moral and Political Philosophy*. Stanford University Press, pp. 29–49.

Berk, J. B. and Green, R. C. 2004. "Mutual fund flows and performance in rational markets," *Journal of Political Economy* 112(6): 1269–95.

Berle, Adoplh A., Jr. 1933. "For whom are corporate managers trustees: a note," *Harvard Law Review* 45: 1365–72.

Berle, Adolph A., Jr. and Means, Gardiner C. 1932. *The Modern Corporation and Private Property*. London: Macmillan.

Bitner, Richard 2008. *Confessions of a Subprime Lender: An Insider's Tale of Greed, Fraud and Ignorance*. New York: Wiley.

Blackburn, Simon 2003. *Ethics: A Very Short Introduction*. Oxford University Press.

Blake, David and Timmermann, Allan 2003. "*Performance persistence in mutual funds*." Financial Services Authority.

Boatright, John R. 2008. *Ethics in Finance*, 2nd edn. Oxford: Blackwell.
   (ed.) 2010. *Finance Ethics*. New York: Wiley.

Bornstein, David 2012. "An attack on Grameen Bank, and the cause of women," http://opinionator.blogs.nytimes.com/2012/08/22.

Bowie, Norman E. 1998. "A Kantian theory of capitalism," *Business Ethics Quarterly*, Special 1: 37–60.

Branch, Ben S. and Taub, Jennifer S. 2010. "Bankruptcy," in Boatright (ed.), pp. 509–29.

Brummer, Alex 2009. *The Crunch: The Scandal of Northern Rock and the Escalating Credit Crisis*. New York: Random House.

Chang, Ha-Joon 2010. *23 Things They Don't Tell You About Capitalism*. London: Allen Lane.

Cheung, Steven 1983. "The contractual nature of the firm," *Journal of Law and Economics* 26 (April): 1–21.

Chisholm, Andrew 2010. *Derivatives Demystified*, 2nd edn. New York: Wiley.

Choudhury, Masudul Alam and Malik, Uzir Abdul 1992. *The Foundations of Islamic Political Economy*. Basingstoke: Macmillan.

Connor, Steven 2011. *A Philosophy of Sport*. London: Reaktion Books.

Consumer Financial Protection Bureau 2012. "Private student loans. Report to the Senate Committee on Banking, Housing, and Urban Affairs, the Senate Committee on Health, Education, Labor, and Pensions, the House of Representatives Committee on Financial Services, and the House of Representatives Committee on Education and the Workforce," http://files.consumerfinance.gov/f/201207_cfpb_Reports_Private-Student-Loans.pdf.

Cornwell, John 2010. "MacIntyre on money," *Prospect*, October 12, available at: www.rustat.org/media/documents/MacIntyre2010.pdf.

Cuthbertson, K., Nitsche, D. and O'Sullivan, N. 2008. "UK mutual fund performance: skill or luck?" *Journal of Empirical Finance* 15(4): 613–34.

Davies, Howard 2001. "Ethics in regulation," *Business Ethics: A European Review* 10(4): 280–7.

  2010. *The Financial Crisis: Who is to Blame?* Cambridge: Polity Press.

Davies, Howard and Green, David 2010. *Global Financial Regulation: The Essential Guide*, updated edn. Cambridge: Polity Press.

Deetz, Stanley 1992. *Democracy in an Age of Corporate Colonization*. State University of New York Press.

Deigh, John 2010. *An Introduction to Ethics*. Cambridge University Press.

Dodd, Merrick E. Jr. 1932. "For whom are corporate managers trustees?" *Harvard Law Review* 44: 1049–74.

Dollar, David and Kraay, Aart 2002a. "Spreading the wealth," *Foreign Affairs* 81(1): 120–33.

  2002b. "Growth is good for the poor," *Journal of Economic Growth* 7(3): 195–225.

Donaldson, Thomas and Dunfee, Thomas W. 1999. *Ties that Bind: A Social Contracts Approach to Business Ethics*. Cambridge, MA: Harvard Business School Press.

Douglas, Tom 2000. *Scapegoats: Transferring Blame*. New York: Routledge.

Dunbar, Nicholas 2000. *Inventing Money: The Story of Long-Term Capital Management and the Legends Behind It*. New York: Wiley.

Durbin, Michael 2010. *All About Derivatives*, 2nd edn. New York: McGraw-Hill.

Duska, Ronald, Duska, Brenda Shay and Ragatz, Julie Anne 2011. *Accounting Ethics*, 2nd edn. Oxford: Wiley-Blackwell.

Dworkin, Ronald 2000. *Sovereign Virtue: The Theory and Practice of Equality*. Cambridge, MA: Harvard University Press.

Elstrom, Peter 2000. "Jack Grubman, the power broker," *Business Week*, May 15, available at: www.businessweek.com/archives/2000/b3681212.arc.htm.

Engelen, Peter-Jan and Van Liederkerke, Luc 2007. "The ethics of insider trading revisited," *Journal of Business Ethics* 74: 497–507.

  2010. "Insider trading," in Boatright (ed.), pp. 199–221.

Ezzamel, Mahmoud and Watson, Robert 1998. "Market comparison earnings and the bidding up of executive cash compensation," *Academy of Management Journal* 41(2): 221–31.

Fay, Stephen 1996. *The Collapse of Barings*. New York: Norton.

Ferguson, Charles with Beck, Chad and Bolt, Adam 2010. *Inside Job*. Sony Classics (DVD).

Financial Crisis Inquiry Commission 2011. *The Financial Crisis Inquiry Report*. New York: Public Affairs.

Fine, Donald I., Ferrell, O. C. and Fraedrich, John 2005. "The fall of Michael Milken," in Gini, Al, *Case Studies in Business Ethics*, 5th edn. Upper Saddle River: Prentice Hall, pp. 184–90.

Finn, Margot C. 2003. *The Character of Credit: Personal Debt in English Culture, 1740–1914*. Cambridge University Press.

Fox, Loren 2003. *Enron: The Rise and Fall*. New York: Wiley.

Frank, Robert H. 1985. *Choosing the Right Pond: Human Behavior and the Quest for Status*. Oxford University Press.

   2004. *What Price the Moral High Ground? Ethical Dilemmas in Competitive Environments*. Princeton University Press.

   2011. *The Darwin Economy: Liberty, Competition and the Common Good*. Princeton University Press.

Freeman, Kevin D. 2009. "Economic warfare: risks and responses," www.scribd.com/doc/49755779/12/How-Bear-Raids-Froze-the-Capital-Markets-and-Harmed-the-Economy.

Freeman, R. Edward and Evan, William M. 1990. "Corporate governance: a stakeholder interpretation," *Journal of Behavioral Economics* 19: 337–59.

French, Kenneth R. 2008. "The cost of active investing," *Journal of Finance* 63(4): 1537–73.

Frey, Bruno S. 1997. *Not Just for the Money: An Economic Theory of Personal Motivation*. Cheltenham: Edward Elgar.

Frey, Bruno S. and Stutzer, Alois 2001. *Happiness and Economics: How the Economy and Institutions Affect Human Well-Being*. Princeton University Press.

Friedman, Milton 1970. "The social responsibility of business is to increase its profits," *New York Times Magazine*, September 13, pp. 32–3.

Friedman, Benjamin M. 2012. Review of Smith, Hedrick (2012), *New York Review*, 59(15): 36–9.

Frydman, Roman and Goldberg, Michael D. 2007. *Imperfect Knowledge Economics: Exchange Rates and Risk*. Princeton University Press.

Geisst, Charles R. 2002. *Wheels of Fortune: The History of Speculation from Scandal to Respectability*. New York: Wiley.

Gibbard, Alan 1990. *Wise Choices, Apt Feelings*. Cambridge, MA: Harvard University Press.

Gill, Matthew 2009. *Accountants' Truth*. Oxford University Press.

Girard, René 2004. *Oedipus Unbound: Selected Writings on Rivalry and Desire*. Stanford University Press.

Goldstein, Itay and Guembel, Alexander 2008. "Manipulation and the allocational role of prices," *Review of Economic Studies* 75: 133–64.

Greenspan, Alan 2007. *The Age of Turbulence: Adventures in a New World*. London: Penguin.

Gutmann, Amy and Thompson, Dennis 2004. *Why Deliberative Democracy?* Princeton University Press.

Habermas, Jürgen 1990. "Discourse ethics," in *Moral Consciousness and Communicative Action*. Cambridge: Polity Press.

Hamilton, Tyler and Coyle, Daniel 2012. *The Secret Race: Inside the Hidden World of the Tour de France: Doping, Cover-Ups and Winning at all Costs*. London: Bantam.

Hancock, Matthew and Zahawi, Nadhim 2011. *Masters of Nothing*. London: Biteback Publishing.

Hare, Richard M. 1981. *Moral Thinking: Its Levels, Method and Point*. Oxford: Clarendon Press.

Hayek, Friedrich A. 1937. "Economics and Knowledge," *Economica* 4: 33–54.

1945. "The use of knowledge in society," *American Economic Review* 35: 519–30.

Hendry, John 2001a. "Economic contracts versus social relationships as a foundation for normative stakeholder theory," *Business Ethics: A European Review* 10: 223–32.

2001b. "Missing the target: normative stakeholder theory and the corporate governance debate," *Business Ethics Quarterly* 11: 159–76.

2002. "The principal's other problems: honest incompetence and management contracts," *Academy of Management Review* 27: 98–113.

2004. *Between Enterprise and Ethics: Business and Management in a Bimoral Society*. Oxford University Press.

2012. "CEO pay, motivation and the meaning of money," SSRN 2021972, available at: http://papers.ssrn.com/sol3/papers.cfm?abstract_id=2021972.

Hendry, John, Sanderson, Paul, Barker, Richard and Roberts, John D. 2006. "Owners or traders? Conceptualisations of institutional investors and their relationships with corporate managers," *Human Relations* 59: 1101–32.

Hinde, Robert A. 2002. *Why Good is Good: The Sources of Morality*. Cambridge University Press.

Hudon, Marek 2008. "Norms and values of the various MFIs," *International Journal of Social Economics* 35: 35–48.

2009. "Should access to credit be a right?," *Journal of Business Ethics* 84: 17–28.

Iqbal, Zamir and Mirakhor, Abbas 2011. *Introduction to Islamic Finance*, 2nd edn. New York: Wiley.

Jennings, Marianne M., 1999. "A primer on accounting issues and ethics and earnings management," *Corporate Finance Review* 3(5): 39–41, reprinted in Jennings 2011, pp. 262–72.

2011. *Business Ethics: Case Studies and Selected Readings*, 7th international edn. Nashville: Southwestern Publishing.

Jensen, Michael C. and Meckling, William H. 1976. "Theory of the firm: managerial behavior, agency costs, and ownership structure," *Journal of Financial Economics* 3: 305–60.

Jensen, Michael C. and Murphy, Kevin J. 1990. "CEO incentives: it's not how much you pay, but how," *Harvard Business Review* 68(3): 138–49.

Jickling, Mark 2006. "CRS Report for Congress: Regulation of Energy Derivatives," Congressional Research Service, available at: www.policy-archive.org/handle/10207/bitstreams/3682.pdf.

2009. "Causes of the financial crisis," R40173, Congressional Research Service, available at: http://digitalcommons.ilr.cornell.edu/key_workplace/600.

Kahneman, Daniel 2011. *Thinking Fast and Slow*. London: Allen Lane.

Kahneman, Daniel, Slovic, Paul and Tversky, Amos 1982. *Judgement Under Uncertainty: Heuristics and Biases*. Cambridge University Press.

Keynes, John Maynard 1920. *A Treatise on Probability*. London: Macmillan.

[1936] 1964. *The General Theory of Employment, Interest and Money*. New York: Harbinger.

Kline, John M. 2010. *Ethics for International Business*, 2nd edn. New York: Routledge.

Knight, Frank 1921. *Risk, Uncertainty and Profit*. London School of Economics.

Kornbluth, Jesse 1992. *Highly Confident: The Crime and Punishment of Michael Milken*. New York: William Morrow.

Korsgaard, Christine 1985. "Kant's formula of universal law," *Pacific Philosophical Quarterly* 66(1–2): 24–47. A version of this paper is also available online at: http://dash.harvard.edu/handle/1/3201869.

Korten, David C. 2001. *When Corporations Rule the World*. West Hartford: Kumarian Press.

Kosowski, Robert, Timmermann, Allan G., Wermers, Russ R. and White, Halbert L., Jr. 2006. "Can mutual fund 'stars' really pick stocks? New evidence from a bootstrap analysis," *Journal of Finance* 59(6): 2551–95.

Krippner, Greta R. 2005, "The financialization of the American economy," *Socio-Economic Review* 3(2): 173–208.

Lamont, Julian and Favor, Christi 2012. "Distributive Justice," available at: http://plato.stanford.edu/archives/win2012/entries/justice-distributive.

Lanchester, John 2010. *Whoops!: Why Everyone Owes Everyone and No-one Can Pay*. London: Penguin.

Layard, Richard 2005. *Happiness: Lessons from a New Science*. London: Penguin.

Leeson, Nick and Whitley, Edward 1996. *Rogue Trader: How I Brought Down Barings Bank and Shook the Financial World*. Boston: Little, Brown.

Lewis, Lionel S. 2012. *Con Game: Bernie Madoff and His Victims*. Piscataway: Transaction.

Lewis, Michael 2011. *Boomerang: The Meltdown Tour*. London: Allen Lane.

Lowenstein, Roger 2000. *When Genius Failed: The Rise and Fall of Long-Term Capital Management*. New York: Random House.

MacIntyre, Alasdair 1981. *After Virtue*. University of Notre Dame Press.

Madison, James, Hamilton, Alexander and Jay, John 1788. *The Federalist Papers*, available at: http://thomas.loc.gov/home/histdox/fedpapers.html.

Madrick, Jeff 2011. *Age of Greed: The Triumph of Finance and the Decline of America, 1970 to the Present*. New York: Knopf.

Mandelbrot, Benoit B. and Hudson, Richard L. 2008. *The (Mis)Behaviour of Markets: A Fractal View of Risk, Ruin and Reward*. London: Profile.

Martin, Justin 2000. *Greenspan: The Man Behind the Money*. New York: Perseus.

Mason, Richard 2006. *Oppenheimer's Choice: Reflections from Moral Philosophy*. State University of New York Press.

McCabe, Douglas M. and Trevino, Linda K. 1995. "Cheating among business students: a challenge for business leaders and educators," *Journal of Management Education* 19: 205–14.

McDonald, Lawrence G. and Robinson, Patrick 2009. *A Colossal Failure of Common Sense: The Inside Story of the Collapse of Lehman Brothers*. New York: Crown.

McLean, Bethany and Elkind, Peter 2004. *The Smartest Guys in the Room*. New York: Portfolio.

McLean, Bethany, Elkind, Peter and Gibney, Alex 2005. *The Smartest Guys in the Room*. Magnolia Pictures (DVD).

Milgrom, Paul and Roberts, John 1992. *Economics, Organization and Management*. Upper Saddle River: Prentice Hall.

Mill, John Stuart [1863] 1998. *Utilitarianism*. Oxford University Press.

Miller, David 1990. *Market, State, and Community: Theoretical Foundations of Market Socialism*. Oxford University Press.

Mills, D. Quinn 2003. *Wheel, Deal and Steal: Deceptive Accounting, Deceitful CEOs, and Ineffective Reforms*. Upper Saddle River: Prentice Hall.

Monks, Robert A. G. and Minow, Nell 2011. *Corporate Governance*, 5th edn. New York: Wiley.

Moore, Jennifer 1990. "What is really unethical about insider trading?," *Journal of Business Ethics* 9: 171–82.

Moreton, Patrick 1992. "Salomon and the Treasury Securities Auction," Harvard Business School Case 9-292-114.

Moriarty, Jeffrey 2009. "How much compensation can CEOs permissibly accept?" *Business Ethics Quarterly* 19: 235–50.

Morris, Charles R. 2008. *The Trillion Dollar Meltdown*. New York: Public Affairs.

Muolo, Paul and Padilla, Mathew 2010. *Chain of Blame: How Wall Street Caused the Mortgage and Credit Crisis*. New York: Wiley.

Myners, Paul 2001. "Institutional investment in the UK: a review," http://archive.treasury.gov.uk/docs/2001/myners_report0602.html.

Nagel, Thomas 1979. *Mortal Questions*. Cambridge University Press.

Nasser, Alan and Norman, Kelly 2011. "The student loan debt bubble," *Global Research*, available at: www.globalresearch.ca/the-student-loan-debt-bubble/22711.

Nelkin, Dana K. 2008. "Moral luck," http://plato.stanford.edu/archives/fall2008/entries/moral-luck.

Noah, Timothy 2012. *The Great Divergence: America's Growing Inequality Crisis and What We Can Do About It*. London: Bloomsbury.

Nozick, Robert 1974. *Anarchy, State and Utopia*. New York: Basic Books.

Nussbaum, Martha C. 2000. *Women and Human Development: The Capabilities Approach*. Cambridge University Press.

OECD 2011. *Divided We Stand: Why Inequality Keeps Rising*. Paris: OECD.

Owens, David 2012. *Shaping the Normative Landscape*. Oxford University Press.

Parfit, Derek 2010. *On What Matters. Volume I*. Oxford University Press.

Perold, Andre F., Musher, Joshua and Alloway, Robert 2002. "Unilever Superannuation Fund vs. Merrill Lynch," Harvard Business School case study 203034-PDF-ENG.

Phillips, Michael M. 2010. "Senators seek, fail to get an 'I'm sorry'," *Wall Street Journal*, April 28.

Phillips, Robert A. 1997. "Stakeholder theory and a principle of fairness," *Business Ethics Quarterly* 7: 51–66.

Pickett, Kate and Wilkinson, Richard G. 2010. *The Spirit Level: Why Greater Equality Makes Societies Stronger*, revised edn. London: Penguin.

Pogge, Thomas 2002. *World Poverty and Human Rights*. Cambridge: Polity Press.

2011. "The Achilles' Heel of competitive/adversarial systems," in Dobos, Ned, Barry, Christian and Pogge, Thomas (eds.), *Global Financial Crisis: The Ethical Issues*. Basingstoke: Palgrave Macmillan, pp. 120–31.

Posner, Richard A. 2009. *A Failure of Capitalism*. Cambridge, MA: Harvard University Press.

Public Citizen 2001. "Blind faith: how deregulation and Enron's influence over government looted billions from Americans," www.citizen.org/cmep/article_redirect.cfm?ID=7104.

Putterman, Louis and Kroszner, Randall S. (eds.) 1996. *The Economic Nature of the Firm: A Reader*, 2nd edn. Cambridge University Press.

Rainer, William J. 2000. "Testimony before the U.S. Senate Committee on Agriculture, Nutrition and Forestry and Committee on Banking, Housing and Urban Affairs," www.cftc.gov/opa/speeches00/oparainer-7.htm.

Rawls, John 1964. "Legal obligation and the duty of fair play," in Hook, Sidney (ed.), *Law and Philosophy: A Symposium*. New York University Press, pp. 9–10.

   1971. *A Theory of Justice*. Cambridge, MA: Harvard University Press.

   1999. *The Law of Peoples, with The Idea of Public Reason Revisited*. Cambridge, MA: Harvard University Press.

   2001. *Justice as Fairness: A Restatement*. Cambridge, MA: Harvard University Press.

Reddy, Sanjay 2005. "Just international monetary arrangements," in Barry and Pogge (eds.), pp. 218–34.

Reddy, Sanjay and Pogge, Thomas 2009. "How not to count the poor," in Stiglitz *et al.* (eds.), pp. 42–85.

Roberts, John D., Sanderson, Paul, Barker, Richard and Hendry, John 2006. "In the mirror of the market: the disciplinary effects of company – fund manager meetings," *Accounting, Organization and Society* 31: 277–94.

Rodin, David 2005. "The ownership model of business ethics," in Barry and Pogge (eds.), pp. 235–52.

Saez, Emmanuel and Piketty, Thomas 2003. "Income inequality in the United States, 1913–1998," *Quarterly Journal of Economics* 118: 1–39.

   2009. Updated tables and figures to Saez and Piketty (2003), available at: http://elsa.berkeley.edu/~saez, cited in Pogge (2011).

Salverda, Wiemer, Nolan, Brian and Smeeding, Timothy M. (eds.) 2009. *The Oxford Handbook of Economic Inequality*. Oxford University Press.

Sandberg, Joakim 2012. "Mega-interest on microcredit: are lenders exploiting the poor?," *Journal of Applied Philosophy* 29(3): 169–85.

Sandel, Michael 2012. *What Money Can't Buy: The Moral Limits of Markets*. London: Allen Lane.

Santoro, Michael A. and Strauss, Ronald J. 2013. *Wall Street Values: Business Ethics and the Global Financial Crisis*. Cambridge University Press, pp. 117–55.

Scanlon, Thomas M. 1998. *What We Owe to Each Other*. Cambridge, MA: Harvard University Press.

2008. *Moral Dimensions: Permissibility, Meaning, Blame*. Cambridge, MA: Harvard University Press.

Schwartz, Peter 1991. *The Art of the Long View: Planning for the Future in an Uncertain World*. New York: Doubleday.

Seaford, Richard 2004. *Money and the Early Greek Mind: Homer, Philosophy, Tragedy*. Cambridge University Press.

Sen, Amartya K. 1985. *Commodities and Capabilities*. Oxford University Press.

1992. *Inequality Reexamined*. Cambridge, MA: Harvard University Press.

Shafer-Landau, Russ 2011. *The Fundamentals of Ethics*, 2nd edn. Oxford University Press.

Shiller, Robert J. 2008. *The Subprime Solution: How Today's Global Financial Crisis Happened, and What to Do About It*. Princeton University Press.

Shleifer, Andrei 2000. *Inefficient Markets: An Introduction to Behavioral Finance*. Oxford University Press.

2004. "Does competition destroy ethical behavior?," *American Economic Review* 94(2): 414–18.

Shleifer, Andrei and Vishny, Robert 1997. "A survey of corporate governance," *Journal of Finance* 52: 737–83.

Simmel, George 1990 (1907). *The Philosophy of Money*, 2nd edn. New York: Routledge.

Simon, Herbert A. 1955. "A behavioral model of rational choice," *Quarterly Journal of Economics* 69: 99–118.

1997. *Administrative Behavior: A Study of Decision Making Processes in Administrative Organizations*, 4th edn. New York: Free Press.

Skidelsky, Robert and Skidelsky, Edward 2012. *How Much is Enough?: The Love of Money and the Case for the Good Life*. New York: Other Press.

Smith, Adam 1776. *The Wealth of Nations*.

Smith, Greg 2012. "Why I am leaving Goldman Sachs," www.nytimes.com/2012/03/14/opinion/why-i-am-leaving-goldman-sachs.html.

Smith, Hedrick 2012. *Who Stole the American Dream?* New York: Random House.

Sorkin, Andrew Ross 2010. "At Goldman, e-mail message lays bare conflicts in trading," *New York Times*, January 13.

Soros, George 1995. *Soros on Soros: Staying Ahead of the Curve*. New York: Wiley.

1998. *The Crisis of Global Capitalism: Open Society Endangered*. New York: Public Affairs.

Sorrell, Tom and Hendry, John 1994. *Business Ethics*. Oxford: Butterworth-Heinemann.

Soule, Edward 2010. "Regulation," in Boatright (ed.), pp. 179–98.

Sternberg, Elaine 2000. *Just Business: Business Ethics in Action*, 2nd edn. Oxford University Press.

Stewart, James B. 1991. *Den of Thieves*. New York: Touchstone Books.

Stiglitz, Joseph 2003. *Globalisation and its Discontents*. London: Penguin.

2010. *Freefall: Free Markets and the Sinking of the Global Economy*. London: Penguin.

2012. *The Price of Inequality: The Avoidable Causes and Invisible Costs of Inequality*. London: Allen Lane.

Stiglitz, Joseph, Anand, Sudhir and Segal, Paul (eds.) 2009. *Debates in the Measurement of Poverty*. Oxford University Press.

Stone, Dan G. 1990. *April Fools: An Insider's Account of the Rise and Collapse of Drexel Burnham*. New York: Dutton.

Taleb, Nassim Nicholas 2004. *Fooled by Randomness: The Hidden Role of Chance in Life and in the Markets*. London: Penguin.

Tett, Gillian 2009. *Fool's Gold: How the Bold Dream of a Small Tribe at J. P. Morgan was Corrupted by Wall Street Greed and Unleashed a Catastrophe*. London: Abacus.

Turner, Adair 2012. *Economics After the Crisis*. Cambridge, MA: MIT Press.

Visser, Wayne A. M. and MacIntosh, Alastair 1998. "A short review of the historical critique of usury," *Accounting, Business and Financial History* 8(2): 175–89.

Walsh, Adrian and Lynch, Tony 2008. *The Morality of Money: An Exploration in Analytical Philosophy*. Basingstoke: Palgrave Macmillan.

Werhane, Patricia E. 1989. "The ethics of insider trading," *Journal of Business Ethics* 8: 84–115.

1991. "The indefensibility of insider trading," *Journal of Business Ethics* 10: 729–31.

Wilkinson, Rorden and Clapp, Jennifer (eds.) 2010. *Global Governance, Poverty and Inequality*. New York: Routledge.

Williams, Bernard 1981a. "Persons, Character, and Morality," in *Moral Luck*. Cambridge University Press, pp. 1–19.

1981b. "Moral luck," in *Moral Luck*. Cambridge University Press, pp. 20–39.

[1985] 2006. *Ethics and the Limits of Philosophy*. New York: Routledge.

Williamson, Oliver E. 1985. *The Economic Institutions of Capitalism*. New York: Free Press.

Willman, Paul, Fenton-O'Creevy, Mark, Nicholson, Nigel and Soane, Emma 2006. "Noise trading and the management of operational risk: firms, traders and irrationality in financial markets," *Journal of Management Studies* 43: 1357–74.

Wright, Paul C. 2010. "Looming crisis: America's credit card debt bubble-burst," *Global Research*, available at: www.globalresearch.ca/looming-crisis-america-s-credit-card-debt-bubble-burst/17903.

Young, S. David 1985. "Insider trading: why the concern?," *Journal of Accounting, Auditing and Finance* 8(3): 178–83.

Zalta, Edward N. (ed.) Ongoing. *Stanford Enclyclopedia of Philosophy*, available at: http://plato.stanford.edu.

Zorn, Dirk, Dobbin, Frank, Dierkes, Julian and Kwok, Man-shan 2004. "Managing investors: how financial markets reshaped the American firm," in Knorr Cetina, Karin and Preda, Alex (eds.), *The Sociology of Financial Markets*. Oxford University Press, pp. 269–89.

Index

Abacus deals, 217, 220, 222, 232
accountability and agency, 186–8, 194, 199
Ace Cash Express, 137
active fund management, 210–14
active fund managers, 233
Adoboli, Kweku, 193, 194, 197, 199, 200, 201
adjustable-rate mortgages *see* ARMs
agency relationships, 186–8, 253, 258, 259
agency theory, 44, 185, 186, 188, 207, 253,
     255, 260, 263
agent discretion, 259
agents in philosophy and economics, 185
AIG, 11, 17, 23, 24, 221, 222, 272, 279
Alchian, Armen, 255
Amazon, 227, 252
American Institute of Certified Public
     Accountants, 247
American Insurance Group *see* AIG
Appiah, Kwame Anthony, 54
Argandoña, Antonio, 148, 152
Aristophanes, 31, 32, 33
Aristotle, 31, 32, 33, 70, 71
ARMs, 7, 25, 282
Armstrong, Lance, 174
Arthur Andersen, 27, 33, 134
asset-backed commercial paper, 19, 22, 283
asset-backed securities, 6, 282, 287, 288
     see also mortgage-backed securities
asset managers, 82
auditors, 27, 33, 134, 193, 241, 244, 245
Augur, Philip, 169

Bainbridge, Stephen M., 181
Baldwin, Robert, 266

Bales, Kevin, 137
Bank of America, 22, 24, 81, 279
Bank of England, 81, 95, 96, 143, 192, 269,
     273, 276
bankers' bonuses, 29, 34, 188, 199, 202–7,
     260
Bankers Trust, 217, 218, 232, 237
banking sector, 3
     deregulation, 3
     size of, 3
bankruptcy, 153–6
Bankruptcy Code, 155
Barberis, Nicholas, 161
Barings Bank, 191, 192, 193, 194, 196, 200
Barker, Richard, 179
Basel II, 4, 275
bear raids, 168, 169, 172
Bear Stearns, 22, 23, 24, 263, 279
behavioral finance, 38
Benhabib, Seyla, 68
Berk, J. B., 212
Berle, Adolph, 253, 254, 255
Bernanke, Ben, 272
Big Bang, 95, 185
big bath accounting, 241
Bitner, Richard, 2
Blackburn, Simon, 56
Blake, David, 212
blame, 195, 196
Boatright, John R., 155
Boesky, Ivan, 176, 177, 178, 184
bonds, 10
     corporate, 85, 86, 133
     government, 85, 86, 133, 170